THE DEVIL

ALSO BY PETER STANFORD

Lord Longford—An Authorised Life

Catholics and Sex

*Cardinal Hume and the
Changing Face of English Catholicism*

Believing Bishops

THE DEVIL

A BIOGRAPHY

PETER STANFORD

A Marian Wood Book

HENRY HOLT AND COMPANY   NEW YORK

Henry Holt and Company, Inc.
Publishers since 1866
115 West 18th Street
New York, New York 10011

Henry Holt ® is a registered
trademark of Henry Holt and Company, Inc.

First published in the United States in 1996 by
Henry Holt and Company, Inc.
Originally published in Great Britain in 1996 by
William Heinemann Ltd.

Library of Congress Cataloging-in-Publication Data
Stanford, Peter.
The Devil: a biography / Peter Stanford.
p.   cm.
Includes bibliographical references and index.
1. Devil.   2. Devil—History of doctrines.   I. Title.
BT981.S7   1996   96-19337
235'.4—dc20   CIP

ISBN 0-8050-3082-4

Henry Holt books are available for special promotions and
premiums. For details contact: Director, Special Markets.

First American Edition—1996

Designed by Kate Nichols

Printed in the United States of America
All first editions are printed on acid-free paper. ∞

10 9 8 7 6 5 4 3 2 1

For Siobhan

CONTENTS

x   *Contents*

PART III: TOO SOON FOR AN OBITUARY

On a Fast Track to Hell

At the age of thirteen, I was convinced I was going to hell to meet the Devil. I remember the day all too clearly. It was the summer of 1975 and I was on a train from Liverpool to Brighton.

Had it been an airline, I would have been called an unaccompanied minor and given a plastic tag to wear announcing the fact. But this was British Rail in the pre-privatization age, that is, before passengers became customers and guards senior conductors. So, *faute de mieux,* my parents entrusted me to the care of a kindly looking middle-aged man in the seat opposite reading the *National Geographic.*

I agreed to this chaperon only after extensive research—peering through various carriage windows all along the platform. It wasn't that I was adverse to some kind of adult supervision—indeed there was scarcely a rebellious bone in my body. Nor was I a precocious teenager aware of the threat that men of a certain age in anoraks posed to my innocence. The important thing was to find someone obviously good, virtuous, and certainly

God-fearing. However ludicrous it may seem today, I had grown obsessed in the nights preceding this great trek by the idea that when the train headed into one of the many tunnels that litter the line, there was a grave danger of being sucked down to hell. My imaginary scenario was that, once engulfed in darkness in an enclosed space, those passengers who had sinned repeatedly and without recourse to confession would be singled out by the Devil, whose natural habitat was—of course—tunnels, and spirited away on a fast track to his subterranean domain of fire and brimstone.

I can't quite recall what terrible crimes I had committed— pushing into the lunch queue at school, economy with the truth over my homework, a couple of Glory Be's short of a Rosary, even (and I still blush with Catholic guilt at such a post hoc admission) the odd impure thought, and the even odder irregular motion of my flesh. But never mind. The point was that I had somehow to attach myself to one of the righteous who would escape the Devil's clutches so as to emerge with him or her at the other end of the tunnels. The kindly gent in the seat opposite, to my untrained eye, couldn't possibly have sinned, so I grabbed on to his coattails. I would be saved by association. It proved a successful ruse, though I fear my traveling companion may have felt otherwise. His peaceful browse through a photo-shoot of extinct African volcanoes was constantly interrupted by my mindless chatter. Anything to keep the thought of the next tunnel and who might be lurking in its midst at bay.

All children have vivid imaginations and teenagers perhaps are more prone than most to this affliction. But my brush with the Devil speaks volumes of my Catholic education at the hands of the Irish Christian Brothers. It was a loving and warm-hearted, if not stunningly intellectual school, but black-and-white notions of right and wrong, good and evil, loomed large on the curriculum. The Devil was as much a part of classroom culture as Shakespeare, Pythagoras, and Lady Antonia Fraser's *Mary Queen of Scots.*

The Irish Christian Brothers were an odd bunch, the last

remnant of a lost age of muscular Catholicism and its attendant certainties and control. Dotted around Liverpool, one of the few English cities where dog collars and the Angelus are part of everyday life on the streets and in the bars, they were still teaching the *Penny Catechism* years after even the strictest convent schools had phased it out in favor of something that allowed for a little more discussion. Biology was sidelined in favor of Russian. It was a traditional Catholic education built on centuries of unchanging practice with only the smallest concessions to the wicked secular world. Mass once a day and occasionally twice; prayer groups to fill the intervening spaces; huge funerals every few weeks for one of the brothers, who would not be replaced because the seminary was empty; religious education in pride of place on the curriculum; and a rich tapestry of images—the Virgin Mary in her blue cloak fixing us with her all-knowing eye at the turn of every well-scrubbed corridor, the Sacred Heart in replica on every wall, pumping out plastic profusions of Christ's blood that had been spilled for us, and skulking in the shadows, hidden around the next corner, lurking at the school gates, inspiring those who would sneer at our uniforms on the bus home, was Satan.

This school, in its time capsule, provided me with a last glimpse of the by then tattered majesty of a figure who had once haunted the imaginations of countless Christians. At a time when most branches of Christendom, save for the most extreme, unattractive, and evangelistic, had effectively declared the Devil dead and buried, my alma mater still saw Satan as an ever-present threat. To stray from what was presented as the norm was to take the Devil's shilling. It was a message that once kept the Catholic Church united, that certainly traumatized my adolescent psyche, but that, as I grew older, I realized had, down the ages, fallen into disrepute.

For the classroom audience, the specter of the Devil may have been enough to provoke a frisson of fear. But in Catholicism at large, the Devil became the equivalent of one of those fresh-faced television personalities who burst on to our screens, attract the public and the headlines for a few months, and then fade when we see them in every program we tune in to. For Satan the process took centuries rather than months, but the basic drift was the same. Moreover, my childhood memories of the Evil One proved so powerful that during my spell as editor of the *Catholic Herald* I tried to commission a series on the Devil and whether the Church and the faithful still believed in him or saw any role for him. It was a thankless task. Writers said what an interesting idea, but no. Priests quizzed me as to why I was interested, and then said no. When I told them of my train ride, they suggested I was out of the ordinary. One even offered to recommend a good counselor. Even the few "licensed" exorcists still permitted to operate by the Church authorities were reluctant to be interviewed. Talk of the Devil has become taboo.

There I might have left it, had it not been for the sight that greeted me during a trip to Rome. Queues and queues of people were waiting outside an obscure and unremarkable church office on the outskirts of the city. They were hoping, my guide told me, for an audience with an African archbishop and exorcist who now lives in the Vatican. Archbishop Emmanuel Milingo, who had once led the Catholic Church in his native Zambia, has become a thorn in the flesh of the ecclesiastical bigwigs. His insistence on raising the question of Satan—and worse his willingness to perform public exorcisms as once Christ had—so angered the powers that be at God's business address on Earth that he was exiled to Rome. People still sought him out by the busload. For them the Devil is real and official silence that borders on disapproval cannot consign Lucifer to limbo. Perhaps they too went to a Christian Brothers' school. I hope they will find this book enlightening as it attempts to pinpoint quite what it is that the Church feels about Satan today. It is written by a fellow inquirer. I am not a theologian; a church, literary, or social historian; an anthropologist; or a psychiatrist, but this biography touches on all those areas. My perceptions are those of a journalist eager to make sense of a figure who has always puzzled me.

In researching this book I have been asked many times whether I believe in an incarnate Devil. While the question of my own beliefs is not the topic of this study, it is at least germane to what follows. For ninety-nine percent of the time I am coldly rational about the whole question. I can trace the development of the idea of a devil, see why it happened, why it caught on, how it was manipulated. Indeed, offering the Devil as a face to put to the abstract reality of evil has been one of Christianity's most impressive and popular policies. In that other one percent, my Catholic upbringing makes itself felt. There are things, events that I cannot explain, that defy reason. I count myself lucky never to have been confronted by the Devil. Only once, many years ago, was I disturbed by an unquiet spirit in a haunted cottage in Devon. There was definitely something there and no amount of reason will convince me otherwise. Occasionally I have sensed a presence, particularly on some of the more unusual research trips undertaken for this biography. During the writing of this book there have been unaccountable noises, doors slamming, bouts of lethargy that defy all previous precedent, that I have been tempted to put down to the Devil doing the equivalent of denying me access to his papers and friends.

So although I end up firmly on the rational side of the fence, there is a single thread that remains caught on a nail on the other side. It is so far proving resistant to attempts to cut it, an umbilical cord back to the Catholicism of my childhood.

This book has been entitled *The Devil: A Biography*. Aside from straining for something snappy on the front cover, the title does reflect what is inside—namely, a very personal exploration of the highs and lows of the Devil's influence. Christianity created the monster that became the Devil, and I have devoted the greater part of the text to the Christian Devil. However, he—and despite my personal penchant for flaunting the Vatican's ban on inclusive language, that erstwhile masculine pronoun in this case will have to be read as encapsulating both male and female—has not grown up in isolation. Throughout the book detailed reference is made to how other credos and cultures have dealt with the problem of evil without recourse to a solution as gruesome as Satan. The specific episodes and eras I have chosen to illustrate more general points may not please everyone. The Devil has indeed been such a part of civilization that every period could have been mentioned. The same applies to the selection of authors, philosophers, and painters. The choice is mine, a kind of *Desert Island Discs* of Satan's extraordinarily long life.

There are many other people whom I should thank for their inspiration. Though this biography is definitively unauthorized and the subject has not cooperated—as far as I am aware—I did at least manage to track down not one but three exorcists. I had been looking in the wrong place all those years ago. The liberal English Catholic Church is far too discreet to admit to harboring such characters. But the Vatican is not shy about having its own experts—Father Gabriele Amorth and Monsignor Corrado Balducci—while the Church of England's open-minded toleration gave me Canon Dominic Walker.

Among those who spared the time to share with me their expertise on the Devil and the question of evil were Karen Armstrong, Bronwen Astor, Fernando Cervantes, Edward Chesser, Father Tony Churchill STL, Peter Clarke, Vicky Cosstick, John Costello, Brian Davies, Clare Dixon, The Reverend Neil Dixon, Dr. Paul Doherty, Bishop Graham Dow, Paul and Patricia de Berker, Susan Greenwood, Canon Peter Humfrey, Professor Leslek Kolakowski, Professor Jean La Fontaine, Professor Simon Lee, Celia Lowenstein, Paul Owens, Rabbi Norman Solomon, Dom Henry Wansbrough OSB, and Nigel Wright.

Simon Banner, Virginia Barton, Lucinda Coxon, Simon Denison, Carla Masera Evans, Michelle Field, Viviane Hewitt, Christine Morgan, Kasia Parham, Kathy Walsh and the team at Inform, Caroline Willson, and Georgina Wyman all provided much needed practical assistance. My agent, Derek Johns, my editors Tom Weldon (in London) and Marian Wood (in New York), and my copy editor, Kate Goodhart, were endlessly supportive. And my wife, Siobhan, was patient, encouraging, and tolerant as I filled our house with the strangest books, manuscripts, and—sometimes—people.

No author trying to understand the development of the personality of the Devil can overlook the pioneering work of the American academic Jeffrey Burton Russell. He has spent almost two decades putting together his four-volume study of Satan, and it is a towering achievement that may well never be equaled. Though his books sat on or near my desk during my labors, my own aim was very different—a concise, accessible biography that brings out the colorful as well as the chilling aspects of the Prince of Darkness, that is rational and well-informed, something indeed that might be read comfortably and without fear on a train journey, tunnels and all.

A Life in the Public Eye

> From the beginning of my career I knew that I
> should win in the long run by sheer weight of
> public opinion, in spite of the long campaign of
> misrepresentation and calumny against me. At
> the bottom of the universe is a constitutional
> one; and with such a majority as mine I cannot
> be kept permanently out of office.
>
> —The Devil in George Bernard Shaw's
> *Man and Superman*

This is not a conventional biography, but then the Devil is a thoroughly unconventional—many would say unreal—character. Even if you put to one side for a moment widespread skepticism about his very existence, Satan is by any standards an unusual subject.

For a start he makes Methuselah, at 969, look like an adolescent. The Devil has been around for some 2,000 years in the New Testament and maybe for a good deal longer in various other guises and incarnations. Indeed exact details of the birth, parentage, and education of this doughty time-traveler are impossible to come by. Like so much else about him they can only be guessed at. There are as many estimates as there are people who feel that he has touched their lives.

Yet, however blotted his copybook, the Devil is very much a part of the Christian viewpoint. Other creeds may have toyed with malign gods and spirits, but none has carved out a similar role—a figure who is the name and the face to put to the abstract reality of evil. On his relationship with the Christian God—

reportedly once very close, almost that of a favored son before they had an almighty falling out—it is hard to arrive at an accurate portrait. Are they equal and opposite ends of the spectrum, principles of good and evil locked in a cosmic battle like Batman and the Joker? Or is the Devil not a free agent? Is he still in some fashion under God's control? "Official" theology appears to endorse the second viewpoint, while the practice and iconography of the churches down the ages backs the first.

It is just one of the murky areas of ambiguity that confront the biographer. The question of ancestry is another. The Devil has no conventional family tree but does appear to have forebears in the ancient civilizations of the Near East and in Judaism and Islam. None begins to approach his prominence and powers but the resemblance is too close to be ignored. The notion of resemblance raises another issue. Though his name in all its various forms—Satan, Lucifer, Beelzebub, Belial, and so on—is after 2,000 years universally recognized and planted in every dictionary and encyclopedia, his face and even his form remain an enigma. Is he, for example, an angel or an animal—the serpent who tempts Eve in the Garden of Eden, the flying pig who was banished from a church by Pope Gregory the Great, or the black cat who lurks in the hell of Mikhael Bulgakov's *Master and Margarita*? Or is he a strange-looking human—the hook-nosed gargoyle on the facade of Chartres Cathedral, the black bewinged imp in Brueghel and Bosch scenes, the fool of medieval mystery plays, easily outwitted by anyone with an ounce of sense and godliness, or the helpless, three-headed colossus of Dante's *Inferno*, encased in ice and weeping tears of bitter frustration?

Others who have tried to convey a glimpse of the Prince of Darkness have strained to find something redeeming about this reviled character. Milton saw the Devil as a magnificent untamed, though ultimately doomed, rebel in *Paradise Lost*. Byron and the Romantics made him their hero, the ultimate overturner of convention, the free spirit. William Blake showed him as a kindly old gentleman in one of his engravings. The Devil, it seems, has a million and one disguises. What are taken as his telltale signs—the horns, the cloven hoof, the tail, the breath that smells of sulfur, the black skin and red eyes—are just several of his many masks. He could be anybody or nobody. That is what beguiles.

Reported sightings also trouble the biographer. It is impossible to find independent verification for any of them. Are they, as Professor Anthony Clare is fond of remarking, all in the mind? Martin Luther was so sure that the Devil was in the room at Wartburg Castle that he threw an ink-pot at him but no one else witnessed the event. The stain remains. Those who have participated in exorcisms will report that the Devil spoke through his victim. Yet psychiatrists are wary of such claims. And the witches who were burned at the stake in the late medieval period after being found guilty by the Inquisition of making a pact with the Devil are today viewed as victims of a miscarriage of justice. Unconfirmed contemporary reports suggest that the Devil is at last starting to feel his age and contemplate retiring from the limelight. Like one of those film stars who suddenly disappears from our screens without any explanation, his name is remembered as if it were part of the furniture, yet many are unsure if he is dead or alive.

There are many who would not shed a tear if he had descended to hell and closed the door firmly behind him. The Devil's starring role came as the "baddie" in the Christian view of the world but many Christian churchmen today, especially in the mainstream Anglican, Catholic, and Protestant denominations, offer a polite "no comment" when challenged as to his fate and try to change the subject. When pressed, however, they will admit that the Devil still lurks on the fundamentalist and superstitious margins of their otherwise thoroughly bright, shiny, and modern churches. His congregation is much reduced, they stress, little more than a twilight zone of those hankering after a lost past. Yet the party line sits rather unhappily with a whole bevy of indicators that suggest that in the long-established Christian churches, the Devil is alive and kicking. The *Catechism of the Catholic Church*, published by Pope John Paul II amid great pomp and circumstance in 1994, makes explicit reference to Satan's continuing role. And exorcisms—expelling the Devil from those he has possessed—continue though at a reduced rate. According to one of his senior aides, Pope John Paul II himself exorcised a young woman in the Vatican, the first pontiff in modern times to perform the rite.

For the most part, however, mainstream Christianity has passed the Devil on to fringe evangelical sects. These "new" churches, with their tendency to take every word of the Bible literally, and their corresponding lack of theological or ethical sophistication, thrive on talk of the Devil.

If news of the Devil's retirement has then been exaggerated in Christian circles, his regular appearances on stage, in films, and even in television advertisements promoting "naughty but nice" products suggest that secular twentieth-century Western society still has a place for him, albeit a cameo that hints at an ill-defined force of evil and malice.

Demonizing, a process carried out by the Romans on the early Christians and then adapted to terrifying effect by the Church itself, remains one of the blights of a supposedly enlightened and tolerant era. The Nazis built on centuries of demonization of the Jews—which had seen the stereotypical Jewish physical features mixed up with those of the Devil to produce in medieval art a beady-eyed goblin with a hooked nose—to carry out the Holocaust that claimed six million lives. Western governments are fond of blaming economic troubles on an alleged army of welfare state scroungers, the job-shy, and single mothers. On the international stage Saddam Hussein becomes the Devil incarnate with every act of terrorism in the world laid at his door, regardless of the evidence.

The Devil is with us and causing trouble. Quite how he does this—or how it is done in his name—is one of the questions that is at the heart of this biography. Not the least among the others is to define the exact nature of the Devil's shadowy existence. Does he in fact have a physical form? Is he a popular metaphor for the abstract reality of evil? Or is he something between the two—a myth, powerful and omnipresent in the collective psyche down the ages?

The Eternal Scapegoat

We live in an age that approaches religion and religious belief with skepticism and places ever greater onus on science to provide the answers to those issues of life and death and destruction that have always perplexed humankind. Even within the churches, doubting Thomases have been elevated from the pitiable to the theologically correct. Yet many scientists will freely admit that they do not have all the solutions and never anticipate being in a position to replace God. Sir Karl Popper, the Austrian-born philosopher and scientist, has said that science offers no truths, only approaches. These approaches are of limited use when applied to those specific human needs that science most conspicuously fails to satisfy. Bereavement, suffering, pain, natural disasters, the various apparently random crises of life remain as puzzling in the late twentieth century as they were to the farmers of ancient Egypt who despaired when the Nile destroyed their crops.

In an age where the faith that saw God as a kind of universal Father Christmas has been destroyed, the myths and symbols of religion retain a unique (though now increasingly undervalued) capacity for helping in negotiating and navigating the inexplicable blows of fate. Rites and rituals can still bring comfort and spiritual growth. Among the most enduring features of the Christian landscape is the Devil. His realm, granted, has been steadily eroded by science as many of the phenomena that were once put down to his wicked hand are irrefutably ascribed to other sources. If, for example, a man had collapsed with an attack of epilepsy in the Near East in the first century A.D., his behavior would have been put down to possession by the Devil or his demons, and he would have been exorcised. In the Middle Ages, such a diagnosis would still have held good—but the patient would have been bled as well. Today the same behavior is understood in terms of an uncoordinated discharge of motor neurones and the patient is treated with diazepam.

Much remains, however, where Lucifer cannot be replaced by a pill. Natural disasters—the suffering that results from the processes of nature—still horrify and prompt talk of evil abroad in the world. So too does what is termed moral evil—that which occurs when a human being knowingly and deliberately inflicts suffering on another. Scientists have impinged on these fields. Climatic changes, global warming, misuse and mismanagement of natural resources have all been shown to have a say in events that were once seen as the actions of evil spirits and gods. Psychiatry now has names and remedies to explain actions that were once simply called "evil." It is no accident that the growth of Freudian psychoanalysis in this century has coincided with a decline in formal attachment to religion. Where once people would have sought counsel from their priest in the confessional and succor in the symbols of good and evil in their churches, today they resort to therapy.

There are many more natural and moral occurrences that still have no name and no explanation. The word "evil" is sometimes questioned in relation to such occurrences. It is considered too abstract, too judgmental. Philosophers will argue that ours is a morally neutral universe with neither good nor evil. Yet many can still almost daily point to actions they would deem as evil— from violent crime, child abuse, and rape to acts of terrorism and the development of nuclear weapons. The important thing is that evil, otherwise an abstract and allusive metaphysical concept, can be identified.

In the modern mind it is located within each individual— what Jung called our "shadow." Historically, the tendency was to place it outside—on the Devil, who exploited a weakness in the human makeup. Of the two placements, the contemporary option is harder to deal with since it imposes a responsibility on each and every individual. The traditional route, while emphasizing that God gave each man and woman free will—the capacity to choose right or wrong—did have the bonus of off-loading some of the burden onto an external force. That is why the Devil still attracts a following. He represents the easy option when we are confronted with evil.

Attempts to introduce concepts of right or wrong, good or evil have always brought in their wake some form of imagery or iconography. As Neanderthal man struggled to survive in the face of what he saw as hostile forces, the notion of an evil force took shape in the form of animals who escaped capture and in some cases posed a physical threat. Cave paintings, among the earliest known illustrations, show humankind in conflict with horned animals. Out of such depictions evolved the half-man, half-beast figure of the horned god of the north. This in turn influenced the Teutonic, Norse, and Celtic deities and ultimately the Christian Devil. Tracing such links has been one of my tasks.

Once good and evil were slotted into the model of some sort of deity, there were then efforts to sort out the exact relationship between the two. Ancient civilizations tended to see them as two sides of the same coin. In Egypt, for instance, Seth and Horus were often worshiped and even depicted together, the generally benign sky god and the usually malevolent god of the desert. The key to a good life was to achieve harmony—or *ma'at*—between these conflicting forces.

The deities of Egypt, and of Canaan and the various peoples of Mesopotamia, were monist—where only one overall divine principle encompassed within its pantheon both good and bad. A different model of organizing the relationship between good and bad came with Zoroaster, who is thought to have lived in current-day Iran around the seventh century B.C. His good god—Ahura Mazda—was in direct conflict with Ahriman, the god of war. This was dualism in its purest form, though some of Zoroaster's followers later were to dilute it and in time the whole tradition more or less died out with only the tiny sect of Parsees upholding its tenets today in the Middle East and India.

Judaism took the monist approach. Yahweh was the almighty, all-powerful one, equally responsible, the Old Testament makes clear, for good and bad events and actions, even at one stage egging Moses on to rape and pillage. This monism began to be eroded in the Book of Job, as eloquent and comprehensive a statement of the many dilemmas and doubts afflicting human-kind as any contemporary, or indeed subsequent document. There Satan makes his first appearance, still very much under Yahweh's wing, as a kind of chief prosecutor at the heavenly court, but at odds with his master over the human capacity to do or be good for its own sake.

It was in the apocryphal literature that blossomed between the writing of the final books of the Old Testament and the time of Christ that a sustained challenge was mounted to official monism. For a variety of social, political, and religious reasons to do with the upheavals and disappointments that God's chosen people were experiencing, the figure of Satan, the fallen angel, found a place as Yahweh's rival in a cosmic battle, the scapegoat for the Jews' misfortunes. In a pattern to be repeated through-out history, the Jewish people tried to understand why their God could have—apparently—abandoned them and hit upon the wiles and temptations of Satan as the reason. All that was evil or negative in the world was ascribed to this angel of darkness as a complex and intertwined series of stories about the "Watcher Angels" who had accompanied Satan on his fall from grace was developed. They were the source of much of the imagery that surrounds the Devil in the New Testament and later in the main-stream of Christian thought.

The Devil is second only to Jesus in the New Testament, but distinct and different approaches to the question of good and evil can be seen between the would-be eyewitness accounts in the gospels of Matthew, Mark, and Luke, the more philosophical and Greek-influenced writings of Saint Paul, and the colorful and apocalyptic Book of Revelations. No single line emerges from the New Testament about Satan, though his status is increased enormously and the official monist line is maintained. It was left to subsequent generations of theologians and churchmen to flesh out that character, to give him a recognizable shape and form, a function in day-to-day Christian life, and an exact relationship with God. From the days of the early Church when the Christian gnostics tried to introduce a more explicit dualism—making this world with all its problems the Devil's creation and the next world, allegedly perfect, that of God—the question of the limit of Satan's influence kept coming back to threaten Church unity. Only at the cost of considerable internal disruption was the slide toward dualism halted.

The problem was to integrate two apparently contradictory ideas—a God who was all-powerful and all-knowing and thus who allowed humanity to suffer, and a God who was also apparently all-loving. The eighteenth-century Scottish philosopher David Hume summed up the dilemma succinctly when he wrote of God: "Is he willing to prevent evil, but not able? Then he is impotent. Is he able, but not willing? Then he is malevolent. Is he both able and willing? Whence then is evil?"

It is a circle the Christian Churches have been trying to square for centuries. Theological debate—around such concepts as free will and original sin as the source of evil in the world—has produced its own blueprint, set in stone at the Lateran Council of 1215 and largely unaltered since. At a popular level, however, the cosmic battle between God and the Devil has continued to rage, often with official encouragement. During the witch craze of the late-medieval period, there was backing at the highest level for the view that the world offered a choice between the two polar opposites. Those unfortunate men and women who were burned at the stake had made a pact with the Devil and chosen the wrong option. In its ruthless and too often misguided pursuit of Cathar heretics, Albigensians, and then those who performed witchcraft and magic, the Inquisition reinforced this picture. Literature and the arts also gave their support while popes, including Gregory the Great, made their own distinctive contribution by promoting saints whose lives were one long battle with Satan as the Church's heroes and heroines.

Whatever the limits imposed by official teaching, the Devil became an essential part of the Christian fabric, someone to blame when trouble and dissent cast a cloud, the eternal and convenient scapegoat. When the Reformation shattered the hope of one, holy, apostolic Europe under the papacy, both sides were quick to see the Devil's hand manipulating their rivals. Luther had only to think of Rome to see a hellish city full of demons parading around in the scarlet robes of cardinals, while one of the most popular depictions of the Protestant reformer among Catholics had him listening attentively as the Devil whispered in his ear.

The Devil became synonymous with the deities of any rival creed to Christianity. With the rise of Islam in the eighth century and its spread into continental Europe and especially into Christendom's "lost province," Spain, Muslims were targeted as the Devil's disciples. Later, the language of the Crusades—whatever their true political purpose—was all about defeating the Infidel and winning back the Holy Places in Jerusalem from the powers of darkness.

In its fight in northern Europe, especially with older and longer-established pagan codes of belief, Christianity was quick to turn the deities it encountered into devils and witches. In assimilating these creeds into Christianity, the Devil became a bridge, close in purpose and in imagery to some of their malevolent spirits. Pagan peoples were used to having malign spirits to blame for their misfortunes. If Christianity had only the one omnipotent God, faceless and remote, and abstract teachings about original sin to offer instead, it might never have succeeded in winning them around. By stressing the image of Christ and his mother as models of the good life, as well as holding up saints as dead spirits to be beseeched with prayer in times of need, the missionary church went part of the way to assuring a flood of conversion. The Devil was an essential part in putting a face to evil. He was also useful in the Roman Church's attempts to outlaw practices it objected to on moral grounds. Since Augustine in the fifth century, it had enforced a strict code of sexual morality. Those who broke it—and particularly those women who were seen by clerics as following in the footsteps of Eve by seducing men into wrongdoing—ran the risk of being tainted with the Devil. His copulating demons—*incubi* and *succubii*—were allegedly always on the lookout for a willing and wanton harridan to lead astray. Indeed documents like the notorious *Malleus Malificarum*, the fifteenth-century witch-hunter's bible, went so far as to suggest that women were genetically more predisposed to do the Devil's deeds than men.

The witch craze was part of a long-running conspiracy theory, a collective fantasy particularly prevalent among Christians—though seen in recent times in social workers and therapists who endorse allegations of satanic-ritual abuse—that there is a group within society breaking all the rules and subverting all the norms. Since one of the Devil's roles down the ages has been that of revolutionary—he was after all the first rebel—his name has become linked with such charges. These usually include nocturnal meetings—symbolizing the path of darkness, not light—inversion of Christian images, orgies, incest, sexual depravity, blood sacrifice. A variety of combinations of these—often accompanied by the Devil's name as endorsement and final "proof"—has been leveled at different groups down the ages—the witches, the Freemasons, the Cathars, and so on. Little that would stand up in a court of law as evidence has ever been produced as substantiation. Self-avowed satanists remain for the most part people who are either sick or who feel in some way rejected, marginalized, or cast out by society and who turn to the Devil as a channel to express their own alienation.

The Reality of Evil

The activities of contemporary satanists and the widespread and troubling allegations of satanic-ritual abuse will be examined in part three. The first part deals with the evolution of the Devil in Christian thought, in the Bible, and beyond. Comparisons are drawn between emerging Christianity and those belief systems in the Near East that are thought to have influenced it most. Since the Devil is largely a Christian preoccupation—though Islam and Judaism toyed with the character before rejecting him—this biography does not explore the treatment of evil in some Eastern faiths. They are for the most part monist—in Hinduism, Braham is the ultimate reality, creator, and destroyer of all things—and have no time for a Devil as an independent or quasi-independent force of evil. Part two changes the emphasis from the theological and scriptural to looking at how the Devil was perceived by Christians in history and his role in some of the best-known episodes of Christian history. Integral to this examination is a history of the development of the Devil in popular culture—in art, literature, and drama—in this age of superstition. Part three deals with the twentieth century and charts the efforts of the mainstream churches to distance themselves from their own terrible creation, while maintaining some sort of teaching on the question of evil. The task has been made more difficult by the rapid growth of the science of the mind with Freud and Jung in particular leading the way in locating evil within the human psyche.

The churches have tried a variety of approaches from the folksy wisdom of evangelicals who tell you cheerfully that "everything God has made has a crack in it," to more scholarly attempts to recast the whole theological treatment of evil without the looming presence of Satan. It was a Jewish writer, Martin Buber (in *Good and Evil*), who came up with one of the more enduring definitions of evil as "the yeast in the dough," the ferment placed in the soul by God to allow it to grow and be tested. It is not a new idea but rather a recasting of an approach that has been around for centuries. Milton, the Puritan poet, was particularly scornful of what he called cloistered virtue, the goodness that has never been put to the test. Evil, he believed, was there to stretch humanity to the limits.

The search to understand, quantify, and even negate that evil—so much a part of the Devil's story—is part of this biography. It makes no pretense to have the answers that have eluded humanity since the beginning; it merely observes the role the

Devil has played—and continues to play—in an endeavor to make sense of the inexplicable.

Few educated people today believe in the Devil as a reality. Yet, those who deny the existence of evil altogether remain a minority. The rest inhabit various staging posts on the way from one position to the other—that there are evil actions but not evil individuals, or that people can be evil but that evil is within them. Such formulas can seem thin and inadequate when faced by daily news reports of terrible and terrifying acts of cruelty and barbarity around the world. Can the hatred that created Auschwitz be found only within humanity or is there a greater force of evil out there? The fundamental question of evil remains—and with it the Devil.

PART ONE

"A MURDERER FROM THE START" —JOHN 8:43

> Who, or what he is, his origin, his habitation, his destiny, and his power are subjects which puzzle the most acute theologians and on which no orthodox person can be induced to give a decisive opinion. He is the weak place of the popular religion, the vulnerable belly of the crocodile.
>
> —Percy Bysshe Shelley, *On the Devil and Devils*

ONE

The Family Tree

> The cultures of Egypt, Mesopotamia and
> Canaan stand directly behind those of the
> Greeks and Hebrews and so exercised at least an
> indirect influence upon the Judeo-Christian
> concept of the Devil.
>
> —Jeffrey Burton Russell

Though the blackest of black sheep, the Devil is seen today as a member of the extended Christian family. Yet the Devil who is such a menacing figure in the New Testament and beyond can trace his lineage back not just to Judaism but to pre-Christian times and to other creeds and cultures that had an influence—sometimes obvious and profound, other times more circuitous—on the authors of the Bible. Satan did not suddenly appear from nowhere as a fully grown adult to traumatize Job, tempt Jesus in the desert, and terrorize generations of Christians. There were precedents, parallels, and a universal need for a figure or formula to explain away what might loosely be termed evil. He came from a long line of demons and evil spirits that had fulfilled just such a role for the peoples of the Near East for four millennia.

The lands of the Bible, of God's covenant with the Jewish people, and of the first Christians, were in a region that was every bit as turbulent as it is now. Abraham's descendents coexisted with powerful and often belligerent nations and tribes, who traded with them in good times, and took up arms against them, subjugated them, and at one stage exiled them to Babylon in bad times. With such economic and military contact came a two-way traffic in cultural and religious influences. There are myriad references in the books of the Old Testament to the gods, spirits, and legends of other belief systems while in the New some of the most graphic passages chronicling Satan's fall from grace among the angels—in Saint Peter's Second Epistle to the Romans and in the Book of Revelation, for example—carry an unmistakable echo of the combat myths of Canaan and Greece.

While none of Israel's neighbors could boast among their own well-developed credos a single personification of evil to rival the Devil, they did worship and fear characters who bore a striking physical resemblance to him, in the different guises under which he is to be found in the Bible. It is a likeness that is more than skin deep. Just as the Judeo-Christian tradition turned—and on its fringes continues to turn—to the Devil as a way of understanding the evils and woes that afflict humankind, so too the other peoples of the Near East struggled to comprehend their environment and the forces of nature that dictated their existence. They followed each other in subscribing to the combat myth—a cosmic battle between good and evil, between benevolent and malevolent spirits, that was played out on earth with human flesh and toil and blood as cannon fodder. These malevolent spirits held the genes that later made up the Devil.

While most traditions saw their gods as monist, two-faced, angels of munificence and kindness one minute, and the next, for no reason, demons of cruelty and destructiveness, there was a growing trend in the immediate pre-Christian era toward what became known as dualism. Good and evil were increasingly seen as opposite and even independent forces. Plato labored to separate evil from the creator, body from spirit, the one base, earthbound, and morally neutral, the second purer and capable of choosing between good and evil. The Jews, in the wake of their exile in Babylon, followed this fashion for creating separate principles of good and evil. While they were later to revert to a more ambiguous position—officially at least, evil spirits have always had a role in popular Judaism—the Christians implicitly enshrined opposite poles of good and evil in their gospel through the character of the Devil.

In examining the cross-fertilization of ideas between various cultures and peoples, the Devil should not be seen as a character invented by one civilization and handed on to others. There are many influences and no single line of development. The personification of evil was not an isolated phenomenon, the preserve of any one corner of the globe. Unconnected but contemporary groups grappled with trying to make sense of a cosmos that was at once benign and hostile, cruel and kind. They faced up to their own death and questioned what eternal reward, if any, there would be for the righteous and what punishment for the wicked.

Independently and at different speeds they came up with the same answer—a system of divine opposites. How far it spontaneously occurred to them and how far they borrowed from their neighbors can only be guessed at when one is projecting back tens of thousands of years without the comfort of extensive primary texts. What is beyond dispute, however, is that for some a personification of evil became an article of faith. Different cultures fashioned their own devils and demons. Some defined them theologically, others through myths and legend, images and folklore. Some wrote down their ideas, others passed them on by mouth.

Therefore there cannot be a single starting point to this biography. The Devil has not one birthplace but many. As many, in fact, as there were human imaginations trying to understand their existence and their environment. The great attraction of evil spirits remains that they put a face to the irrational and can explain away the abstract reality of evil in the world.

Where Christianity has a single Devil, earlier creeds had a cast of characters who, while individually lacking his power and scope, approximated the different roles that we now associate with Satan. They would, perhaps, have one malign god to oversee the underworld, another to wreak destruction over the planet, and a third to represent the darker side of humankind. For Christians, all three functions were unified in Satan. Tracking down the Devil's forebears among pre-Christian gods is therefore not an exact science. There are hints and allusions, fragments and thoughts, but there was no one blueprint.

Egypt

The civilization that thrived along the Nile and its delta from the fourth millennium B.C. until the time of classical Greece and Rome was a model for all that followed. Those who came into contact with the Pharaohs' realm were impressed and inspired by Egyptian religious life. Herodotus (c. 485–425 B.C.), the historian and traveler, believed that his fellow Greeks had acquired the names of their gods from Egypt.[1] He was mistaken, but the fact that a celebrated and widely influential writer could put forward such a thesis demonstrates the influence of Egyptian culture. Even in the present century there remains a fascination with the beliefs of ancient Egypt that has seen scholars puzzling over coded mystical messages in the topography of the pyramids.

Religion was not organized in any institutional form with churches and priests and rule books but was nonetheless an integral part of Egyptian life, as much taken for granted as the ebb and flow of the Nile. Egyptians searched in their religion for something beyond the cycles of everyday existence, for a timeless, unchanging cosmos. The afterlife was a great obsession, as the mummies and grave goods in the death chambers of the pyramids make abundantly clear. Each Egyptian sought to prepare his or her case to put to the gods when he arrived on the threshold of the underworld.

Tuat, the underworld, bears a passing resemblance to the hell that was later to become the Christian Devil's lair. While its location is not so much under the earth as all around it, Tuat's undisputed master of ceremonies is the black, jackal-headed god

Anpu, or Anubis. Represented in tomb paintings like the rest of the Egyptian deity as half-man, half-beast, Anpu has a tail and horns and is sometimes shown with the scales that weigh the souls of the dead. Those who are judged to have been righteous in life pass on to an eternal rest in the Abode of Bliss, while the wicked are consumed by fire and tormented by demons. These spirits are described in lurid details in the *Book of the Dead* (c. 1580–1090 B.C.) in terms that echo later designations of the Devil—Embracer of Fire, Swallower of Shadows, Breaker of Bones, Dweller of the Pit, Eater of Blood, Eater of Entrails, Lord of the Horns. Reference is also made to the serpent spirits that roam about Tuat.

The Egyptians believed in many gods but saw them all as manifestations of the One God. There was no other figure to rival the One God. However, within this pantheon individual gods could be helpers and hurters. When the crops flourished and life was sweet, the Egyptians would worship the sun god, Ra, or Amon-Re, but when there was drought and famine, plague or infestation, they would pray to Seth—associated with scarcity, aridity, and the desert that lay in wait beyond the drawn-out straggling oases that made up ancient Egypt.[2]

If any one god was popularly associated with evil it was Seth, who was usually depicted with Horus, the hawk-headed sky god, as part of a two-faced creature. Seth appears in a variety of guises—sometimes a serpent or a black pig—but most often he is a tall, upright figure with boxed-off ears and a proboscislike snout. He is also sometimes portrayed as red—the inhospitable hue of the scorching sands that threatened Egypt's farmlands. Black, by contrast, was a positive color, the tone of the rich river deposits that nourished the crops. Jeffrey Burton Russell suggests that "it is possible that the redness of Seth helped make red the second most common color, after black, of the Christian Devil."[3]

In many Egyptian myths, Seth and Horus are locked in mortal combat. In one story, Seth traps Horus in a box and tries to drown him in the Nile, only to be thwarted by a timely intervention from Isis, Horus's sister/wife. In another, Seth tries to kill Horus when he is a baby. Having failed then, the two spend their adulthood with daggers drawn, with Horus castrating Seth, symbolically depriving him of power. Seth, by way of response, tears out Horus's eye and buries it. In yet another tale, Seth tries unsuccessfully to sodomize Horus.⁴ These gruesome stories are significant in terms of the issues that affected Egyptians' lives and prosperity. Sterility fails to conquer fertility when Horus resists buggery. The ongoing battle represents disharmony, lack of *ma'at*. Both sustain injury through their lack of harmony, just as the earth and its inhabitants suffer when they fail to strive for *ma'at*. The impression of a devil as we would understand the term is then transitory and on the whole deceptive. If a devil exists it is in an impersonal sense as the absence of *ma'at*. Indeed, it would be a mistake to see Seth as wholly, irredeemably bad. Some of his deeds are heroic. He rescues Ra, the sun god, from Apep, the serpent, by throwing a chain around the creature's neck and forcing it to vomit the contents of its stomach. Some Egyptians even worshiped Seth as their protector in war.

Mesopotamia

The civilization of Mesopotamia is as old if not older than that of Egypt. Both were based on river valleys—in the case of Mesopotamia, the crescent of land between the Euphrates and the Tigris in modern-day Iraq. Like the Egyptians, the Mesopotamians had an overriding concern with the cycle of the seasons on whose whims survival depended, and developed a deity to explain the inexplicable in these events.

The Mesopotamians were the pioneers of the written word, their script predating the Egyptian hieroglyph. Appropriately the Mesopotamian *Epic of Gilgamesh* is the oldest story in the world and its subject the original literary hero. The most complete version of the text only dates back to the seventh century B.C. but the bare bones of the tale are known to have been written down around 2100 B.C., well before the first books of the Bible. Since the idea of a devil or demons as responsible for earthly misfortune and "sin" is one that is as old as humankind, it is fitting that *Gilgamesh*, the first cosmic drama, should mark the debut of the first truly diabolical literary character, Huwawa.[5]

The *Epic of Gilgamesh* is part of the religious, political, and cultural tradition that links the various closely related groups and dynasties that ruled the flatlands of Mesopotamia from 3000 B.C. to 500 B.C. The Sumerians developed the first observable civilization in this region. Their conquerors and spiritual heirs were the Akkadians, Assyrians, and Babylonians, who expanded their domains and conquered new lands. This aggression culminated in 587 B.C. in the capture of Jerusalem, which carried the Hebrew people into slavery in Babylon with profound consequences for Jewish thought and for the later books of the Old Testament that were composed during and after the exile.[6] However, the interchange of ideas between the Israelites and the Mesopotamians had been going on for generations as the two traded, and the similarity between some of the most enduring and celebrated stories of the two peoples is striking. Mesopotamia, for instance, had its own Moses in the legend of King Sargon I. The *Epic of Gilgamesh* was part of the cultural and religious heritage that the warlike people of Mesopotamia carried with them on their travels and trading missions. It was largely passed on through the oral tradition and there are many different variations on the theme, but the core epic, based on a real-life benevolent king of Uruk who reigned around 2500 B.C., concerns a god-man who attempts to overcome death.

In the earliest surviving Sumerian version of the epic, dating back to 2100 B.C., there is the poem "Gilgamesh and Huwawa." Gilgamesh goes with his companion Enkidu to the cedar forest, which is guarded by Huwawa. This monster cuts a terrifying, devilish figure: "His roaring is the flood-storm, his mouth is fire, his breath is death." Quite what Gilgamesh's motives are in going on this trip remain open to debate. In some versions, it is a simple case of collecting the timber that his people need. Mesopotamia was an intensely farmed and treeless region and its misfortune in being short of wood was put down to evil spirits. In later versions, Gilgamesh is seeking to free his land from the more general malaise of villainy and evil, which are, significantly, laid firmly at the door of Huwawa. As the story was passed on from generation to generation, the struggle between the two took on a broader cosmic significance and the character of Huwawa became more and more demonic, mirroring the later transformation of the menacing but manageable Satan of the Old Testament into the all-pervading "Evil One" of later literature.

> *In the forest resides fierce Huwawa*
> *Let us, me and thee, slay him,*
> *That all evil from the land we may banish.*[7]

When they arrive in the cedar forest, depicted as a dark, lawless, intimidating place, Gilgamesh and his companions start felling trees. Huwawa defends his domain, attacks them, and puts Gilgamesh into a deep sleep. Some time later Gilgamesh comes back to life, seeks out, and slays Huwawa, thereby freeing his people from evil. The parallels are obvious between such a sequence of events in this first recorded story and the classic combat narrative of good versus evil, with evil getting the upper hand initially but good ultimately triumphing. However, in this instance Gilgamesh then goes to visit Enlil, lord of heaven and king of the gods, and presents him with Huwawa's head on a platter. Enlil is less than overwhelmed with gratitude—the Mesopotamian deity, like the Egyptian, had both good and bad faces. Huwawa was a servant of the darker nature of Enlil. To punish Gilgamesh, Enlil unleashes a terror over the land.

Demonology, and indeed the whole notion of a cosmic battle between good and evil, was well developed in Mesopotamia. The people, much more pessimistic and superstitious than the Egyptians, believed they lived on the battleground between the gods and the demons. The demons tended to be secondary to the gods, able to cause trouble, pain, and suffering, but ultimately unable to take on and defeat them—but this did not stop them from trying. The Mesopotamians were great believers in amulets and charms to protect themselves against these grotesque, beastly demons.[8] "No other ancient society," writes Professor John Roberts, "left men feeling so utterly dependent on the will of the gods. Lower Mesopotamia in ancient times was a flat, monotonous landscape of mudflats, marsh, and water. There were no mountains for the gods to dwell in like men, only the empty heavens above, the remorseless summer sun, the over-turning winds against which they had no protection, the irre-sistible power of floodwater, the blighting attacks of drought."[9]

Canaan

Like other peoples of the Near East, the Canaanites—or Phoeni-cians, as the Greeks called them—fashioned gods and demons to help them to understand the challenges and blessings thrown up by their environment. Many of the Canaanites were fishermen and traders. Rather than depending on a river like the Egyptians and Mesopotamians, they were at the mercy of the sea.

The Bible has a very specific strip of land in mind when it talks of Canaan, but the Canaanites spread out along and inland from the coastal strip that is today Lebanon, Syria, and Israel. From around the third millennium onward, this seafaring people developed their sphere of influence. While their achievements pale into insignificance with those of Mesopotamia and Egypt—and indeed Greece—the Canaanites had a highly developed reli-gious tradition whose influences can be seen in the Old Testament and most clearly in the Book of Job where Satan makes his fascinating debut.

The archaeological discovery in 1928–1929 of the ancient city of Ugarit on the Syrian coast revealed details of the religious beliefs of the Canaanites and evidence of the extent of their contact with the Egyptians and the Mesopotamians. Among the finds that have been dated around 1400 B.C. are a series of epic poems, chronicling the primary Canaanite fertility myths. The key characters are the storm god, Baal, and his sister—or perhaps wife—Anath. Baal was the son of the high god of the Canaanites, El, ruler of sky and sun, often depicted as a bull.

Baal and Anath were both symbols of fertility—a central pre-occupation in Canaan as in Egypt and Mesopotamia. Their great enemy was Mot, lord of death and sterility. (The Bible presents Baal as evil, but that may just have been Jewish prejudice against what they regarded as the false and therefore wicked gods of Canaan. Certainly for those who worshiped him, Baal was a savior.) Just as Huwawa initially triumphs over Gilgamesh, Mot defeats Baal and swallows him, ushering in an era when the crops die in the fields. After seven years Anath has her revenge on Mot, killing him and grinding his body into seed to make the fields blossom once more.

> *She seized El's son, Mot,*
> *With a sword she sliced him;*
> *With a sieve she winnowed him;*
> *With a fire she burnt him;*
> *With millstones she ground him;*
> *In the field she scattered him.*[10]

Anath's victory liberates Baal, who comes back from the dead and inspires a new age of plenty. Thereafter he and Mot continue their fight, locked in eternal battle.

In the Canaanite myth, as in those of Egypt and Mesopotamia, while opposites are important, the idea of dualism is missing. The struggle between Baal and Mot is tempered by an ongoing battle between Baal and Anath. Though they are brother and sister (or husband and wife), Anath too can be destructive. And there are other characters who take on something approximating to the role of the evil one. Yam, the Canaanites' god of the sea, represents the chaotic, disintegrating power of water, and is described at one stage of the myth as El's son but bitter enemy of Baal.[11]

Greece

The Greek pantheon is enormously complex and amorphous, a mixture of outside influences from other Near Eastern civilizations with the myths and legends that belonged to the various groups who lived around the Aegean Sea. Brought together by their common language, the Dorians, Ionians, Aeolians, and other Hellenic peoples who history groups together as the Greeks, held sometimes self-contradictory views on cosmic powers and their own fate after death.

At a popular level there existed superstitions and rituals redolent of those described already in Mesopotamia and Egypt. But what distinguished Greece was that its writers and thinkers attempted, with the birth of schools of philosophy in the fourth century B.C., to rationalize human existence and death. Rather than throw themselves on the mercy of ill-defined gods and demons, these philosophers subjected ancient beliefs to logic and reason. The Greeks invented the philosophical question and were no longer content to believe that the gods moved in mysterious ways, one minute sending floods and earthquakes, the next rains and fertile soil. They began the search for a coherent explanation to the world that did not rest upon arbitrary whims and ritualistic sacrifices but that placed the emphasis on human acts and a divinely ordained plan of right and wrong. Though the admiring gaze of hindsight now rests on these thinkers, they worked in a society where the majority had great faith in oracles and omens. While the elite of philosophers strove to empty the folklorish treasury and replenish it with science, morals, and reason, state governments were busy consulting the oracle at Delphi on matters of high politics and lavishing it with gifts in return.

One characteristic in particular distinguished the gods of

Greece from the monsters of Mesopotamia and the tyrants of Egypt—they were made in the human mold and subject to human passions. In Homer's *Odyssey* during the Trojan War the gods take sides in a manner that is all too human. They compete shamelessly and Homer, the philosophic poet Xenophanes was later to complain, attributed to the gods everything that was unpleasant in humankind—theft, adultery, deceit. However, Homer's attempt to give a recognizable form to religious beliefs cannot be taken as a blueprint for the faith of society at large. He made little distinction between gods and demons.[12] All had ambiguous characters, a heavenly side as well as traits that belonged in the underworld. Hades, ruler of the underworld, and held responsible for the death of crops in the field, was linked to Pluto, the god of wealth or abundance of harvests. Zeus, the most revered of the gods as the ruler of the skies, the source of light and fertility, was also held responsible for the destruction wrought by storms and his trademark thunderbolt. Ultimately all the gods were manifestations of the One God. The Greeks had no one who even aspired to the role later taken by the Christian Devil—when the Greeks spoke of *daimons* (usually translated as "demons") they were in fact referring to something more ambiguous, akin to spirits, potentially either good or bad.

In fashioning their image of Satan, however, subsequent generations of Christian thinkers, writers, and artists owe a great debt to the Greeks. Some of Lucifer's best-known characteristics are to be glimpsed in the players in the Greek celestial drama. Hermes, for example, was both the messenger of the heavenly court and the god of thieves who led the dead into the underworld. His traditional depiction, with winged sandals, is believed to have influenced medieval artists. Hermes' son, Pan, was the god of sexual desire, a force seen by the Greeks as both creative and destructive. When the Christians, strongly influenced by Augustine in the fifth century, started to condemn anything to do with sex as bad and devilish, they turned to Pan for iconographic inspiration. His horned, hairy, goatlike figure was the model for many a painting of the lusty, bestial Devil.

The Greeks were constantly changing, reassessing, and developing their religious beliefs. Although in the eighth century B.C. Homer saw the underworld as a grove of willow and poplar trees, where no distinction was made between the righteous and the wicked, later writers began to look for some form of divine judgment in death as a way of justifying the fluctuations of fate in this world. Slowly the underworld came to be more and more associated with the character of Hades and took on the features of the pit of suffering and gnashing of teeth, fires forever ablaze, with which later generations of Christians became all too familiar.

Plato (c. 428–c. 348 B.C.)—who in fact made little impact on the majority of his fellow Greeks in his own lifetime—ends his *Republic* with a section on the myth of Er. It tells of a man who comes back from the dead to inform his fellow men of what awaits them after death. "When his soul left his body, he went on a journey with a great company . . . they came to a mysterious place at which there were two openings in the earth; they were near together, and over against them were two other openings in the heaven above. In the intermediate space there were judges seated, who commanded the just, after they had given judgement on them . . . to ascend by the heavenly way on the right hand: and in like manner the unjust were bidden by them to descend by the lower way on the left hand." The final destination of the unjust was a terrible and terrifying place to behold.

Plato's allusion to heaven and hell was part of a broader philosophical search for the meaning of good and evil. Homer had made little attempt to separate the two, but spoke vaguely of a greater cosmic force that assigns to nature and to each his or her destiny, something akin to fate. Homer's contemporary Hesiod (c. 700 B.C.) held that the gods punished you for unholy acts like murder by an inexorable law of Cosmos whose judgments were carried out by the Furies, mythological maidens with serpents twined in their hair. Where Homer had no vision of eternal punishment, Hesiod wrote that divine judgment turned your life into hell. It was not until the time of Plato, however, that the dilemma posed by the existence of evil received its fullest consideration. Plato was influenced by the mystical cult of Orphism. The Orphics based their beliefs on a classic combat myth, in the mold of Gilgamesh and Huwawa, which had Zeus and his son Dionysus engaged in a battle with the Titans, a group dedicated to destroying the gods. Good clashed with evil, but more significantly the Titans were taken to represent man's baser materialist urges, the earthly part of his existence, his bodily needs, while Dionysus represents spirit. The world of the spirit was the domain of the One God.

However, the body, weak and subject to ungodly passions and impulses, could deflect man away from the good and toward evil. Plato defined evil in a variety of ways. One argument he mooted was that evil had no real being at all, but was rather a lack of perfection. He was troubled, however, by the weakness of his theory when confronted with wars, murders, and human violence. How could something so tangible and unjust simply be written off as an absence of good? Plato tried to square the circle by acknowledging such acts as evil, but by absolving the One God of any responsibility. "For the good we must assume no other cause than God, but for the cause of evil we must look for in other things and not in God," he wrote in his *Republic*. It was an idea that, when developed by Plato's followers, was to inspire biblical accounts of the fall of angels from heaven and the birth of the Christian Devil before the world began.

Persia

It was the prophet Zoroaster—literally "golden splendor"—who broke the tradition of numerous nature gods and demons in Mesopotamia and who produced the first character, akin in his powers and aims to the Christian Devil.

Details of the life of Zoroaster are few and far between, but he is believed to have lived between the later half of the seventh century B.C. and the middle of the sixth century in Bactria, the

area known today as Iran. He abandoned the ancient Mesopotamian tradition of two-faced gods, sometimes good and
sometimes bad, exerting their power over their followers
through forces of nature, and taught his disciples instead that
there were two opposite and equivalent forces, the one positive
and the other negative. By relegating existing gods to minor
roles, Zoroaster elevated Ahura Mazda, the god of light, above
all others. Set against Ahura Mazda, who sought to bring law
and order to nature, was the fiendish Angro Mainyush or
Ahriman, the force for war in nature. All good was due to Ahura
Mazda and all evil to Ahriman. Zoroaster was the first recorded
dualist, believing that the world could be divided down the
middle into black and white, with no one omnipotent power in
control.

Many of those who claimed to follow his teachings in later
generations sought to temper such a polarized viewpoint by
reintroducing other gods and trying to bring Ahriman under the
control of Ahura Mazda. They claimed that they were following
the prophet, but since three quarters of the *Avetsa*, the bible of
Zoroastrianism is missing, it is hard to judge who is telling the
truth. However, the *Gathas*—or hymns—that were reputedly
written by Zoroaster, make abundantly clear the general principle of opposites. "Now at the beginning, the twin spirits have
declared their nature, the better and the evil. . . . Of these two
spirits, the evil one chose to do the worst things; But the Most
Holy Spirit, clothed in the most steadfast heavens, joined himself
unto righteousness."[13]

Some of Zoroaster's disciples later talked of this Holy Spirit—
the Spenta Mainyu—as one of two conflicting spirits with the
Ahriman, or evil one. In this system, Ahura Mazda was an overall
power who begat twin spirits of good and evil and then left them
to battle for the soul of humankind. He was then the court of
ultimate appeal, giving them freedom of action but preventing a
final victory for evil. This notion of the supreme god retaining a
final veto over the power of the Devil is present in Christian
teaching.

It is difficult not to spot in the figure of Ahriman a prototype of the Christian Devil. Described as the Evil One, a cosmic force to rival that of the good god, he was likened by Zoroaster to a serpent. As the Devil is held responsible for the seven deadly sins in Christianity, Ahriman was served by seven archfiends—wrong-mindedness, heresy, anarchy, discord, presumption, hunger, and thirst. He inhabited a hell-like void and Zoroastrianism taught that on death the soul passes over a *cinvato peretush* or "accountant's bridge" where those who had sinned could be pulled down into the void for eternal punishment by Ahriman. Those who fall for his wiles are described by Zoroaster as "people of the lie," a phrase later much favored by Christian writers and echoed in John's gospel (8:44). Indeed the whole notion of a bridge has echoes in the Christian concept of a ladder to heaven. There are other parallels between Zoroaster's teachings and those of Christianity. Both warn that a great world crisis is at hand and anticipate a day of judgment. Zoroastrianism talks of a savior, created by Zoroaster's seed, who will come to redeem the world. The interchange of ideas between Zoroastrianism and Judaism—and hence Christianity—has been well established historically, geographically, and culturally.[14] Although a minority cult, Zoroastrianism influenced a diverse range of groups—most notably the various Gnostic groups who undermined mainstream Christianity with their dualistic views of the world.

TWO

A Jewish Childhood

> The Devil's deepest wile is to persuade us that
> he does not exist.
>
> —Charles Baudelaire

There is scarcely a mention of the Devil in the Old Testament. The figure who plays such a leading role in the New Testament is conspicuous only by his earlier absence. However, scattered throughout the Old Testament is a cast of characters who individually and together contain the seeds of the future Prince of Darkness, though they never truly aspire to his role as the apotheosis of evil.

The Jewishness of Christianity makes the Hebrew Scriptures, as the Old Testament is often known, the nursery for the Devil. Without Judaism, many of the notions Christians today take for granted would never have evolved, while in purely practical terms, without the seedbed and protective cover of Judaism, the tiny band of followers of a short-lived messiah from Nazareth could not have managed to found one of the world's great religions. The books of the Old Testament were composed between roughly 900 and 100 B.C., though the texts as we know them today mostly date from the period after the exile of Jews to Babylon from 586 to 538. Carted away from the Promised Land

with their spiritual home, the Temple, destroyed by their conquerors, the Israelites fell back for sustenance and moral courage
on weekly readings of the Scriptures. By the end of the exile, or
soon afterward, the first five books of the Old Testament,
the Pentateuch, had taken on the form we know today though
they detailed events from over 500 years earlier. Though
Mesopotamia boasts some of the earliest written texts, the Jews
were truly the first people of a Book, with the Christians and
Moslems following in their wake.

Such a written source, handed on and interpreted by generation after generation, made possible a greater abstraction and
universalizing of the vision of God and of His creation. Equally,
by giving a variety of authors the chance to expound their
particular viewpoint it introduced a greater degree of debate and
pluralism. When looking at the development of the concept of
the Devil in the Old—and the New—Testament, there is no
point looking for one right answer. The Bible is a collection of
writings by people who use history not simply to report events,
but to put over a particular slant. Without some knowledge of
the background and of the politics of the time, a straight reading
of the Bible is akin to a Martian reading a biography of George
Bush by Bill Clinton without knowing any of the context and
believing it to be gospel.

Contemporary biblical scholars agree that, except for the
oldest fragments in the writings of the prophets, no text in the
Hebrew Scriptures was composed at the same time as the hap-
penings it chronicles. Furthermore, nothing was set in stone.
The Old Testament was shaped and reshaped in the light of the
shifting patterns of Jewish belief and ritual and of the geo-
political fortunes of the Israelites. Any attempt then to discern an
evolution in ideas through the books of the Old Testament is at
best only half of the picture. The Book of Job, for instance, central to the development of the Devil, comes in the chronology of
the Old Testament before the exile, yet it was, scholars now
believe, written after the event and was subsequently added to
and amended.

The exile was a crucial experience in the molding of Jewish identity. It challenged the Israelites to rethink what they had previously taken for granted—their status as God's chosen people. How could Yahweh have allowed them to be enslaved and humiliated? Had he abandoned them? Or had some other force intervened to direct them away from the path of righteousness? Human sinfulness did not seem an adequate explanation for so great a suffering. The arbitrary nature of Yahweh's anger was disorientating and demoralizing and led not only to a return to the scriptures but to a parallel surge of interest in superstition, folklore, and myth. This extant oral tradition offered one way forward in the darkness of abandonment and confusion. As we have already seen in ancient Greece and will later witness in the Europe of the later middle ages, "official" religion is rarely exclusive in practice, with witchcraft, astrology, ghosts, and fairies existing alongside the doctrines of seemingly all-powerful churches.

Among the Israelites of the immediate pre-Christian times, this expressed itself in the cult of the fallen angels. Developed in books and writings now largely outside the canon of the Hebrew Scriptures and known collectively as the Apocrypha, this parallel movement of popular superstition contained a fledgling dualism. National and individual misfortune were blamed on forces created by the omnipotent and almighty Yahweh, which had somehow escaped his power and sown the seeds of evil in humankind. The cult offered an explanation, a means of redress in times of adversity.

More promising then than depending on chronology is to examine how the Hebrew Scriptures as a whole deal with those same issues of right and wrong, good and evil, death and redemption that preoccupied the neighbors and contemporaries of the Jews and that later gave rise to the Christian Devil. The Apocrypha must be included in any such investigation. Whatever their subsequent provenance and reputation, these holy books had great influence in their time and played their part in shaping the adult Christian Devil of the New Testament.

Yahweh for Better or Worse

The prevailing impression left by the Old Testament is that Yahweh, like the One God of the Egyptians, was responsible for everything on earth, holding it in balance through the law that he had handed down to Moses. "I am Yahweh, unrivalled," boasts Isaiah (45:7). "I form the light and create the dark, I make good fortune and create calamity."[1] On the surface Yahweh leaves no room for anything approximating a personification of evil.

The Book of Joshua, which chronicles the conquest of the Promised Land by Moses' successors, resounds with the Israelites' conviction that Yahweh is the source of everything, no matter how ugly or, to later generations, morally repugnant. Yahweh is the inspiration behind the savagery shown by the Israelites' toward their opponents. When Joshua and his men massacre the citizens of Jericho and of Ai, put the King of Hazor to the sword, and raze the towns of Canaan, they do so in the name of Yahweh. "All these kings and their kingdoms Joshua mastered in one campaign, because Yahweh the God of Israel fought for Israel." (Josh. 10:42–43). In the Book of Numbers, Yahweh is even seen as endorsing rape. "Exact full vengeance for the sons of Israel on the Midianites," he tells Moses (31:1), so Moses and the priests instruct their men, in the name of Yahweh, to "kill . . . all the women who have slept with a man. Spare the lives only of the young girls who have not slept with a man and take them for yourselves" (31:18–19).

This side of Yahweh is a disturbing one to those nurtured on the loving God of the New Testament. Becalmed briefly in Yugoslavia during the Second World War, the Catholic novelist Evelyn Waugh and Lord Birkenhead bet a restless Randolph Churchill ten pounds that he couldn't read the Bible all the way through. Waugh recalls that Churchill did not take to the task, "as quietly as we had hoped." Indeed, he had got no further than the Book of Genesis before he was heard exclaiming with a look of puzzled excitement: "God, isn't God a shit!"[2]

If the Israelites suffered military setbacks, it was because they had violated their covenant with Yahweh. And his wrath with his own people was if anything worse than with their enemies. When Achan holds back some of the booty captured in the Canaan campaign, Joshua, at the instigation of Yahweh, takes him to the Vale of Achor and asks him: "Why did you bring evil on us? May Yahweh bring evil on you today." The Israelites promptly stone Achan to death. "Then Yahweh created his burning anger" (Josh. 7:24–26).

Yahweh is also seen as responsible for the plagues and disasters that were ascribed by the Mesopotamians to their vengeful nature gods. When the Philistines seized the Ark of the Covenant, the sign of Yahweh's special relationship with the Israelites, they carried it off to the city of Gath with disastrous consequences as the First Book of Samuel relates. "After they had taken it there, the hand of Yahweh lay heavy on that town and a great panic broke out; the people of the town from the youngest to oldest, were struck with tumours that he brought out on them" (1 Sam. 5:9–10). It is not only the enemies of the Israelites who are afflicted. Yahweh sent the flood that only Noah and the motley crew of his ark survived because of "the wickedness of man" (Gen. 6:5–6). Likewise it is Yahweh who destroys Sodom and Gomorrah in a hail of brimstone and fire (Gen. 19). The most basic contrast between the Old and New Testaments is that in the first, God is often cruel and willful, while in the second, his all-loving and all-forgiving nature is much more to the fore—albeit with occasional bouts of weeping and gnashing of teeth. At the root of this dichotomy is the fact that for much of the Old Testament Yahweh represents both good and evil while in the New, much of his malign function has been hived off to the Devil.

The Old Testament view in its stories of destruction is not, however, of Yahweh as the absolutely unpredictable force of other creeds. The Egyptians would offer sacrifices in the hope that their gods would protect them from natural disaster, but when such calamities arrived they had no comprehension as to what they had done wrong. For the Israelites, the Hebrew Scriptures make clear, the source of Yahweh's anger is plain. It is unleashed by the sinfulness of humanity, by the Israelites' failure to respect their Covenant with him. Far from ascribing evil in the world to any sort of devil or demon, the Hebrew Scriptures in general place the burden of responsibility on humankind and its faithlessness.

Much of the early part of the Old Testament in particular is concerned with strict adherence to the law and observance of ritual. Obedience was an obligation that went with the Covenant, a response to the love shown by Yahweh. And on a practical level, keeping the law had the advantage of keeping Yahweh good and benign. It was only when the Israelites ignored the Law, as handed down to Moses, that Yahweh showed his darker, more ruthless side. In that sense there are parallels with the ideas of *ma'at* found in Egypt, expressed poetically in the Book of Isaiah (11:6–9).

> *The wolf lives with the lamb,*
> *the panther lies down with the kid,*
> *calf and lion cub feed together*
> *with a little boy to lead them.*
> *The cow and the bear make friends,*
> *their young lie down together.*
> *The lion eats straw with the ox.*
> *The infant plays over the cobra's hole;*
> *into the viper's lair*
> *the young child puts his hand.*
> *They do no hurt, no harm,*
> *on all my holy mountain,*
> *for the country is filled with the knowledge of Yahweh*
> *as the waters swell the sea.*

When the earth is in harmony, Yahweh's dark shadow does not fall across humankind, only his benign munificence. But when his command was thwarted, his vengeance could be terrible.

Occasionally Yahweh's blacker side is given physical expression. In the Book of Genesis (32:23–32), Jacob struggles with an angry stranger at the ford at Jabbok, suffering a dislocated hip in the process. Though this is sometimes presented as Jacob battling with an angel—as, for example in Eugène Delacroix's (1798–1863) large wall paintings in the Chapel of the Holy Angels in the Church of Saint-Sulpice in Paris—it is clear that the encounter was in some sense with Yahweh, as Jacob confirms in naming the place Peniel, "because I have seen God face-to-face." In Exodus (4:24–26), Moses has a chilling encounter. "On the journey, when Moses had halted for the night, Yahweh came to meet him and tried to kill him. At once Zipporah, taking up a flint, cut off her son's foreskin and with it she touched the genitals of Moses. "Truly you are a bridegroom of blood to me," she said. And Yahweh let him live." Such embodiments of Yahweh's malignant nature, however, are rare outside the opening books of the Old Testament which tell of the Israelites' struggle to establish themselves in the Promised Land. These events are thought to have taken place around 1200 B.C., when Yahweh was the tribal god of a warlike people, giving divine respectability to their territorial ambitions.

Once the Israelites had conquered those who stood in their way, they settled and began to organize their community along less military lines. Peace gave them the opportunity to ask questions about social organization and morality and to refine their tribal god into someone more rounded. In particular, the Old Testament books of the prophets, tentatively dated by scholars between the mid-eighth century and the Babylonian exile (save for those fragments mentioned earlier), show a great concentration on questions of right and wrong, good and evil.

In such a climate the dichotomy between an omnipotent and

loving God and his occasional cruelty became harder to live with. Blaming his terrifying show of anger on human weakness seemed inadequate faced with the scale of the punishment. In response to these fundamental questions—issues indeed that have confronted each and every believer who worships a single god—the Israelites attempted to reconcile their Yahweh with the existence of evil in the world by creating a twin. The Egyptians had paired Seth with Horus. The Israelites tried to find a way to distinguish between the good side of Yahweh's nature and his capacity to do harm. In the process they fashioned a series of messengers and servants at the heavenly court who were the infant Devil. While the Israelites' beliefs remained monist in name and in theory, in practice they took the first steps down the road to a *de facto* dualism that was to become increasingly prevalent in the postexilic period.

The Evil Twin

The early books of the Hebrew Scriptures make passing references to evil spirits and demons, hinting that vestiges of polytheism and earlier superstitions may have lingered on before they were expunged by the later Judaic belief in an omnipotent Yahweh. For instance in Leviticus, the third book of the Old Testament, Yahweh instructs Aaron to take goats and draw lots for them. He is to "allot one to Yahweh and the other to Azazel." Aaron is to "offer up the goat whose lot was marked 'For Yahweh' and offer it as a sacrifice for sin. The goat whose lot was marked 'For Azazel' shall be set before Yahweh, still alive, to perform the rite of atonement over it, sending it out into the desert to Azazel" (Lev. 16:8–10).

This legacy of spirits and demons may have contributed to the development of the belief that Yahweh's less acceptable deeds could be ascribed to messengers or what might be called angels. The messenger—*malak Yahweh* in the Hebrew text—starts out by being neutral, a kind of herald or, more practically

Yahweh himself in a form visible to man. Thus when Hagar, the maidservant to Abraham's elderly and barren wife, Sarah, discovers that she is pregnant by her mistress's husband, it is "the angel of Yahweh" who comes to comfort her and assure her that this first-recorded case of surrogate motherhood has divine approval (Gen. 16:7–12). In the Book of Exodus an angel appears to Moses as a flame of fire in the middle of a bush (3:2), prefacing the arrival of Yahweh himself (3:4). The angel or messenger later develops a less ceremonial function. When King Saul, in the First Book of Samuel, is frightened by the battle ahead, his dilemma is put down to the spirit of Yahweh having left him and an "evil spirit from Yahweh" taking its place (16:14–15). In order to exorcise that evil spirit—though the Old Testament does not use such an emotive word—Saul calls upon David, later memorably to vanquish the mighty Goliath, who drives out the spirit by playing his harp. When Yahweh kills the firstborn of Egypt on the night of the first Passover, it is "the destroyer," his messenger, who enters the homes of those who would keep Moses and his people in drudgery and slays their children (Exod. 12:23).

Occasionally the messenger could show flashes of independence. In the Second Book of Samuel, Yahweh is angry with his people (24:16). "It was the time of the wheat harvest. Yahweh sent a pestilence on Israel from morning till the time appointed and plague ravaged the people, and from Dan to Beersheba seventy thousand men of them died. The angel stretched out his hand towards Jerusalem to destroy it, but Yahweh thought better of this evil and he said to the angel who was destroying the people 'Enough. Now withdraw your hand.' " It was a significant moment in the history of the Israelites—the Temple of Jerusalem was erected where the angel stopped his destruction. There is little room for doubt that *malak Yahweh* was a manifestation of Yahweh himself, not something separate. The angel's overstepping of the mark was a device to give Yahweh the chance to repent and show the forgiving side of his nature.

The idea of Yahweh having a messenger to do his dirty work

could only insulate the good God so far. More significant is the suggestion, which first surfaces in the earlier sections of the Old Testament, that there is a heavenly court—*bene ha-elohim*—of other godlike figures who sit with Yahweh in the Israelites' version of Zeus' pantheon. Chapter six of Genesis begins with the story of how these "sons of God" came to earth and married "daughters of men." The concept recurs throughout the Old Testament. Psalm 82, dated by some between the third and second century B.C., starts with the lines "God stands in the divine assembly among the gods he dispenses justice" and ends, "You too are gods, sons of the Most High, all of you but all the same you shall die like other men; as one man, princes, you shall fall." This suggestion, prefacing the Devil's descent from heaven to hell, was to be taken up in the Apocrypha. But in the Hebrew Scriptures, the most explicit development of the idea of a heavenly court comes in the Book of Job.

Job's Comforter

In espousing the idea of a heavenly court in the prologue to the Book of Job, its writer was taking another step along the path of insulating the theoretically omnipotent Yahweh from the messy business of evil. While the text is impeccably monist in tone, the debut in Job of Satan as a character hints at a new focus for the torment and temptation of humankind.

The Hebrew word *stn*—literally, opponent or someone who obstructs—does appear elsewhere in the Old Testament where it is translated into English in a number of different ways. In 1 Kings 11:14 it comes out as enemy—"Yahweh raised an enemy against Solomon." More significantly in the tale of Balaam's donkey in the Book of Numbers (22:22), the *stn* is the angel of Yahweh. "His [Balaam's] going kindled the wrath of Yahweh and the angel of Yahweh took his stand on the road to bar the way." The angel, clutching a sword, is bent on punishing the faithless Balaam, but the donkey spots the danger ahead and ducks and dives to avoid it. Balaam, by contrast, sees nothing and beats his mount because he cannot understand its erratic behavior. It is only when the angel, the *stn*, reveals himself to Balaam that the rider appreciates the donkey's tenacity. Balaam is moved to repent before the messenger of his angry God and is saved.

The Satan of the Book of Job is, however, the first bearer of that name to merit a capital letter. His role, sitting in the heavenly court, is to play what we might today call Devil's Advocate, though his powers are a shadow of those enjoyed by the Devil of the New Testament. Satan is absolutely loyal to Yahweh, but has taken upon himself the role of chief antagonist to humankind. Described in the prologue as having been "round the earth, roaming about" in the manner of *malak Yahweh*, he now contents himself from his privileged position within the pantheon with tormenting Job to see if he will stay true to his God. In the prologue to the Book of Job, Satan argues with Yahweh that humanity is only good because it has received a reward to make it so. Take away that reward, add a little suffering, and you will find that the basic motivation is a good deal less virtuous. Satan predicts that Job, Yahweh's good and faithful servant, "will curse you to your face" if he goes unrewarded. Yahweh begs to differ with his lieutenant and the long dialogue poem illustrates and illuminates this debate. It is the first time in the Old Testament that the fundamental issue of suffering and why a good God allows it is addressed. As a literary approach to a question that has puzzled God-fearing humanity down the ages, Job is without rival.[3] In it are encapsulated all the dilemmas that have afflicted humankind down the ages, all the questions that theologians and philosophers have debated. Why is there pain and suffering; why do the wicked prosper and the good lose out?

The book is in fact a drama in three parts, with the torment and doubts of Job—"a sound and honest man who feared God and shunned evil"—sandwiched between an explanatory prologue and valedictory epilogue, both of which scholars believe were added to the main body of the text after the exile. By the introduction of Satan in the prologue, the dilemma of the eponymous central character is transformed into a discussion in the heavenly court between Yahweh and Satan. By giving Satan such a role, the sufferings of Job were given an extra dimension as an allegory for those of Israel during the exile and heaped, not at Yahweh's door, but at that of his mischievous servant.

A series of terrible misfortunes befalls Job in the prologue. His cattle are stolen, his servants put to the sword, fire destroys his sheep, and a freak storm wrecks his house and crushes his children. But, contrary to Satan's expectations, Job refuses to turn his back on Yahweh.

> *Naked I came from my mother's womb*
> *naked shall I return.*
> *Yahweh gave, Yahweh has taken back.*
> *Blessed be the Name of Yahweh.*
>
> (1:21–22)

Satan, however, will not hold his peace and goads Yahweh into giving him free rein to test his thesis that there is no such thing as a wholly good man. "He is in your power," Yahweh reluctantly concedes Job to Satan. "But spare his life."

The main section of the book is then set on earth, with Job's sufferings picked over in a series of speeches by him and four friends—Eliphaz, Bildad, Zophar, and Elihu. There are moments when Job, acting as a spokesman for humankind, despairs at a Yahweh who can bring such darkness and destruction into his life that previously had been so blessed.

> *Your own hands shaped me, modelled me;*
> *and would you now have second thoughts and destroy me?*
> *You modelled me, remember; as clay is modelled,*
> *and would you reduce me now to dust?*
>
> (10:8–9)

Job never gives way, though in his trials and tribulations he finds it increasingly difficult to understand that the God who loves him can also be the one who is punishing him. Job represents humanity searching for an answer to suffering and evil in the face of their own daily tribulations. Job protests his innocence repeatedly in the face of his friends. Their reliance is on the conventional wisdom of the Old Testament, namely, that Yahweh has two faces and that his harsher actions are the result of humankind's sinfulness. They even recall, in the course of the debate over good and evil, some of the pre-biblical combat myths. For instance, Bildad praises the muscular God:

> *With his power he calmed the Sea*
> *with his wisdom struck Rahab down.*
> *His breath made the heavens luminous*
> *his hand transfixed the Fleeing Serpent.*
>
> (26:12–14)

Rahab is another name for the fierce dragon, Leviathan, of the Canaanite myth, and the fleeing serpent is the servant of Mot, lord of death and sterility. The language of these passages—full of water imagery, monsters, and dragons, awesome power, a God who shapes and orchestrates the physical universe around him—recalls the combat narratives of Gilgamesh and Huwawa and of Baal and Mot.

By voicing but not giving in to his doubts about the role of an omnipotent God in a world of pain and suffering, Job becomes, in the hands of the author of the book, a voice of protest at that prevailing theology, one who can find no comfort in the time-honored notions trotted out by his companions. Eliphaz, for example, holds forth:

> *Happy indeed the man whom God corrects!*
> *Then do not refuse this lesson from Shaddai [God]*
> *For he who wounds is he who soothes the sore*
> *and the hand that hurts is the hand that heals.*
>
> (5:17–18)

Elihu, another of the friends, uses language that hints more at the notion of a hell—*sheol*—literally, an unpleasant place for departed spirits. Yahweh guides his people away from what sounds like eternal damnation.

> *Then it is he whispers in the ear of man*
> *or may frighten him with fearful sights*
> *to turn him away from evil-doing,*
> *and make an end of his pride;*
> *to save his soul from the pit*
> *and his life from the pathway of Sheol.*
>   (33:16–18)

The possibility of hell and judgment at death is first described explicitly in the Old Testament in the Book of Daniel—composed around 165 B.C. and one of its youngest texts. There the prophet sees a vision of a day of judgment, a time when "those who lie sleeping in the dust of the earth . . . will awake, some to everlasting life, some to shame and everlasting disgrace." However, in Job, Elihu's reference to *sheol* is not taken up, though there is a heartfelt appeal for some, as yet undefined, distinction in death between the righteous and the wicked. Why should the innocent suffer, Job asks, when those who flout Yahweh's laws prosper on earth? Again the influence of the exile can be glimpsed.

There is no one message from the Book of Job. The fact that its central text has been added to at the start and finish has led some to argue that it is dangerous to include it in the Old Testament canon at all. Job at least is unarguably restored to favor by the end of the book. The epilogue leaves him with double what he had before as a reward from Yahweh for keeping the faith. Satan, after his appearance in the prologue, is silenced and his thesis gains little credence. After all the debate, the prevailing view that God is all powerful, that evil is from him and somehow part of his plan remains, despite Job's efforts to highlight the shortcomings of such an approach. The Book of Job is in that way a lament at the weakness of the system, without proposing a new way forward.

Though the Book of Job introduces Satan, it does nothing to give him any sort of status as Yahweh's evil side. However, the growing interest in the figure of Satan in the immediate post-exilic period is confirmed by his appearance in the Book of Zechariah. Once again Satan is the adversary of humankind, not of God as in the New Testament. It features the heavenly court, with Satan among its figures. But where, in Job, Satan is described as having been roaming the world, in the manner of *malak Yahweh*, in Zechariah, the angel messenger is a different character who rebukes Satan.

In the vision of Zechariah, "He [Yahweh] showed me Joshua, the high priest, standing before the angel of Yahweh, with Satan standing on his right to accuse him. The angel of Yahweh said to Satan, 'May Yahweh rebuke you, Satan, may Yahweh rebuke you, he who made Jerusalem his very own.' " The implication is that Satan has gone too far in seeking out unjust men. The sense of Satan chomping at the bit, trying to break loose, is tangible, but it is not followed through in the Old Testament. That was to come in a series of extraordinary books that developed out of the Hebrew Scriptures, the product of the national sense of angst that afflicted the Israelites after the exile. They have, however, been excluded by tradition from the canon.

The Fall of Angels

Satan cut his teeth in the outpouring of writing that accompanied the Israelites' soul-searching in the postexilic period. His story—taken up in the New Testament—is that of the fallen angel, cast out of heaven, who sets himself up as a rival to

Yahweh. It is a story that has become part and parcel of the Devil's curriculum vitae in every subsequent age, and which has inspired artists—most notably the Flemish painter Rubens (1577–1640), whose "Fall of Rebel Angels," a heaving mass of flesh and contorted limbs, hangs in the Alte Pinakothek in Munich.[4]

Scribes and prophets tried to provide an explanation for the fate that had befallen the Jewish people in Babylon and since. In the years after the return from exile, Jewish thought and social behavior came under the influence of Greece, with the upper classes in particular Hellenized in their attitudes and looking down on the masses. This widening social gulf led to the great Maccabean revolt of 168–164 B.C., which was only suppressed with great bloodshed. The Israelites remained divided and troubled and though they achieved independence in 142 B.C., they fell under Roman hegemony in 63 B.C., heralding an almost 2,000-year wait for the re-emergence of the Jewish state.

In this climate of political turmoil, fear, and division, apocryphal—from the Greek word for "hidden"—literature flourished. Yahweh's covenant with the Jews and its origins came under detailed scrutiny. The result was the fashioning of what was in effect a Jewish creation epic to rival the Canaanite saga of Mot and Baal. The writers drew heavily on mythological figures, on folklorish traditions that had been briefly glimpsed in the earliest books of the Old Testament.

A renewed emphasis on the idea of a heavenly court came as Israel strove to find a way back to unity under its one-time protector. In times of trouble and strife, there is a tendency to look for scapegoats, someone to blame, and evil spirits are usually high on the list of alternatives. Leading Jewish writers pointed a finger at the sinfulness of Yahweh's chosen people and presented a pessimistic view of humanity always hovering one step away from perdition and immortality—later so central to Christian thought.

A handful of the mythological sagas of the Apocrypha are in the canon of the Old Testament. The Book of Daniel and the

Book of Wisdom both date from this period. Their inclusion as "deuterocanonical" (or of doubtful parentage) books in the Bible has always been controversial. Saint Jerome, the fourth-century Church father whose translation of the New Testament into Latin inspired the Vulgate, considered Wisdom beyond the pale and dangerous. Wisdom was written by a Hellenized Jew in Alexandria in the first century B.C. It is thought his motive was to protest against what he saw as the godless values of that city, and the book contains the Old Testament's only reference to the Devil, though it is usually reproduced with a small *d*.

> *Yet God did not make man imperishable,*
> *he made him in the image of his own nature;*
> *it was the devil's envy that brought death into the world,*
> *as those who are his partners will discover.*
>
> (2:22–24)

Biblical scholars have taken this to be a rare reference to the fall of Adam and Eve in the Garden of Eden and its responsibility for bringing sin and misfortune into the world, which is very much a theme of apocryphal literature. The passage in Wisdom marks an important development for the devil figure as not only the opponent of humankind—as in Job and Zechariah—but also of Yahweh himself. Though the theme is not pursued, or indeed followed up in any other Old Testament text, the events in Eden, featured in the opening chapters of the Book of Genesis, became a central concern for other apocryphal authors.

Representative of this new approach is the Book of Enoch, named after one of Adam's descendants who is described in chapter five of Genesis as living for 365 years and as "walking with God." It has been dated as somewhat earlier than Wisdom, anywhere between 200 and 60 B.C., but has been excluded from the Old Testament. There are in fact several versions of the text, while even in its most complete form—known as Ethiopian Enoch after the language in which it was written—it shows the mark of more than one writer.

The theme of Enoch is an odyssey around the earth and down to the underworld, so that the author can witness God's plan. Such a plot is almost identical to that later used in Dante's *Inferno*.[5] The picture, unsurprisingly in such pessimistic times for the Israelites, was one of ruination. In attempting to explain how things have fallen so low, Enoch returns to the origins of Yahweh's bond with the Jews and reworks the story of Genesis. The heavenly court, the "sons of God" of Genesis 6, lose in Enoch's hands their divine status and become angels. In this capacity they are no longer part of the pantheon of heaven and are free to fall to earth where, by giving vent to their lust and having sex with the daughters of earth, they spawn a generation of evil giants, the "Nephilim." The connection between sex and evil, so much a part of traditional Christian and especially Catholic teaching, has a long vintage.[6]

Collectively known as the Watcher Angels—a phrase used in the Book of Daniel and meaning "the eyes of God"—these rebels are given a variety of names, some of which refer back to shadowy characters who flitted through earlier books of the Hebrew Scriptures. Here they are fleshed out in the search for a reason for evil. There is Belial, mentioned disparagingly in the Book of Samuel; Azazel, the demon from Leviticus; Mastemah; Satanail; Sammael; and Semyaz. All of these names were later to be used by medieval clerics in connection with the Devil and some found their way into popular culture. Present too is the Satan of the Book of Job, though the word at times is used in a collective and general sense, with a lowercase *s*, as an adversary or wrongdoer, and at others, with a capital *s*, as a definite figure.

Semyaz leads the fallen angels. According to Enoch, they came to earth of their own free will at Mount Hermon, descending like stars. This description was to give rise to the name Lucifer—"giver of light"—and was echoed in Luke's gospel (10:18) when Satan is described falling "like lightning from heaven." It is Semyaz who eggs his fellow angels on to sexual excess, until, as Enoch puts it, "all their conduct became corrupt." Others of his company share with their earthbound concubines a variety of dastardly skills. Azazel, for instance, gives instruction in weaponry and "taught all unrighteousness on earth and revealed the eternal secrets." In short, the sins of the world are ascribed to the Watcher Angels for introducing humankind to wicked ways. The giants produced by the unholy union of sons of God and women of earth turn to destruction. Yahweh is moved to intervene and sends four good and true angels to help out—Uriel, Raphael, Gabriel, and Michael—who defeat the giants and cast them into the pit. Enoch, like Daniel, alludes to a hell, but in his *sheol* all the souls of the departed are held together, with the virtuous enjoying a good afterlife but the wicked suffering eternal torment.

Enoch was vague as to why the Watcher Angels abandoned their posts in heaven. The later Book of Jubilees adds a little more precision. Also known as "Little Genesis," it was written sometime between 135 and 105 B.C. by a Pharisee, one of a Jewish sect who in the second century B.C. gathered to oppose the growing influence of Greek culture on Israel and to herald the arrival of Messianic kingdom. Jubilees puts a different gloss on the descent from heaven. The Watchers came to help humankind in the long tradition of benevolent messengers from Yahweh, but they lusted after the daughters of earth and degraded themselves. Again it was sex, and more importantly, womankind, acting in imitation of Eve, who led to their fall.

Jubilees has a novel explanation for Yahweh's attitude to the faithless Watchers. Though he subsequently defeats nine-tenths of them and banishes them to the netherworld forever on account of their perfidy, he allows one-tenth to remain active in tempting humankind. In a variation on the theme of Satan being let loose on Job, Mastemah, the head Watcher, roams the earth luring men and women away from the path of righteousness, while remaining himself always ultimately answerable to Yahweh. The semblance of monism was maintained at the same time as a practical dualism was established.

More than most books of the Apocrypha, Jubilees reworks key passages in the Old Testament to fill its own particular slant. Mastemah becomes a supercharged *malak Yahweh* when he and not God meets Moses in the desert and tries to kill him. Similarly, it is Mastemah, not Yahweh, who puts Abraham to the test and asks him to kill his son Isaac in a re-enactment of the story of Genesis (22:1–9). Jubilees sets up Mastemah as someone instantly recognizable to later generations of Christians, a devil, a force for evil whose power might not quite match that of Yahweh but who remains at least semidetached from the omnipotent God. How that relationship between Yahweh and the adversary worked became a source of endless speculation by theologians and writers. As the historian Jeffrey Burton Russell puts it: "The chief problem with this apocalyptic theodicy is the question with which Friday puzzled Robinson Crusoe: if the Lord has the power to destroy the Devil and wishes him destroyed, why does he wait till the end of the world?"[7]

The fundamental question of Yahweh's omnipotence was blurred, but as the debate continued the figure of the Evil One loomed larger and larger. The Testament of Reuben, another book of the Apocrypha, written around 109–106 B.C., switches the focus to the more traditional Christian targets of Adam and Eve, with Eve tempting Adam to sin and thus setting an example for the daughters of earth who seduced the hapless Watcher Angels. In placing the blame for sinfulness and evil more on women than men, Reuben was anticipating much of what was later to be preached in the name of God. It conjured up the image of the Watcher Angels taking possession of women while they were making love to their husbands with the result that their offspring were poisoned by evil from their first breath.

Lust was one of the main reasons advanced in the apocryphal literature for the fall of angels from heaven and it became firmly rooted in the imagery of the demons. Another explanation was offered by the Book of Secrets of Enoch, thought to be a variation on the theme of Ethiopian Enoch, but existing today only in Slavonic and showing signs of having been written around the first century A.D., with additions as late as the fifteenth century. Here the angels rebelled ón account of their pride, a theme taken up by the influential Church father Origen in the third century.[8] "And one from out the order of angels, having turned away with the order that was under him, conceived of an impossible thought, to place his throne higher than the clouds above the earth, that he might become equal in rank to any power. And I threw him out from the height with his angels, and he was flying in the air continuously above the bottomless." Other apocryphal books develop this notion. The Apocalypse of Moses, dated around 70 A.D., suggests that the angels were jealous not of Yahweh's powers, but of man's, specifically Adam's. It was as if the older children of God rebelled against their new sibling down on earth and tempted him into offending their father.

The rapid development of the idea of the Evil One in apocryphal literature poses the question of where the ideas that took such a hold on writers and thinkers of the time came from. Historians of the period have spotted traces of Belial in Canaanite thought, while a fragment known as the Book of Giants—found with the Dead Sea Scrolls and thought to be of this era—mentions Gilgamesh and Huwawa. The most obvious link, however, is with Babylon and the Zoroastrianism that the Jews encountered during their exile and occupation. Cyrus the Persian, the liberator of the Jews from their Babylonian prison and described as "the anointed of Yahweh" in Isaiah (45:1), was a follower of Zoroaster. The parallels between the dualism of that credo and what appeared in the Apocrypha are striking. The images of light and darkness used to describe Yahweh and the evil one are also found in Zoroaster's descriptions of Ahura Mazda, the force for good, and Ahriman, the force for evil. Ahriman is often depicted as a serpent. The difficulty, as ever, with parallels between the developing demonology of the Near East and that of Zoroastrianism is that the timescale allows for a two-way traffic and it is never entirely clear who is influencing whom.

What is beyond question, however, is that though there

seems a great sea change between the Old and New Testaments and their attitude to the personification of evil, the books of the Apocrypha provide the bridge. They were widely read at the time of Christ and influenced both his disciples and Christian thinkers who later fashioned the Devil as a terrifying adult.

THREE

Head-to-Head with Jesus

Sine diabolo nullus dominus,
Without the Devil, no God.

—Traditional saying

The Devil's clash with Jesus in the New Testament dominates proceedings. The shadowy, uncertain adolescent of the Hebrew Scriptures, who put on such a spurt of growth in the literature of the Apocrypha, matures in the holiest of the holy books of Christianity.

Though it is tantamount to heresy in the mainstream churches today to mention the fact, the New Testament is a story of the war between Jesus and the Devil, between good and evil. The tendency among modern theologians and church leaders is to avoid mentioning the Devil lest they or their creed be dismissed as medieval or superstitious. At best they will concede his repeated appearances in the New Testament are a metaphor, a symbol of evil, though any talk that such an explanation should then be extended to Jesus—suggesting that he is a symbol of good and nothing more—is fiercely resisted. The consequence is that too much study of the New Testament today excludes the Devil. It is as if Doctor Moriarty were edited out of the Sherlock Holmes stories.

The character and actions of the Devil are crucial to the story of salvation of humankind that is at the core of the New Testament. Without the Devil, Christ has nothing and no one to defeat, no way of dispensing with the shortcomings of the here and now and of ushering in the "kingdom of God." Yet the Devil does not rise out of the pages of the New Testament as a rounded character, the ever-eager artful dodger, the con man in working clothes who became central to the Christian tradition. This is perhaps not surprising when one considers that Jesus too is seen more on account of his deeds than as himself. These omissions would seem to confirm the theory that the New Testament is more than a straightforward history and biography, that it should be read on more than one level.

The New Testament contains not a single description of Christ, what color his hair and eyes were. Though it is his humanity that is crucial—a God-made-man—there is little sense of Jesus as a person. His image was later created by generation after generation of artists, down to today's favored rendition of him with blue eyes, hippie hair, and a beard, the erstwhile star of *Jesus Christ Superstar*. Likewise, the Devil can often appear a cipher, a caricature of unpleasantness conjured up to convey a point. When his personality is explored, it is without a single focus. The questions of origins and background are left vague. The conclusion of the New Testament may be a victory for Christ and the powers of light but the Devil's fate is far from crystal clear. He is stranded in a kind of limbo, marauding and threatening but at the same time ultimately doomed come the Day of Judgment. The New Testament writers left it to subsequent generations of Christians—high and low, learned and superstitious—to mold this compelling creature into the apotheosis of evil.

Whatever the different ways of approaching the New Testament, the gospel accounts are presented from the pulpit and in various papal pronouncements as if they are a verbatim transcript of Christ's pronouncements. The truth is rather different. They are the words of God in the words of man and were written up to seventy years after the crucifixion of Jesus. Like the Old Testament, the New is in no particular chronological order and reflects the political and social outlook of its authors. Some of Saint Paul's letters, for example, predate the writing of the gospel accounts. In the New Testament, however, they come afterward. And though the gospels themselves start with Matthew's version, there is a strong, many would say over-whelming, case for saying that Mark's was the first gospel.[1]

Paul, in particular, is characteristic of another too easily for-gotten aspect of the New Testament—the conviction that the Second Coming was imminent. This plays some part in its, at times, catchall and simplistic tendency to put every ill down to the Devil. The authors of much of the New Testament were sure that the Messiah's return in triumph would be any day, and that the people had to be won around. Such Messianic hopes proved illusory and received the first of many setbacks when the Jews fought what was for many of them a holy war against their Roman overlords from 66 to 70 A.D. The Messiah did not descend from on high to rescue his people. Instead Jerusalem was destroyed with Jew turning against Jew as the bitter factional divisions between Pharisees and Sadducees turned into a witch-hunt in the name of purity.

The dominant Old Testament picture of Yahweh as the omnipotent God, as the source of everything good and bad, is still present in the New Testament. With the concentration on the character of the Devil comes a new approach to the eternal question, with Satan positioned as the counter-principle to Christ. Mixed in are some of the notions from apocryphal litera-ture, especially that of the rebel angels. Christianity did more than simply adapt the best of Jewish thought to bolster its own savior. It borrowed from Greek ideas, introducing the split between the body, with its tendency toward sin, and the spirit, pure and the domain of God. The result is a canon that is in theory strictly monist but where dualism can occasionally be glimpsed.

Body and Soul

Without Paul, chief tormentor of Jesus' disciples before he had
the original Road to Damascus experience, Christianity might
well have remained just another apocalyptic Jewish cult. It was
this poacher-turned-gamekeeper who spread Christ's teachings
beyond Israel, nurtured the developing church with a missionary
zeal, gave intellectual vigor to the credo, and debunked the idea
that Jesus came only for the Jews. "All baptised in Christ, you
have all clothed yourself in Christ and there are no more distinc-
tions between Jew and Greek, slave and free, male and female,
but all of you are one in Christ Jesus" (Gal. 3:27–28). As one of
his most celebrated biographers, E. P. Sanders, has remarked:
"Fortunately Paul wrote letters and equally fortunately someone
collected, edited and published some of them. In these letters a
remarkable human being still speaks and it is in them that we
find Paul—a man full of flash and fire, passion and vigour, wit
and charm, pride and humility, enormous self-confidence, and
fear and loathing."[2]

Paul's various letters to the Romans, Corinthians, Ephesians,
and Galatians have been enormously influential in the development of Christianity. They epitomize the sometimes confused
picture the New Testament presents of the Devil. In his Letter to
the Church in Rome, Paul appears to confirm, albeit vaguely, the
traditional idea that God is omnipotent, source of all things
good and bad in the world. "You will ask me 'In that case how
can God ever blame anyone, since no one can oppose his will?'
But what right have you, a human being, to cross-examine God?
The pot has no right to say to the potter: why did you make me
this shape? Surely a potter can do what he likes with his clay?"
(9:19–20). Such an insistence that it is not for us to know why,
simply to know, recalls the closing passage of the Book of Job
and much of the Hebrew Scriptures.

Paul also writes extensively of the Devil and his role in a
world that is teetering on the brink of moral and physical dis-

aster. "Every time Paul uses the word Satan," says literary historian Neil Forsyth, "he is referring to the opponent of human salvation, not to the figure who does battle with Michael in the Book of Revelation."[3] The cosmic dualism that came later in the Book of Revelation, which concludes the New Testament with a vision of a war in heaven, has no place in Paul. Neither does talk of evil spirits and demons, though occasionally there are flashes of apocalyptic imagery and its accompanying penchant for opposites in Paul's repeated predictions of the imminence of the Second Coming. "The night is almost over, it will be daylight soon. Let us give up all things we do under cover of the dark; let us arm ourselves and appear in the light" (Rom. 13:12).

Paul's overriding imperative, however, is to spread the good news of the promise of salvation and eternal life far and wide in the shortest possible time. It is in that context that Satan becomes one of the stumbling blocks standing in the way of humankind. He is an obstacle, an adversary in the literal and Old Testament meaning of the word *stn*. Writing to the Church at Thessalonica, Paul, in regal mood, says: "A short time after we had been separated from you—in body but never in thought, brothers—we had an especially strong desire and longing to see you face to face again, and we tried hard to come and visit you; I, Paul, tried more than once, but Satan prevented us" (1 Thess. 2:17–19).

It is not only Satan who performs this role of obstructing, "After that will come the end, when he [Christ] hands over the kingdom to God the Father, having done away with every sovereignty, authority and power. For he must be king until he has put all his enemies under his feet and the last of the enemies to be destroyed is death, for everything is to be put under his feet" (1 Cor. 15:24–26). The enemies—what earlier translations of the Bible rendered ringingly as principalities and powers[4]—may include Satan but this is not made explicit. He is certainly not thought the only source of discord and disharmony on earth.

Paul casts his net wider and has harsh words to say about human sinfulness. The notion of evil being the result of an external force preying on humankind (which is the dominant theme of the gospels of Matthew, Mark, and Luke) finds little space in Paul's theology. Rather than blame everything on the Devil, he attempts instead to draw up a new version of Yahweh's original covenant with the Jews that could include everyone. It was as if Paul was trying to update the law, the moral code of the Old Testament, in the light of Christ's teachings.

Paul includes sex among the distractions from the Second Coming. He sees it as open to abuse and therefore a way for Satan to make mischief. "Do not refuse each other except by mutual consent," he advises married couples (1 Cor. 7:5), "and then only for an agreed time to leave yourselves free for prayer; then come together again in case Satan should take advantage of your weakness to tempt you." The link between sex and Satan was once more explicit. Sexual excess had been the downfall of the Watcher Angels in the Book of Enoch, but there is another dimension here. Plato suggested in some of his writings that evil might be deemed the absence of good, and Paul could be seen as holding that by avoiding conjugal sex, couples were leaving a void where the Devil could thrive. Paul's concerns about sex are part of a wider tendency in his writings to develop what echoes the Greek line of dividing the body and the soul. In Galatians, he writes (5:16–24): "Let me put it like this: if you are guided by the Spirit you will be in no danger of yielding to self-indulgence since self-indulgence is the opposite of the Spirit. . . . When self-indulgence is at work, the results are obvious: fornication, gross indecency and sexual irresponsibility, idolatry and sorcery, feuds and wrangling, jealousy, bad temper and quarrels, disagreements, factions, envy, drunkenness, orgies and similar things. I warn you now, as I warned you before, those who behave like this will not inherit the kingdom of God. What the Spirit brings is very different: love, joy, peace, patience, kindness, goodness, trustfulness, gentleness and self-control."

The association of the spirit with God and the flesh as open to the wiles of the Devil was not yet made, but Paul's high moral tone on sexuality was to be taken up by those who saw anything to do with the body as the work of Satan. However, in drawing a distinction between flesh and spirit in the same way that Christ is set against Satan, Paul was giving a clear signal. The flesh was one source of sinfulness. In his First Letter to the Church at Corinth, Paul suggests another when he compares the destruction that Adam brought through his infidelity in the Garden of Eden—"death came through one man" (15:21)—with the harmony that Christ later restored—"the resurrection of the dead has come through one man" (15:22). Adam is then the enemy by his original sin—a legacy passed on to all who came after him. There is no mention of the Devil, though later he, and not Adam, became the snakelike villain of Eden.

The Exorcist

The Evil One has many names in the New Testament. Usually he is either the Hebrew Satan or the Greek Devil. In the three "synoptic" gospels—the accounts by Matthew, Mark, and Luke of Christ's life, written after Paul—the Devil also appears as Beelzebub. The Pharisees, confronted with Jesus' capacity to cure a blind and dumb demoniac, respond: "The man casts out devils only through Beelzebub, the prince of devils" (Matt. 20:24). Jesus denies the charge. "If it is through the Spirit of God that I cast devils out, then know that the kingdom of God has overtaken you" (Matt. 20:27). Though the origins of the name are unclear, Beelzebub—literally, "Lord of the Flies"— seems to be a derogatory form of Prince Baal, the Canaanite god.

Jesus' retort makes clear that his overriding purpose in all three synoptic gospels is to bring about the Kingdom of God. Where Paul quotes Christ very little and prefers to make his own observations and offer his own teaching, the gospels concentrate on Jesus and present sound bites from his life. The tone is that of an almost military account of Christ's victory over the Devil, with preliminary skirmishes between the two during Jesus' forty days and nights in the desert—traditionally the preserve of evil spirits—building up to the final battle on the hill of Calvary on the first Good Friday. Jesus' death, however, and his return from the grave are not treated in any explicit way in the synoptic gospels as part of his fight with Satan. That interpretation of the events came later.

In his three-year public ministry, Jesus' principal weapon in fighting the Devil is exorcism. Though today exorcism is a rare and to some an exotic practice, more the preserve of Hollywood than mainstream churches, it was a fairly routine procedure for coping with sickness among the Jews at the time of Christ. When challenged by a synagogue official after healing a woman bent double who the crowd believed to be possessed by a demon, Jesus did not buck popular wisdom. He defended his exorcism of a woman "whom Satan has held bound these eighteen years." The Jews, as has been remarked upon before, were a profoundly superstitious people and talk of evil spirits fed into their own view of the world.

Exorcism is one of the key features that distinguishes the synoptic gospels from the writings of Paul and John. Paul scarcely spares a thought for demons and devils, and then only as a way of poking fun at the beliefs of those he deems heathens. By contrast, in Mark the author rushes through Jesus' early life and his period in the desert in order to include, in the first chapter, an exorcism. The tone is set. "That evening, after sunset, they brought to him all who were sick and those who were possessed by devils. The whole town came crowding round the door and he cured many who were suffering from diseases of one kind or another; he also cast out many devils" (Mark 1:32–34). Mark recounts that it was through his exorcisms of evil spirits that Jesus' fame spread. In a literal sense such encounters were cures. But on another, much more significant level, they are one of the distinctive ways in which the New Testament approaches the question of good and evil. What is inside the possessed person comes out when faced down by Christ. Jesus makes it clear that the true source of disharmony in individuals and, by association, in the world is an external agent—evil spirits who are in the pay of the Devil.

There is, however, an intrinsic confusion even within the three gospels concerning the source of evil. In Jesus' sermons, he appears to be saying that individuals must take responsibility for the world around them and can choose to be good or bad. This dichotomy is not resolved even within the New Testament as a whole—rather it was left to a subsequent generation of thinkers, writers, and theologians to add their own spin to whichever part of the biblical text suited their purpose. "In each act of exorcism," wrote Anton Fridrichsen in his essay "The Conflict of Jesus with the Unclean Spirits," "Jesus saw a defeat of Satan, a presage of the final triumph that was soon to come to pass. . . . Jesus actualised Satan, just as he actualised God. Just as he treated with full earnest the coming of Divine Kingdom, so he treated also the present dominion of Satan."[5]

In perhaps the most graphic passage in the gospels about the Devil's power to possess, the story of the Gerasene demoniac (Luke 8:26–39), the theme of opposites is unmistakable. When Jesus asks the possessed man his name, he replies: " 'Legion' because many devils had gone into him. And these pleaded with him not to order them to depart into the abyss." Trying to escape Jesus' exorcism, the devils left the man and possessed a herd of pigs grazing nearby but could find no hiding place. The herd charged down the cliff into a lake and drowned. The story is built on contrasts: between the upper world and the lower world, between clean and unclean, man and animal, two sides of the lake that separate the Jews of Galilee and the Gentiles of Gerasene. The language and symbolism of the whole episode reflects the central act of driving out what is inside the possessed man, of rooting out the external agent that spreads chaos and evil in the world.

When they talk of expelling evil spirits, the synoptic gospels have only one person in mind. In their Greek form the New Testament writings still make a distinction between *daimons*—which could be good or bad—and *diabolos*, or devils. Such subtleties were later lost in translations that follow more the general thrust of the gospels in grouping spirits and demons together as part of the army of evil under Satan's command. The battle motif is further confirmed when Jesus passes the gift of exorcism on to his disciples. "Then he summoned the Twelve and began to send them out in pairs, giving them authority over unclean spirits" (Mark 6:7). Luke gives the same episode more of an apocryphal edge: "The seventy-two [disciples] came back rejoicing. 'Lord,' they said, 'even the devils submit to us when we use your name.' He said to them, 'I watched Satan fall like lightning from heaven. Yes, I have given you power to tread underfoot serpents and scorpions and the whole strength of your enemy; nothing shall ever hurt you. Yet do not rejoice that the spirits submit to you; rejoice rather that your names are written in heaven' " (Luke 10:17–20).

The impression that all of humankind is vulnerable to possession—and that they must not therefore be judged culpable if they succumb to such a fate—is emphasized by Jesus' angry exchange of words with his favorite apostle and the future Pope Simon Peter. "From that time Jesus began to make it clear to his disciples that he was destined to go to Jerusalem and suffer grievously at the hands of the elders and chief priests and scribes, to be put to death and to be raised up on the third day. Then taking him aside, Peter started to remonstrate with him. 'Heaven preserve you Lord,' he said, 'this must not happen to you.' But he turned and said to Peter, 'Get behind me Satan! You are an obstacle in my path because the way you think is not God's way but man's' " (Matt. 16:21–23).

It is a curious run-in, made all the more intriguing by the fact that Jesus' words are almost identical to those he uses earlier when he resists the Devil in the desert. "Be off, Satan" (Matt. 4:10). The significance of the episode is not entirely agreed. On the one hand, it seems that if Peter can momentarily be an instrument of the Devil's work, so can any mortal soul. It could equally be that the word "Satan" is being used in the generic

Hebrew sense of the word as an obstacle, an adversary, one who blocks the path.

The synoptic gospels leave open the questions of how Satan fits into the Divine Plan of an all-knowing, all-seeing God and the Devil's indispensability in bringing about Christ's passion and death and resurrection. The possibility that the Devil could still in some dark way be God's servant, the tempter of humankind after the fashion of Job, is not entirely exhausted. The writings of the Apostle John and his circle, however, sought to put any such suggestion out of court.

Revelations of Future Infamy

Christ lived at a time when apocryphal literature and the popular cults that surrounded it were at their height. Both the content and the style of this particular movement left their impression on Paul and the synoptic gospels, albeit to a limited extent. In Mark, for example, there is a passage often labeled the "Markan Apocalypse," which conjures up the imagery used to describe the Watcher Angels of the Book of Enoch without ever explicitly mentioning their fall from grace. "But in those days, after that time of distress, the sun will be darkened, the moon will lose its brightness, the stars will come falling from heaven and the powers in the heavens will be shaken. And then they will see the Son of Man coming in the clouds with great power and glory" (Mark 13:24–26). Such cosmic language, prosaic and image-laden, is, however, comparatively rare in Matthew, Mark, and Luke and is more usually found in the New Testament writings ascribed to John and his followers. John, one of the first twelve apostles, gives the only eyewitness account of Christ's life, but it was not "published" until the death of its author. It is an attempt by John to draw out the significance of Christ's deeds rather than a straight narrative. Hand in hand with his gospel go the three letters he wrote to the early Christian communities.

The last entry in the New Testament, the extraordinary Book of Revelation, is also associated with the apostle John—either the work of the evangelist himself, or of one of his immediate circle somewhere between 70 and 95 A.D.

John is less interested than the synoptics in agents of the Devil, in evil spirits and demons, than in Satan himself. Of the four gospels, it is the most dualist, a precursor to the high point of the battle between God and the Devil in Revelation. Only in John's account of the last week of Christ's life are the events of the crucifixion put in the context of the cosmic battle. At the Last Supper, Jesus tells his apostles: "Now sentence is being passed on this world; now the prince of this world is being overthrown. And when I am lifted up from the earth, I shall draw all men to myself" (12:31–32). Later, before he is arrested, Jesus again describes his coming ordeal in terms of a cosmic battle. "I shall not talk with you any longer [he tells his apostles], because the prince of this world is on his way. He has no power over me, but the world must be brought to know that I love the Father and that I am doing exactly what the Father told me" (14:30–31).

John is preoccupied with why the Jews failed to recognize Jesus as their savior. He mixes Old Testament ideas about the sinfulness of human nature—echoing Paul's writings and per-haps influenced by them—with the suggestion in the other gospels that the Devil possesses humans and makes them do evil deeds. "If God were your father, you would love me," Jesus tells the crowd (8:42–44), "since I have come here from God; yes, I have come from him; not that I came because I chose. No, I was sent, and by him. Do you know why you cannot take in what I say? It is because you are unable to understand my language. The devil is your father and you prefer to do what your father wants. He was a murderer from the start; he was never grounded in the truth. There is no truth in him at all; when he lies, he is drawing on his own store, because he is a liar, the father of all lies." The epigram "father of lies" has become a standard term in various Christian rituals when referring to the Devil and it is in John's writings that Satan can be said first to achieve the power and the dastardly majesty that was later ascribed to him by Christian writers. There is no hedging with talk of demons, no avoiding the issues. Only the Devil and those who follow him, John warns, will be denied eternal life. No one will be lost, Jesus promises, "except the one who chose to be lost" (17:12). Quite what being lost means is not immediately made clear.

The Book of Revelation develops John's gospel and the concept of eternal life. It becomes a powerful vision that recalls in words and details a whole range of influences from apocryphal literature to the monsters of Canaan, Egypt, and Babylon. Revelation is final confirmation that the Christian Satan is a direct descendant of the cosmic adversaries of the Near Eastern credos. For the Devil's life story, the most significant section of Revelation is chapter 12, which tells, for the first and only time in the Bible, of a battle royal in heaven. It is a vision that has contributed enormously to the picture of the Devil presented in learned articles and classrooms around the globe. Satan starts off as a "huge red dragon" with seven heads and ten horns, immediately recalling both the Greek hydra and Labbu, the monster of Canaanite mythology. The dragon's tail then sweeps one-third of the stars in the sky down to earth—a description that echoes a passage in the deuterocanonical Book of Daniel (8:10)—before turning its attention to a woman about to give birth to a child. The dragon tries to eat the child.

> The woman brought a male child into the world, the son who was to rule all the nations with an iron spectre and the child was taken straight up to God and his throne, while the woman escaped into the desert.

The text then abruptly changes direction—evidence, some scholars suggest, that Revelation is the work of more than one author—and focuses on the war in heaven with the dragon and

"his angels" slogging it out with the Archangel Michael and the
virtuous angels. The latter prevail and the dragon and his band
are driven out of heaven.

> The great dragon, the primeval serpent, known as the
> Devil or Satan, who had deceived all the world, was hurled
> down to the earth and his angels were hurled down with
> him. . . . [The woman is then once again in the Devil's
> sights.] But she was given a huge pair of eagle's wings to
> fly away from the serpent in the desert . . . so the serpent
> vomited water from his mouth, like a river, after the
> woman to sweep her away in the current, but the earth
> came to her rescue. It opened its mouth and swallowed
> the river thrown up by the dragon's jaws. Then the dragon
> was enraged with the woman and went away to make war
> on the rest of her children, that is, all who obey God's
> commandments and bear witness for Jesus.

The narrative continues with the dragon becoming a sea-
monster with the mouth of a lion, the paws of a bear, and the
look of a leopard, screeching blasphemies and making war
"against the saints" and all humanity. "There is need for shrewd-
ness here: if anyone is clever enough, he may interpret the
number of the beast: it is the number of a man, the number
666." In one vision are collected many of the characteristics that
continue to shape the image of the Devil to this day—the serpent, the wild beast, the deceiver, the utterer of blasphemies,
even the would-be satanic epigram 666.

This and the other numbers in these passages have a symbolic
meaning bound up with the politics of the time, and with the
Jewish obsession with driving out their Roman · overlords.
Though Revelation tends to speak of Babylon and hark back to
the events of the exile, it does so in symbolic terms. Its real concern was the contemporary battle with Imperial Rome. The Jews
had a tendency to project their political unhappiness onto a
cosmic stage, with dreams of revenge and vindication as

Yahweh's chosen people being the balm they applied to the wounds of defeat at the hands of the Romans in 70 A.D. The woman in Revelation can be read as Israel, her adversary the Roman Emperor, and her child the promise of divine favor. The monster's seven heads, according to biblical scholars, represent a succession of seven Roman emperors, its ten crowned horns are ten subject kings. The number 666 is more of a puzzle. One theory is that letters were given a numerical significance so that messages could be passed in code between the anti-Roman groups. By an obscure calculation, 666 has the number value of Nero, who ruled until 68 A.D.[6]

The symbolism of Revelation, however, is never one-dimensional. The number seven was used in other credos to convey malevolence. Ahriman, the Evil One in dualist Zoroastrianism, was supported by seven archfiends. Significant too is the fact that the Devil/serpent/dragon figure is held responsible in Revelation for natural disasters on the earth in the same way that earlier races had blamed the dark shadow of their gods for earthquakes and floods. Revelation is the only New Testament book to consider "natural" evil. The rest of the canon is concerned largely with personal morality and "social" evil.

As befits the final book of the New Testament, Revelation attempts to answer some of the significant questions left unanswered by the four gospels and by Paul. What, for instance, happens to Satan on the much anticipated Day of Judgment?

> Then I saw an angel come down from heaven with the key of the abyss in his hand and an enormous chain. He overpowered the dragon, that primeval serpent which is the Devil and Satan and chained him up for a thousand years. He threw him into the abyss and shut the entrance and sealed it over him to make sure that he would not deceive the nations again until the thousand years had passed. At the end of time he must be released but only for a short while.
>
> (Rev. 20:1–3)

Once freed, Satan "will come out to deceive all the nations in the four quarters of the earth . . . his armies will be as many as the sands of the sea. . . . But the fire will come down on them from heaven and consume them. Then the Devil, who misled them, will be thrown into the lake of fire and sulphur, where the beast and the false prophet are, and their torture will not stop, day or night, for ever and ever" (Rev. 20:7–10).

A vision of the Last Judgment follows, when Hades and Death "were emptied of the dead that were in them; and every one was judged according to the way in which he had lived. Then Death and Hades were thrown into the burning lake. This burning lake is the second death, and anybody whose name could not be found in the book of life was thrown into the burning lake.

The promise is that God will be triumphant—that is one of the safeguards that prevents the Devil being an equal and equivalent power to God. In the meantime the Devil is left with some latitude to work his spell on humankind.

FOUR

Leader of the Opposition

We have on the surface at least our
bisymmetrical bodies; our right and left and our
right and wrong. We live in a world of heat
and cold, of night and day. In such a world there is
both good and evil, God and Devil.

—R. L. Thompson

Whatever its other ambiguities concerning the Devil's life
and work, the New Testament makes it abundantly clear
that his driving ambition was to defeat Christ and bring down
the Church. It is ironical therefore that when the first Christians
found themselves under attack first from the Jews, then the
Romans, and finally dissidents within their own ranks, they
turned to the Devil as a way of safeguarding the future of the
Church. By making Satan the author of all the woes that were
afflicting them—and in the process demonizing all who sought
to put down the fledgling Church—the founding fathers created
an opponent with a unique power to unite Christians and
strengthen their resolve in fighting the good fight.

In the decades that followed Christ's death, the original band
of apostles remained the focus of the ever-expanding cult that
worshiped his name. They ensured that a single teaching line was
maintained and instilled discipline by dint of the authority that
came with their firsthand knowledge of the Messiah. However,
their deaths deprived the Church of such a focus and soon there

were as many different interpretations of his teaching as there were new Christian communities springing up.

The optimism and sense of expectation created by promises of an imminent second coming turned to disappointment and disagreement when it failed to materialize. As outside threats multiplied, the Devil was a handy scapegoat and his malevolent status grew accordingly. The early Church fathers discovered, however, that blaming your fate on Satan had a downside. Soon different groups—known by a variety of names but collectively called the Gnostics—were ascribing every challenge they met to the Devil and denying that the earth was God's creation. Many suggested that a place so hostile and unwelcoming could only have been made by Satan. Their solution was to turn in on themselves and actively seek martyrdom as a way of escaping a living hell for the safety of life after death in heaven with God.

The more clear-sighted fathers quickly recognized that this was a recipe for disaster, carrying with it the threat of self-destruction. As Professor John Roberts puts it, they faced the possibility that the Church "might develop into just another cult of the kind of which many examples could be seen in the Roman empire and, in the end, be engulfed like them in the magical morass of ancient religion. All over the Near East could be found examples of the 'mystery religions' whose core was the initiation of the believer into the occult knowledge of a devotion centered on a particular god."[1] To avoid such a fate, they had to draw up boundaries for the Devil. He could not be an equal and opposite force to God, the master of this world against the master of the next. The framework that they developed as a response—a halfway house between a theological monism and a practical dualism—has remained the bedrock of Christian belief ever since.

When in Rome

Ironically for a Church that in subsequent eras perfected the art of demonizing its opponents, Christianity began the second century more sinned against than sinner. The early Christians found themselves charged by the Romans with precisely the sort of foul ritual—incest, orgies, cannibalism—that was subsequently attached by Christians to the name of Satan and those alleged to be have sold their souls to him.

In Rome, religion was a national cult, cement to bind the far-flung empire together. Christians had the effrontery to demur and their refusal to take part in "official" worship was seen as a threat to the very fabric of the empire. The Christians' claim that Christ—and not the godlike Emperor—was Lord of the Universe was seen as subversive. Eagerly awaiting the second coming, they had a habit of decrying everything about the here and now. As the Romans turned an increasingly critical eye on the Christian communities, they saw a group speaking out defiantly against their political overlords as a Second Babylon.

The charges dreamed up by the Romans against the Christians were more than a match for whatever foul and baseless accusations Church leaders later leveled at their opponents. All they lacked was the figure of the Devil, an ingredient clerics were only too ready to add to the mix when they became the oppressor. The source of many of the wild and disgusting stories put about by the Church in the medieval age concerning Jews and witches can be glimpsed in contemporary accounts from this early period.

Intrigued by the Christians' secret gatherings, the Romans let their imaginations get the better of them. There were accusations of incest, of cannibalism, and even of worshiping a god who was a donkey. "Others say that they reverence the genitals of the presiding priest himself, and adore them as though they were their father's," the early Christian apologist, Minucius Felix, wrote in his *Octavius*, of the charges leveled against his fellow believers by the Romans. "As for the initiation of new members, the details are as disgusting as they are well known. A child, covered in dough to deceive the unwary, is set before a would-be novice. The novice stabs the child to death with invisible blows; indeed he himself, deceived by the coating of dough, thinks his stabs harmless. Then—it's horrible—they hungrily drink the child's blood, and compete with one another as they divide the limbs. Through this victim they are bound together; and the fact that they all share the knowledge of the crime pledges them all to silence. Such holy rites are more disgraceful than sacrilege." Such accusations echo down the centuries up to and including our own times with allegations of ritual satanic abuse. Minucius Felix—writing as if he were a disinterested but horrified onlooker describing these vile Christian ceremonies—continues: "On the feast-day they foregather with all their children, sisters, mothers, people of either sex and all ages. When the company is all aglow from feasting, and impure lust has been set afire by drunkenness, pieces of meat are thrown to a dog fastened by a lamp. The dog springs forward, beyond the length of its chain. The light, which would have been a betraying witness, is over-turned and goes out. Now, in the dark, so favourable to shame-less behaviour, they twine the bonds of unnameable passion, as chance decides. And so all alike are incestuous, if not always in deed at least by complicity; for everything that is performed by one of them corresponds to the wishes of all. . . . Precisely the secrecy of this evil religion proves that all these things, or practically all, are true."[2]

These accusations were treated by the early Christians with a mixture of scorn, humor, and outrage, but the fact they were made at all reveals a side of the human psyche that is all too ready to demonize a group within its midst, to believe the most heinous of accusations that have little basis in fact.

In short, the Christians learned from their misfortunes to redirect the fire of their onetime opponents on to their own adversaries. First targets of this new form of demonization were the Romans. Where the Jews had long regarded their Roman overlords as evil, the Christians took this one stage further by describing the empire as the work of the Devil. A good example of this comes in contemporary accounts of the pogrom at Lyon in 177 A.D. This civil strife was well documented and indeed relived by Bishop Eusebius (260–339 A.D.) in his *History of the*

Church. He told how both Christian-Greek immigrants to the French city and native converts, high- and low-born alike, were attacked on account of their faith.

"The severity of our trials here," Eusebius quotes from accounts written at the time,

> the unbridled fury of the heathen against God's people, the untold sufferings of the blessed martyrs, we are incapable of describing in detail: indeed no pen could do them justice. The adversary swooped upon us with all his might . . . he left no stone unturned in his efforts to train his adherents and equip them to attack the servants of God . . . but against them the grace of God put itself at our head, rescuing the weak and deploying against our enemies unshakeable pillars, able by their endurance to draw upon themselves the whole onslaught of the Evil One.[3]

The language is unmistakably biblical—the adversary, the Evil One. The notion of a cosmic battle between good and evil stands in a long tradition, but seeing the Devil's face behind every attack on the Church, secular, political, or theological, gave a terrifying new dimension to Satan's character.

Down but Not Out

The early Church was clearly capable of standing up for itself. With formulation of responses came a broader drive toward definition of the Christian position on various central questions of dogma and belief—among which was the role of Satan.

There was nothing that equated to the canon of the New Testament, and a whole host of apocryphal literature was in circulation alongside the writings of Paul, John, and the other apostles. In this melee, Satan became a key player. As the literary historian Neil Forsyth puts it: "The struggle between competing versions of Christianity lent some of its characteristics and a vital theological function to Satan. As the Prince of Error and the Father of Lies, he became the arch-heretic, the name under which rival teachers were denounced."⁴

Despite the ringing tones of the Book of Revelation, at the dawn of the second century of Christianity the Devil remained decidedly enigmatic. The Book of Enoch was well known and its story of the Watchers, with Satan the leader of the fallen angels, enjoyed widespread credence in the Christian communities. However, beyond that general consensus loomed larger unresolved issues. If Satan was a fallen angel, he must have been created by God in the first place. Why then did he go astray? Pride, lust, envy had all been suggested by various apocryphal writers. How far could God then be held responsible for the Devil's deeds? Was the Evil One a full-blown adversary, a loose canon, or simply an agent of an omnipotent God?

Behind all these questions lay the fundamental clash of dualism against monism, or rather of what degree of dualism the emerging Christian Church could tolerate. The solution appeared to be a two-pronged approach. An ethical dualism was largely taken as read—that good and evil were the two choices facing humankind. This indeed predated Christianity. Some Christian writers favored a theological dualism to match the day-to-day beliefs of the faithful. They therefore presented an ever more polarized view of the cosmos, at odds with Old and New Testament monism, with God and the Devil slogging it out with their respective armies. It was left to the leaders of the early Church to find an uneasy compromise to answer this new—and to their mind—dangerous trend.

God is wholly good, they decreed, and knows more than we do. The Devil lies at the root of many of the mysteries—suffering, natural disasters, destructive human behavior, rejection of God—and continues to wage a rearguard action in a battle with God that ultimately is lost. Hand in hand with this developing theodicy—or vindication of God in a world where evil exists—went a fleshing out of the character of the adult Devil. Christians wanted to put a face on the adversary that was attacking them, and created a Devil who captured the popular imagination, fashioned a world around him, gave him a costume and characteristics. While the theologians debated such—to them—central questions as where he existed—in the air, the earth, or the underworld—Christians at large were content to fix an image of the Devil in their mind.

The Smack of Firm Government

The Devil's role was not limited to demonizing opponents and detractors. Faced with a divided Church with little concept of central authority, those who would mold it into a uniform body with a hierarchy and an agreed set of ideas soon realized Satan might be a useful ally. The extent to which the question of authority and dissent within the early Church was intricately linked with talk of the Devil can be seen in the crucial First Epistle of Saint Clement to the Church at Corinth. By tradition the third or fourth bishop of Rome, and a follower of Saint Peter, Clement in 96 A.D. tried to put an end to disagreement in the local Church by insisting that its elders stood in due succession to the apostles and thereby carried the authority that Christ had given the twelve. In the course of his letter, Clement describes those who dissent from the elders as acting on "the promptings of the adversary." The Devil was causing disharmony in Christian ranks and only by subscribing to a structure of authority could he be resisted. The Devil became a scapegoat, someone against whom to rally the faithful. Unpopular or contentious policies could be ushered in under the pretext that to oppose them was to leave the Church open to Satan and all his works.

The theme was taken up and expanded by the most influential writer of this period, Ignatius, the Bishop of Antioch, who was martyred in 107 A.D. and who believed that the bishop was the fount of all authority in the community. Ignatius developed the biblical idea of two kingdoms to argue that everything to do with the current age was evil and had been since the fall of Adam and Eve. Christ's death and resurrection had shattered the Devil's power, but until the second coming and the birth of the new kingdom, the world remained in the grip of an *archon*—literally, an "evil spiritual prince." That prince cast a "stench" over the whole world in his attempt to divert people from Christ's purpose. "Do not let yourselves be anointed," he wrote to the Ephesians, "with the foul smell of the teaching of the prince of this world lest he capture you and rob you of life to come."

Ignatius's rejection of everything to do with this world as the work of the Devil had much in common with the view of the Christian Gnostics. In his case, it shaped his attitude to his own fate. Ignatius had long expected to be martyred for his outspoken stance against the Romans, but his response was a passive one. "I long to suffer," he wrote, "but I do not know whether I am worthy . . . I need the meekness in which the prince of this world is undone."[5]

The link between heresy and the name of Satan was quickly established in early Christianity. It became a distinguishing feature of Christianity that kept Satan forever in the forefront of believers' minds. The Devil and heresy were ever more closely associated as Christianity faced in the third century the greatest threat yet to its survival—the rise of Gnosticism, which gave the Devil a role equal to that of God.

An Evil World

The very ambiguity of Christianity on the subject of the Devil has meant that down the ages, groups of believers have seen Satan as an equivalent and opposite power to God. The first such "heretics" were the Gnostics. The term Gnosticism, based on the Greek word *gnosis*, meaning "knowledge," is used in many contexts. As Paul Johnson remarks in his *History of Christianity*: "No one has yet succeeded in defining 'Gnosticism' adequately, or indeed demonstrating whether this movement preceded Christianity or grew from it."[6]

There were two separate phenomena—a widespread spiritual and philosophical movement known as Gnosticism, which may predate Christ but which certainly existed in his time and afterward, and a substantial minority within the emerging Christian Church who took on broadly Gnostic ideas. It was this second group who, in their determination to pin the blame for evil on someone other than God, intensified the debate about Satan throughout the second and third centuries.

Christian Gnosticism should not be underestimated either in terms of its geographical spread and influence, or in its effects on the early Church fathers. The high point of Gnosticism in the second and early third centuries proved to be a cathartic moment for Christianity, forcing it to establish a canon and define what was and what was not an acceptable doctrine. Gnosticism was an amalgam of ideas borrowed from the Greek philosophers, from Judaism and from Zoroastrianism. Its fundamental principle, salvation, was based on a secret knowledge revealed to the elect by God. These chosen few became the source of Gnostic thought and account for its shapelessness. Their "revelations" of the divine were diverse in the extreme.

All Gnostics rejected the here and now as irredeemably evil. They borrowed from Plato and his followers the notion that the soul has to turn inward, away from the world of senses and matter toward a higher spiritual plane. From Zoroastrianism, the Gnostics inherited a separate but complementary idea of two opposite but equal cosmic spirits in conflict, one benign and the other malevolent. Run together, these two legacies led the Gnostics to believe that the visible world of flesh, earth, and water was in the grip of an evil creator. Only the spirit, coming from the invisible world of light, was good. Gnosticism became a deeply pessimistic credo, a counsel of despair totally at odds with its environment, fragmented by the excesses and idiosyncrasies of its chosen few, disorganized, and overburdened with theories and mystical notions.

The most influential Gnostic thinker and writer was Marcion of Pontus. A Syrian by birth and a disciple of Saint Paul, Marcion joined the Christian community in Rome in the 130s only to be expelled as a heretic in 144. Thereafter he lived off his personal fortune in the Near East and attracted a devoted band of followers. Marcion, deeply influenced by Gnostic pessimism, became obsessed with the question of evil in the world and detected the influence of a Devil-like figure called the Demiurge in the Old Testament. Meaning literally "world-maker" or "partial mover," this was a favorite creation of the Greek-speaking Gnostics. The Demiurge was the creator of this world and stood—to an ill-defined degree—in the shadow of God, the prime mover who was the creator of the world to come.

Marcion found it impossible to reconcile the God of the Hebrew Scriptures—the tormentor of Job, the Yahweh who gave his blessing to the Israelites as they raped and pillaged— with the loving, forgiving, healing God of Paul. The two could not be the same, he surmised, and with a characteristic Gnostic flair for iconoclasm suggested that there were two different gods—one, the Demiurge, the God of the Old Testament, responsible for the sufferings of this world, and the second, the true God, Paul's inspiration. Marcion believed Yahweh to be a malevolent spirit who created the flawed universe, the "author of evils." He set this Yahweh/Demiurge figure against the God who had been unknown to humankind before Jesus came to reveal him. Marcion denied humanity a link with the good God and put its creation down to the Demiurge. God had always been there, remote and observing the world, but it was only when he sent his son Jesus that he chose to interfere in the affairs of the world and show his power. Jesus' blood had, Marcion argued, been the ransom that would ultimately be the salvation of humankind.

The Church fathers were not prepared to countenance his claims. Their reluctance had little to do with sensitivity for the feelings of the Jews—rarely a preoccupation of Christianity until modern times.[7] Because of their passionate attachment to the

Demiurge, the Gnostics risked, in the Church fathers' view, compromising God and his creation and turning Christianity into a vague, mystical, and inward-looking sect. They had to be driven out, and the chosen method was to brand them heretics and servants of Satan.

Back from the Brink

Irenaeus (140–202), Bishop of Lyon, was an ardent refuter of the Gnostic proposition that the world was made evil. In *Against the Heretics* he outlined his own version of the creation story. The creator of the world was the Logos, the word of the good God—a term much used by the Gnostics. As part of that creation God made angels, but some turned against him on account of envy and fell. Among their number was the Devil. As God's creation, however, he was inferior in power.

Irenaeus was suspicious of the whole pessimistic Gnostic tendency to shift the blame for everything that was wrong in the world onto an evil force—he thought that this let humanity off the hook and he preferred to invoke human responsibility for sin. Without that there would be a free-for-all, with any sort of morality put off until death.

Irenaeus was the first outspoken advocate of Original Sin, a concept hinted at in Saint Paul, given its most persuasive treatment by Augustine and a dogma that remains a central part of Christianity to this day. Adam and Eve represented the goodness of God's creation, but Satan entered the garden either as, or using, the serpent and tempted them. Since God, Irenaeus said, had given humanity the freedom to choose between good and evil, Satan was able to exploit its Achilles' heel. All humans carry the baggage of Adam and Eve's original sin. However, according to Irenaeus, Christ came as the second Adam to make good, by his death and resurrection, that first failure. Whereas previously Christ's death had been seen as a gesture of reconciliation between God and humankind, Irenaeus put forward a whole new theory of atonement. Christ's death atoned for past sinfulness. God was offering his son as ransom to liberate those who had died and those who were to come from the grip of the Devil, into which they had been delivered by Adam. The Devil, however, tried to overstep his authority and killed Jesus who, being unaffected by Adam's sin, was able to descend to hell and inflict a mortal wound on Satan.

Irenaeus's Devil was therefore a compromised, if not crippled, force but one who nonetheless was intent on some form of revenge. The Gnostic notion that the Devil had any claim over humankind as its creator was rebutted but Irenaeus warned that Christians would be the target of the Devil's continuing anger. The evidence of that, he said, could be seen in the attacks the Church was currently suffering—from the Romans, the Jews, and even internal dissenters. Again, the message was clear in Irenaeus's writings. If you're not with us, you're with the Devil. To fight off such attacks, Irenaeus prescribed praying to God.

Tertullian followed Irenaeus in pulling the early Church back from the brink of Gnosticism. One of the growing number of wealthy converts to Christianity, he was born around 155 in Carthage in North Africa and lived there all his life, becoming bishop of the city in 220. One of the first theologians to write in Latin, Tertullian was a fervent advocate of living a strictly moral life and emphasized that it was how you lived your life on earth that you would be judged in the world to come. According to Tertullian, God had made the world good, and human sin and Satan's sin had distorted it. The Devil was less a creator than a creature of God who had rebelled and fallen from grace. Tertullian took up the notion that humanity had been given a choice between good and evil. What God creates, the Devil is seeking to destroy or pervert. "Thus Tertullian thought the Devil's function," writes the American scholar Jeffrey Burton Russell, "similar to that of the shadow of God, the destroying *malak Yahweh* of the Old Testament, with the fundamental distinction that the

Devil was a creature rather than a manifestation of divinity. The Devil had taken God's beautiful creation and filled it with lies."8

Warming to his theme, Tertullian identified various demonic activities: astrology, necromancy, magic, horse races, baths, taverns, theaters, brothels, makeup, fancy clothes. For Tertullian it was a lie for a woman to dress herself up as anything other than she was and since the Devil was the prince of lies, any attempt to improve on nature was to play into the hands of Satan. While much of Tertullian's theology would have gone over the heads of the early Christians, he contributed greatly to the composite picture of Satan that was to be passed down from generation to generation.

A Place in the Sun

The fight back launched by Irenaeus and Tertullian initially only showed mixed results. Gnosticism had touched a popular chord with a Christian community losing faith in promises of a Parousia. Recent discoveries in the Upper Nile Valley, for instance, show that a decidedly Gnostic form of Christianity was the norm there, while down river at Alexandria, the second city of the Roman Empire, the prevailing belief was a form of Jewish Christianity, using the *Gospel of the Hebrews*, later declared heretical. Alexandria resisted the claims of Rome to hegemony and authority in the emerging Church.

The picture at the end of the second century was not a homogeneous one. There was no one orthodoxy. It was only in the third century that the different varieties of Christianity were blended into one recognizable whole, and it took well into the fourth century for that uniform message to take hold, with isolated pockets of dissent remaining. To ensure itself as great a chance of success as possible, the official line was a broad and tolerant one, amalgamating and accommodating as many different opinions as was possible. Only the most extreme varieties were ruled heretical, including both Marcion's explicit dualism and Tertullian's increasingly obsessive asceticism that led him into the Montanist cult.

One of the most important tools in fashioning a single Christianity was the change from an oral tradition to a written one. With his genius for creating an image in the popular imagination the Devil weathered the transition, but not without difficulties. Once the Devil was the stuff of theological tomes, the debate quickly petered out. His domain was in the stories passed by word of mouth to demonstrate his power and the threat he posed. Folklore mixed with the oral tradition to fashion a living, breathing Devil, far removed from the dry abstraction of the theologians and scholars.

The New Testament canon emerged around this period in the written form we know today partly as an exercise in bringing together the divergent communities within the wider Christian family. The special pleadings of one group were balanced against those of others. Greek-speaking Christians who urged the exclusion of the Book of Revelation were thwarted by the desire to appeal to those nearer to Judaism who appreciated its apocryphal overtones. The great compiler was Bishop Eusebius and by 367, Athanasius (c. 298–373), Bishop of Alexandria, was able to give a list of approved texts in his Easter letter that approximate what is in the canon today.

Parallel to this development was the growth in the power and prestige of the bishops, which contributed to the process of giving Christianity an intellectual underpinning. Thus far it had been based on popular rituals—shared celebrations, a great outpouring of love, and an immovable conviction that the second coming was imminent. Those who had begun to dabble with what might be called theology had embroidered on to this base a patchwork of different ideas. Origen provided the first all-embracing definition. "If Paul brought to the first generation of Christians the useful skills of a trained theologian," writes Paul Johnson, "Origen was the first great philosopher to rethink the new religion from first principles. As his philosophical enemy, the anti-Christian Porphyry, summed it up, he 'introduced Greek ideas to foreign fables'—that is, gave a barbarous eastern religion the intellectual respectability of a philosophical defence."[9]

Origen (c. 185–c. 254) was born in Alexandria and his scholarship—he knew Greek and Hebrew and studied Platonism and Gnosticism as well as Christianity under Clement of Alexandria (c. 150–210)—was matched by a fanatical disposition. Today he is perhaps best remembered for castrating himself in an uncharacteristically brutal and literal attempt to live up to the passage in Matthew's gospel where Christ urges his followers to be eunuchs for the sake of the kingdom of heaven. Origen's writings— notably his *On First Principles*—were hugely influential, though the book's author himself was often regarded with suspicion by his fellow Christians. Origen followed Irenaeus and Tertullian in arguing against the Gnostics that the world was good. But in order to be truly good, you have to have a choice and hence God had also created freedom that included the freedom to do evil. Evil was then part of creation.

When he turned his attention to the problem of evil in this world which was created good, Origen came up with a theory that owed much to Greece and Plato. The purpose of the world, he suggested, was to learn to love God. Not to do this was to lack purpose, to lack Being. "Those who have given up their part in the Being by depriving themselves of Being have become Non-Being." Evil in this plan is Non-Being, nothingness, an absence or a void. Logically, the Devil as the apotheosis of evil is also Non-Being. In spite of his own act of gospel-inspired self-mutilation, Origen challenged the sometimes literal-minded interpretation of scripture favored by his contemporaries. He argued that the opening chapters of the Book of Genesis should be read allegorically. Rather than slavishly follow the order of Adam and Eve's fall from grace in Eden and then the descent of the Watcher Angels, Origen suggested that the angels had rebelled first and that God had created Adam and Eve as compensation after such a great disappointment. But Adam and Eve then fell prey to the fallen angels and joined them in their rebel-

lion. The Devil's fall, Origen concluded, was not to do with lust
for the daughters of earth, but on account of pride. He wanted
to be God.

It was a radical suggestion that placed human suffering and
evil in the broader context of a cosmic battle between God and
the Devil. After Adam and Eve went the way of all flesh, demons
and good angels—or intelligences—were left to fight it out. That
struggle was going on in each and every human, Origen said,
two rival forces pulling us between Being and Non-Being. Adam
and Eve by their sin had tipped the balance in favor of evil, he
went on, and it required Christ's suffering and death to restore
the equilibrium and give good angels the upper hand. In his
Commentary on Matthew, Origen took up Irenaeus's ransom
theory. "But to whom did Christ give his soul as a ransom for
many? Surely not to God. Was it then the Evil One? For he had
power over us, until the soul of Jesus was given as a ransom for
us, since he let himself be deceived, thinking he could have
power over that soul and not recognizing that to keep him
would require a trial of strength that he was not equal to." Jesus
was a kind of bait for Satan, who imagined that he could destroy
him. Having done so, he finds that Jesus has slipped into hell to
break his power over humanity. Origen's was an optimistic doctrine at odds with the Gnostics. The Devil had been defeated
and though he continued to snap at humankind's heels, what
power remained to him after Christ's victory could be crushed
by individual Christians simply invoking the name of Jesus.

Origen's belief that even the Devil could be saved on the final
day, in universal redemption—apocatastasis, from the Greek
word for "restoration"—was, however, an unpopular one.
Though his writings were much quoted and copied, he himself
was posthumously condemned for heresy in 543 and again at the
Second Council of Constantinople in 553. The pessimistic
Jerome (340–420), who started off as a fan but later grew to distrust anything that smelled of Greek philosophy, was in the vanguard of those who would put down Origen, but his sternest
critic was Augustine.

Eminence Grise

Augustine was born in 354 into a new kind of Christian Church. Rather than hovering on the margins, a mystical, populist, but divided and often persecuted sect, it had become a major force in the Roman Empire. In 313, the Emperor Constantine's Edict of Milan prescribed toleration for the new religion. In 392, Theodosius (379–395) made Christianity the official religion of the Empire.

The authorities hoped that by harnessing the dynamism and exuberance of the Christian community to the state, the collapse in the fabric of the Roman Empire could be reversed. It proved a forlorn hope. Augustine lived long enough to see the sack of Rome by the Visigoths in 410, and just before his death the Vandals overran his native North Africa. In such a period of uncertainty, the Christians saw the Devil all around them, in those who plundered the Empire and destroyed their newfound security.

The rape of Rome in particular turned Augustine's thoughts to the evil forces within the world and their origin. In his writings he came increasingly to see Christianity as the heir-apparent to the Roman Empire as the bastion of civilization. Often described as "the dark genius of imperial Christianity,"[10] he staked out the Church's claim to such an elevated status and laid the intellectual foundations for the medieval power of the Papacy and the Holy Roman Empire.

Augustine was born into a middle-class home in what is today Algeria. Though his mother, Monica, was a woman of extraordinary piety, Augustine did not formally join the Church until he was a young man in Milan. Previously he had lived what he later came to see as an appallingly dissolute life. Aside from his sexual license, Augustine was a Manichaean for nine years. This cult, which existed on the fringes of Christianity, revolved around the personality and thoughts of Mani, a late third-century Mesopotamian ecstatic. He combined the asceticism of Montanism with the insights of the Eastern religions. From Zoroastrianism, Mani copied dualist ideas and pessimism from Gnosticism. A controversial figure, Mani was executed at the behest of the Zoroastrians after being condemned by the Emperor Diocletian as "like the poison of a malevolent snake."

Augustine's early writings on joining the Christian Church were taken up with rebutting Mani's claims with Jewish and Greek notions of a beautiful created universe. "In their mouths [the Manichaeans] were the Devil's traps and a birdlime compounded of a mixture of the syllables of your name," he wrote in his *Confessions*. In particular, he demonized the Manichaean leader in Carthage, Bishop Faustus, and accused him, like the serpent in the Garden of Eden, of trapping the wayward in the snares of Satan through "flesh's morbid impulse and lethal sweetness." The equation of sex with sin and the Devil was a powerful and recurring theme in Augustine's writings, and Christianity's residual sexual pessimism owes a great deal to his particular outlook.

Augustine's great theme was the sinfulness of humanity and hence he was more interested in individuals' responsibility for the evil that he perceived in the world than the Devil's. However, he wrote in one of his earliest works, *On the Free Choice of the Will*, that he had "always believed in the vast power of the Devil."[11] Satan, Augustine held, was under God's control, but each individual had demons battling to seize possession of his or her soul. The human race he described as a fruit tree, made as good by God but providing something for the Devil to pluck at and play with.

In *Confessions*, Augustine lumps together human sinfulness with the Devil's as if they are different sides of the same coin, rather than one being caused by the other. "The deceiving mediator [as Augustine refers to Satan in this section] . . . has one thing in common with human beings, namely sin. He wishes to appear to have another feature in common with God: since he is not clothed with mortal flesh, he boasts that he is immortal.

But because 'the wages of sin is death,' he in common with mankind is condemned to death."

When confronted with the barbarity that followed the fall of Rome in 410, Augustine's thinking took a decidedly negative turn. He no longer saw evil as an abstraction, something sent to instruct and guide us. Instead it became a punishment. In *City of God*, he reflects on the Visigoths' triumph and describes the pain and suffering it brought as something sent by God to teach wisdom. He asserted that there is a divine plan that is beyond human imagination. Part of that plan is the freedom to choose good or evil. With evil comes punishment. Yet, Augustine puzzled, how can humankind be free to choose, since God, who is all-knowing, must already be aware of what choice will be made. Augustine struggled to square this circle. His chosen concept was that of predestination—that God knows and plans everything in advance. Yet he tried to integrate such a scheme with free will, which he saw as humankind's way of putting a stick in the spokes. In this foolish human endeavor, the Devil played a leading and encouraging role. "If even he [Satan] began as a good angel and became devil by a perversion of the will," Augustine asked in *Confessions*, "how does the evil will by which he became devil originate in him, when an angel is wholly made by a creator who is pure goodness?"

Augustine believed that Satan was the chief of the fallen angels who became demons. They too had been given free will but had sinned because of a defect in their wills that God did not know about but which he permitted. The Devil could not be saved on the final day, Augustine wrote, contrary to Origen's most controversial teaching, but rather had lost both his intelligence and his capacity to love when he chose evil. His whole existence was, as Augustine put it in his *Confessions*, "darkened by folly." This theory, however, did not quite match up with predestination. In his later works, Augustine returned to the topic and suggested that pride had been the reason, if not the cause, of Satan's fall. The Devil wanted to be God. When he failed in that, the Devil took his revenge by polluting Adam and hence through Original Sin (which Augustine endorsed) the rest of humankind. Jesus broke this hold. In his tract *On the Trinity*, Augustine wrote of Christ's passion, death, and resurrection as God offering his son to the Devil as the food in the mousetrap. Satan made a grab for Jesus but overestimated his own powers, for Christ was not only a man but God incarnate. The Devil was thus defeated but will stay with humanity until the second coming.

In his often abstract theorizing on the Devil, Augustine did not neglect to nod in the direction of the popular trend to develop the "personality" of Satan and especially of the demons that assisted him. He presented a picture of these onetime angels hovering in the atmosphere about the earth like wasps, ever-ready to swoop and sting humans whose guard was temporarily down. Since angels possessed ethereal bodies, made up of light and air, Augustine wrote in his *On the Divination of Demons*, demons must be similarly composed. Their extraordinary form gave the demons special powers, enabling them to move with alarming speed and to read the human mind at will.

Augustine gave the Devil a central, if restricted, role. He built on the writings of those who had sought to explain Christ's death and descent into hell. He gave eloquent expression to the atonement theory, to Original Sin, to Christianity's rejection of dualism. Yet there is still a flirtation with dualism in Augustine's thought, a failure to separate out ethical dualism—good versus evil—from cosmic dualism—two opposite poles. His concept of the two cities could easily fall into both—a problem that Christianity has never resolved.

The essential events and personality traits of the adult Devil are in place—his dispute with God his creator; his rebellion; his perversion of the Garden of Eden; the breaking of his hold over humanity after Christ's passion; his subservience to God but continuing role as a source of evil within a world created good.

Most of his best-known features are there too—the sulfur; the brimstone; the torment; the association with the serpent. The Devil had come of age and taken on the mantle of leader of the opposition.

As the Church began to grow in power and influence, as its political ambitions multiplied and hopes of the second coming faded, Satan loomed large in its thoughts both as an adversary to be feared and, increasingly, as a potential rallying point for bringing and holding the faithful in line when outside forces or internal dissidents threatened to sweep the See of Peter on to the rocks.

PART TWO

THE WHOLE WORLD'S SEDUCER

> The Devil has been one of the organising
> principles of world politics for as long as
> Christian civilisation has existed. The Devil
> serves to identify what evil is and became an
> entity who was responsible for evil that let God
> and ourselves off the hook. That has been the
> function of the Devil in history.
>
> —Leslek Kolakowski

FIVE

The Horned God of the North

There is an old tale that goes, that Herne the hunter,
Some time a keeper here in Windsor forest,
Doth all the wintertime, at still midnight,
Walk round about an oak, with great ragg'd horn

—William Shakespeare, *Merry Wives of Windsor*

If you glance at any history of Christian doctrine, you will find that the Devil merits a surprisingly brief entry given his reputation as God's opposite number. As far as theologians are concerned, this reputation is undeserved. God is almighty and tolerates no rival. However, theologians and thinkers have never been the Devil's main constituency. He is a popular figure, not a dogmatic abstraction, and has come alive not in learned tomes or seminary debates, but in the minds of the faithful, terrifying, omnipresent, and grotesque, evil incarnate.

As the early Church expanded throughout Europe from the fifth century onward, its missionaries discovered Satan to be a useful ally in making new converts. Preaching that God was both loving and the ultimate source of every misfortune in the world was a handicap when addressing people with an existing deity of benevolent and malign spirits. So the missionaries began to talk up the Devil's role. From the pulpits and in the mosaics, sculptures, and illustrations that were the principal teaching tools in an age of illiteracy, Satan's reputation as the enemy grew and grew.

When looking at the role the adult Devil played in society from the era of the early Church until the dawn of the twentieth century, it is vital to picture a very different world. Fear, insecurity, and pessimism were determining factors in shaping people's lives and expectations. There were doctors with rudimentary skills in the latter part of the period under review, and village healers with supernatural and sinister powers. Yet what are today regarded as trivial diseases were then a death warrant. Colds and flu could not be dealt with by antibiotics. The more unusual afflictions were unequivocally put down to the work of evil spirits.

The society of the first millennium and at least half of the second was largely agricultural and rural. It was only at the end of this period that urbanization, literacy, and wider availability of books made an impact. Despite advances in farming techniques over the centuries, there was little that might now qualify as famine relief measures or harvest controls—a storm or a flood could wipe out the crop and bring widespread misery. With no banks and no concept of financial insurance, people kept their wealth, their guarantee of food on the table, in flimsy barns that could easily be destroyed by fire or torrent. People teetered on the brink of disaster in a way that is now hard to imagine and that might easily induce a state of despair. To ward off such feelings, they indulged in a shared belief in supernatural powers, be they pre-Christian, pagan, Jewish, Gnostic, or—as the Church increasingly spread its influence across Europe—Christian. Such supernatural powers were thought to be at play in even the most trivial events—an animal's sickness or health, a hen's fecundity, a dog barking in the night. They could only be placated by corporate ritual by the local community. "Such is to me," said Thomas Carlyle, "the secret of all forms of paganism. Worship is transcendent wonder; wonder for which there is now no limit or measure; that is worship. To these primaeval men, all things and everything they saw exist beside them were an emblem of the godlike, of some god."[1]

Individual communities were isolated and introspective. Though there were widespread patterns of belief in groups of gods—the Celts and the Teutonic peoples, for instance, had their own pantheons—different regions, towns, and villages had their own local deities, genius loci, as they are sometimes deemed by academic historians.[2] These deities were honored and entreated by an annual festival. Travel was the preserve of the very few. The majority of the population of any village believed that beyond the outskirts of the dwellings lay a vast expanse of space where the most terrifying forces and demons had their headquarters. Until the 1570s, for example, the Fruili villagers in the hinterland of Venice held that malevolent spirits gathered several times a year to attack crops and murder children. In response to such sallies, it was believed that the spirits of the good men of each village, the *benandanti* as they were called, rose at night from the earthly bodies of their owners as they slept and went out to drive away the spirits from the fields.[3] Such beliefs and rituals were an odd ragbag. When Christianity came into contact with pagans, other creeds and rebels in its own ranks, new ways to ward off evil spirits evolved. A constant element was the importance of acting together. Those who refused to participate or who expressed doubts often found themselves branded and stigmatized—an early form of demonization.

The Missionary Impulse

Christianity understood significant missionary sallies into northern Europe during the papacy of Gregory the Great (c. 540–604). With his active encouragement, the Word spread northward and westward beyond the Alps to modern-day France, Germany, Scandinavia, and—under Augustine of Canterbury who landed in Kent in 596—to England.

There had been, of course, Christianity in these areas during the time of the Roman Empire. Saint Alban, for example, the first Christian martyr in England, was beheaded by the Roman authorities in 303 for giving shelter to a priest.[4] With the collapse of the Empire, however, the Christian foothold came under threat from the victors' own Norse and Teutonic deities. Gregory's missionaries set out to buttress these threatened outposts of what he had come to see as his own kingdom. He pushed ahead with turning the Church's role into that of a political power, with the papacy uniting Church and state under a kind of divine monarchy. Christ and the saints became weapons for the missionaries to defeat the powers of darkness and paganism. Christ's victory over death and evil became both the rallying point and the promise of eventual success for those who followed in his footsteps. Images of "Christ in Judgment" and "Christ Harrowing Hell"—always defeating the Devil and his legions—are among the most common representations to be found in medieval churches.

This missionary push was partially successful, but many held on to their old ways of magic and superstition at the same time as embracing Christianity. Gregory did not attempt to wipe out all traces of paganism straightaway. A pragmatist and a politician, he permitted that in some missionary areas there should not be any immediate attempt to displace existing religious systems and expressions of community solidarity. Instead he realized that to take root, the new faith had to follow a three-pronged strategy. First coexistence and toleration, later transformation—adapting existing rituals to Christianity's practices and calendar—and finally persecution. Sometimes, where the missionaries felt themselves on fertile ground, all three would come together in one great push. In other areas it was a much slower progress. For the greater part of the first millennium and beyond, Christianity lived grudgingly in parallel with older beliefs and superstitions.

Behind the various spirits and belief systems that the missionaries encountered lay an ancient northern European culture of gods that can be traced back to earliest times. The menacing figures of the Teutonic Thor and Woden and the Celtic Cernunnos shared a mutual ancestor in the shadowy horned god of the north. The earliest trace of a primitive deity has been found in a cave drawing of a masked human wearing the horns of a stag and a horse's tail in the Caverne des Trois Frères, at Ariège in France. It is believed to be over 9,000 years old. As later representations found across western Europe confirm, the horned god came to be worshiped through sacrifice as a way of warding off misfortune. Even in his prehistoric form, he shows a recognizable likeness to the Satan of early medieval Europe. In both traditions, the bringer of evil is represented as either an animal or half-man, half-beast. Among the Teutonic gods of northern Europe the missionaries met the figure of Loki, the father-figure of a dynasty of evildoers. Loki's children were a wolf, a serpent, and the queen of the world of the dead. Together this unholy band, with their lieutenants, the frost giants, threatened the world with destruction, a doomsday, or *Ragnarok*. The missionaries realized that the figures of Loki and Satan could be merged as a way of easing the acceptance of Christianity. Both the Devil and Loki resided in the underworld. Both had a mission to spread evil. Both had a fundamental characteristic as a trickster, able to chop and change their appearance, to take over other bodies to deceive their victims.

The extent to which pagan notions and imagery in this process influenced Christian perceptions should not be overlooked. The historian R. L. Thompson—from his own decidedly anti-Church stance—has suggested that: "When we read of the conversion of the west to Christianity, it is well to remember that the change was more apparent than real. It might even be truer to speak of the conversion of Christianity to the West."[5] The keys of Saint Peter began appearing in this period. The fact that Cernunnos's power was traditionally represented by a set of keys may not be a coincidence.

This interchange of ideas can be seen in some early written sources. The old English poem *Beowulf,* dated by some scholars as early as the seventh century, was once regarded as the work of a pagan celebrating ancient traditions in defiance of the "new" Christianity. However, in more recent times[6] it has been accepted as fundamentally Christian with Teutonic imagery, perhaps the work of a Christian monk with a profound respect for the traditions that lived alongside his own faith. The author interweaves elements of Germanic legend and actual events.

The tale of Prince Beowulf's battle against the monster Grendel reworks the theme of a cosmic battle between good and evil. It consciously places that theme in a historical context, encapsulating past, present, and future in its majestic sweep. The tone of the poem is often pessimistic, in line with the spirit of the age. The concept of "wyrd," or fate, is to the fore, though Beowulf battles against such ideas. The temptation to see him as a Christlike figure is rejected by the details of the text. He has a pagan burial in the traditional manner with his body burned on a funeral pyre. And his final speech, full of pathos, offers no glimpse of a heaven. Yet the respect with which it is presented speaks volumes of the Christian author's attitude and of the accommodation of his religion and older beliefs.

The interchange of ideas included trying to superimpose Christian ideas on pagan practices. In reality the old and not quite vanquished left its mark on the new and triumphant. One commonly used stage in transformation came when villagers held weeklong festivals in honor of the various pagan deities who they believed would ensure a good harvest. Christian clerics picked up on the idea and introduced the notion of a patron saint for the community. The festival evolved into celebrating the saint. However, in the minds of their congregations the saint was often just a new name for the spirits they already worshiped. In Luxembourg, the cult of Saint Herbert grew strong, linking in with an existing respect for Diana the huntress, a Roman god borrowed from the Greeks. Saint Herbert's symbol—a full-grown stag with a cross attached to its antlers—deliberately included a reference to Diana. As late as the eighteenth century in the nearby Loire and Somme regions, wine makers were whipping statues of their patron, Saint George, when the harvest failed, another reminder of the curious overlap between Christian and pagan figures.[7]

The symbolism of pagan festivals could be adapted to Christian ends. Saint John's Day was celebrated on the same day that some rural communities—especially in parts of northern Europe and notably in Scandinavia—marked the start of preparations for the harvest. The main thrust of these pagan events was the victory of light over darkness, marked by the lighting of bonfires that blazed in the night sky. This age-old rite was effortlessly assimilated by the Church since it fitted perfectly with its own imagery of Christ, the bringer of light, vanquishing evil. Rather more problematic was what came after the lightning of bonfires—nude swimming, dancing, leaping over fires, lovemaking, and revelry. At first the Church turned a blind eye to such excess, calculating that the essentials of the Christian message had been conveyed concerning Christ's triumph and that all else was of secondary importance.[8] In the late Middle Ages, however, when the continued existence of magic and superstition provoked greater hostility among the ecclesiastical authorities, similar unrestrained merrymaking came to be regarded as satanic.

On the Offensive

The Venerable Bede (c. 673–735) reports in his *Ecclesiastical History of the English Nation* that Redwald, king of the East Saxons, "in the same temple had an altar to sacrifice to Christ and another smaller one of offer victims to devils."[9] He goes on to make clear his own dislike of such ambiguity. In the *Liber Poenitentalis*, Archbishop Theodore (668–690) is deeply disapproving: "If anyone at the Kalends of January goes about as a stag or as a bull—that is making himself into a wild animal and dressing in the skin of a wild animal, and putting on the head of beasts—those who in such wise transform themselves into the appearance of a wild animal, penance for three years because this is devilish."

These voices within Christianity—always strong but increasingly insistent as the medieval period progressed—associated anything that was sacred to the pagan gods with the Devil as a means of debunking indigenous beliefs. Christians were taught by their monks and priests that the Devil lived in pagan temples and that such places had to be sprinkled with holy water, stripped of their decorations, and rebuilt with an altar.

As part of this growing hostility to paganism, the link between gods like Cernunnos and Thor and nature—the trees, the fields, the dark—was turned into something sinister. In Teutonic beliefs, the gods were giants who inhabited or created huge things, especially the large boulders that are found scattered in the low-lying parts of present-day Germany. Christianity adapted this to its own purposes. Big objects were named after the Devil—the origins of the Devil's Dykes, Devil's Bridges, Devil's Gorges, and even the Devil's Nostrils (two vast caverns on the Zetland Islands) that still pepper the Christian countryside.

Force, flexibility, and ingenuity were not enough in the assault on old belief systems. Christianity had also to take into account why they were successful, what purpose they served, and then provide an alternative. Ancient rites were regarded as a guarantee of putting food on the table and corn in the fields. (When the harvest failed and there was famine, the rites themselves were not blamed—people assumed they had not performed them correctly or wholeheartedly.) By contrast, all the local priest had to offer was prayer and resignation to meet calamities. The notion that a supposedly just God hurled torments down was a difficult one to grasp. Original sin—according to theologians the source of all evil in the world—was too abstract. Some priests in a Church where central authority and discipline remained weak tolerated the continuation of magic and superstition that allowed their occasionally bemused flock to take action in the face of adversity. The traditional rituals offered a comfort as can be seen as late as 1594—seventy-seven years after Luther acted out the first drama of the Reformation—in the writings of a German cleric in the county of Nassau-Wiesbaden:

> The use of spells is so widespread . . . that not a man or woman begins, undertakes, does or refrains from doing anything . . . without employing some particular blessing, incantation, spell, or other such heathenish means. . . . All the people hereabouts engage in superstitious practices with familiar and unfamiliar words, names and rhymes, especially with the name of God, the Holy Trinity . . . numerous saints, the wounds of Christ . . . verses from the New Testament. . . . They also make strange signs[;] . . . they do things with herbs, roots, branches or special trees; they have their particular days, hours and places for everything. . . . And all this is done to work harm on others or to do good, to make things better or worse, to bring good or bad luck to their fellow men.[10]

The Church was facing an enormous challenge and it showed—as it has in moments of crisis down the ages—a tenacious strength and capacity to adapt. If one omnipotent God could never replace the supernatural powers, then the medieval Church concentrated on Christ—and his mother, Mary—in an attempt to put a human face on God and goodness. If one omnipotent God was inadequate and plain confusing when it came to dealing with the crises and disasters of life, Satan was waiting in the wings. People who had got used to blaming spirits for ill-fortune did not easily grasp the notion of original sin. The Devil provided an alternative part of the Christian canon and his role grew beyond what the theologians might have wanted. The omnipotent God remained elusive, faceless, and the preserve of the thinkers and the Devil was stretched by clerics to cover many of the functions of the supernatural powers. Only with Satan as part of the package—a practical dualism—could God be accepted by communities as the Almighty.

Gregorian Chant

Before any such extension of the Devil's domain could get under way, Christianity had to explain the Prince of Darkness to its converts. In the fifth and sixth centuries, Saint Augustine's teachings trickled down to the Christian communities where their broad thrust had enormous influence. In their details, though, Augustine's thoughts often went over the heads of an ill-educated congregation—and their priest too. Augustine fashioned a two-dimensional, lifeless structure on which to hang various theories and explanations about evil in the world, a halfway house between dualism and monism that left the Devil powerful but not outside the ultimate control of an omnipotent God. Yet there was little in his writings to prompt the subsequent fear of a black-clad, half-man, half-beast with horns, a tail, and burning-red eyes known as the Devil.

No artist's impression of the Devil exists before the sixth century. The earliest depiction of Satan shows him clad not in black but in red, an angel standing before Christ in a mosaic in San Apollinaire Nuovo in Ravenna, which dates back to 520. It was to be the first of many as the Devil became the source of boundless fascination for Christians and especially the artists and writers in their ranks. Mosaics, illustrations to accompany and explain learned books, stained-glass windows, and sculptures all served in this period of illiteracy to teach and reinforce belief in the Devil. He is everywhere, or rather he is represented everywhere by a menagerie of creatures associated with evil and malevolence. Few medieval artists represented Satan as a person. That came later. He was more often an imp or a grotesque combination of man and beast.

There was no artistic orthodoxy, no single image beyond menace that the Church demanded of the artists, sculptors, and illustrators in its pay. Art historian Luther Link, in his study of representations of the Devil, highlights the discontinuity with two contrasting examples from the first half of the ninth century.[11] Both take what was a standard biblical theme—the temptation of Christ in the desert. The Stuttgarter Psalter shows Jesus' opponent in traditional medieval garb—a winged, dark-skinned, naked, and almost witchlike ghoul. However, a contemporary ivory book cover kept in the University Library of Frankfurt has the Devil looking like Christ's twin. "The graphic attributes and concept of the Devil," writes Link, "were rarely defined in the imagination of artists, unlike, for example, those of Mary or Judas or Samson." Satan was, according to Link, an ill-defined face, hidden by many and disparate masks.

In a ninth-century biography of Saint Afra, Satan is seen in what was one of his most familiar guises—pitch-black and covered with wrinkled skin. But in Fra Angelico's "Last Judgment" in the Convent of Saint Mark in Florence from the fifteenth century, there are devils with horns, tails, wings, fur, feline characteristics, and canine features—and any combination of all of them. There was not even a single motif that pointed straightaway to the Devil, such as those used for each of the four gospel writers. Christ's twin on the book cover does carry a stick that might have been taken for the Devil's apparently ubiquitous pitchfork. Yet in medieval art even this is not a constant. It is there in the Eadwine Psalter, an early eleventh-century manuscript held at Trinity College, Cambridge, but in many other places is replaced either by a rakelike implement or left out altogether.

Saints' lives, passed on by word of mouth, by preachers and in the early manuscripts, were another popular way of explaining the ways and wiles of the Devil to a general audience from the sixth century onward. In many of the tales, the villain was the Devil, with the saintly hero reliving Christ's battle with Satan. Through such tales the Evil One became real and terrifying. Pope Gregory gave this recourse to the dead heroes of Christianity official blessing and even contributed a story or two of his own. In his *Dialogues* Gregory told tale after tale of overactive demons. One of the most often repeated concerned a nun who had succumbed to the deadly sin of gluttony. Wandering around the monastery garden, her eye fell hungrily on a lettuce. She gobbled it up without so much as making the sign of the cross only to discover that in her haste she had eaten a demon who then began to torment her. A holy man was called and the demon was expelled but not before protesting, "What did I do? I was just sitting on a lettuce when along she came and ate me."

Where Gregory led, others followed and tales of saints proliferated. The Devil was always the villain, but not always a menacing or sinister one. Anticipating the comedy of the medieval mystery plays, he was often shown as a fool. In the story of Saint Dunstan (924–988), Abbot of Glaston and later Archbishop of Canterbury, the Devil is made to look particularly stupid. While making a metal chalice for Holy Communion, Dunstan was surprised by the Devil. But he kept his wits about him and seized Satan by the nose with the burning hot pincers he had been using on the cup. The story was commemorated in a once-popular rhyme.

> Saint Dunstan, as the story goes,
> Once pulled the Devil by the nose.
> With red-hot tongs, which made him roar
> That he was heard three miles or more.

Gregory's popular diabology was enormously influential. It was he who first codified the seven deadly sins—pride, envy, anger, sloth, avarice, gluttony, and lust—to "serve as a classification of the normal perils of the soul in the ordinary conditions of life." Where once the Devil had been guilty of just one sin—pride, envy, or lust, depending on which apocryphal author you followed—in Gregory's age all the ills of the world were being heaped at his door with a corresponding decline in human responsibility. It proved an inspired idea. As both a religious and a cultural yardstick, the seven deadly sins remain with us today.

Quite how seriously did people take all this talk of Christ harrowing hell, of saints battling with Satan, of a Devil who was always ready to pounce? How much was belief and how much folklore? Did congregations follow their preachers slavishly or did they play along with what was a colorful and easily assimilated idea? To use a modern analogy—we may go to see films about vampires, but we don't necessarily believe in them. It would be arrogant to judge those who lived in the medieval age any less sophisticated. People may have listened and repeated what they heard in the pulpit, but how far did they believe it to be true?

The Desert War

The growth of monasticism in the fifth and sixth centuries contributed to the cult of saints and to the gloomy preoccupation with the Devil. Monasticism in the Mediterranean basin was initially an experiment by solitary souls, eccentrics exasperated with the world, who went out into the sterile, bleak, and unyielding environment of the desert to relive Christ's struggle with Satan. They attracted disciples, and so the first monastic communities developed. According to legend, one of the pioneers, Saint Anthony (251–356), spent almost ninety years as a solitary, living first in a tomb and then in the Egyptian desert near Thebes. He never changed or washed his face, conserving all his energies for repeated confrontations with the Devil. The image of the saint falling to the ground, defenseless against the marauding Devil save for his cross and the name of Jesus was later to become a standard theme in both religious art and literature. The French author Gustave Flaubert produced his version of events in 1874. Around 360, Anthony's story was spread by Bishop Athanasius and became one of the staples of the cult of saints. Athanasius relates what the Devil did to induce Anthony to sin:

> He harassed him during the night, and he persecuted him sometimes to such a point that Anthony took up the posture of a wrestler. The Devil sent him obscene thoughts;

Anthony repulsed them by his prayers. The Devil made
himself tender and caressing; Anthony, shamefast, pro-
tected his body by faith, prayers and fasts. The Devil took
the form of a woman; he reproduced her gestures. But
Anthony remained faithful to Christ. . . . He who thought
to be able to make himself like God was vanquished by an
adolescent. He who thought himself above flesh and
blood was wrecked against a man clothed in flesh
and blood. . . . Finally, the dragon, seeing that he could
not overthrow Anthony, was seized by rage. He appeared
to Anthony as he is in reality, that is, in the form of a black
child: ceasing to attack by thought alone, he took a human
voice and said: "Many are they whom I have deceived,
whom I have thrown down: but I have been able to do
nothing against thee." Anthony asked him, "Who art
thou—thou who speakst thus?" The Devil replied in a
groaning voice, "I am the friend of fornication. I lay my
snares before the young to make them fall into this vice,
and I am called the spirit of fornication. . . . It is I who
have tormented thee so many times and have always been
repulsed." Anthony, after giving thanks to God, replied to
his enemy confidently: "Thou art utterly contemptible;
thy spirit is black and thou art like a child without
strength. Henceforth I will disturb myself no more
because of thee, for the Lord is my help and I can despise
my enemies." When he heard these words, the black man
fled at once and did not even dare come near this man.[12]

Athanasius includes many of the standard defining characteristics of the Devil. He is an incorrigible tempter dressed in black
and often seemingly as innocent as a child. Yet when confronted
by a man or woman of firm faith, who turns to prayer and fasting
to repulse his advances, he becomes powerless.

Anthony and other saints were raised to hero status by the
Church in this period. The mark of goodness, of winning God's
favor, had nothing to do with practicing the gospel virtues of

loving your neighbor, being charitable, and attending the sacraments, but rather lay in one single feat: repulsing the Devil.

Desert monks who followed in Anthony's footsteps were not
the only or indeed the enduring manifestation of monasticism.
Other Christians like Saint Patrick set sail from Ireland's shores
to assist the spread of a distinctly Celtic form of monasticism
throughout northern Europe. What both Egyptian and Celtic
variations had in common was a suspicion of hierarchy and the
trappings of Church organization. Both aimed, as Paul Johnson
puts it in his *History of Christianity*, to "live as close to the sub-
sistence level as possible, consistent with good health; and they
should preach the gospel on foot 'after the manner of the
apostles.' "[13] Some monks were so hostile to the growing power
of bishops and Rome that they fancied they saw a satanic plot
unfolding there. Saint Martin of Tours (d. 397) believed that
the ecclesiastical authorities were working hand in hand with
the Devil.

It was in response to such independence of mind and spirit
that Gregory encouraged Benedict of Nursia (480–547) to
found at Subiaco (and later at Monte Cassino) an order of
monks more willing to work with Rome. Benedict's *Rule* proved
immensely popular—and continues to be so to this day. In its
simplicity and lack of ornament, it proved attractive to young
men and women in search of commitment in an unstable world.
Benedict was a man of his time. His vision of the Devil as a figure
stalking humankind looking for each and every sign of a chink in
the armor was typical of the age. In chapter fifty-four of the *Rule*
he forbids his monks to exchange gifts, or to receive them from
friends and relatives outside the monastery, "lest occasion be
given to the Devil." In chapter fifty-eight, on the process for
accepting new vocations into the order, he writes: "the clothing
taken from him is to be put away and kept safely in the wardrobe
so that should he ever agree to the Devil's suggestion and leave
the monastery, he can be stripped of the clothing of the
monastery."[14] As Benedict's monks spread across Europe in the
following centuries, founding monasteries and centers of

learning, they played a leading and often dominant part in the arts and education, imbuing them with their own particular viewpoint and their own particular vision of the Devil.

Exorcism

Fundamental to the missionary drive was the imperative to bring the sacraments to pagan people. Although Satan was so much a feature of this expansion across Europe, he had little more than a minor part in any of the Church's formal rituals. Only in the baptism ceremony was his malign influence formally mentioned.

Immersion in water as a ritual ceremony had existed long before Christ. When he was baptized by his cousin John, it is thought that they were imitating a Jewish Essene rite of purification. The formalization of the practice within the Christian Church came from the third century onward when at Easter there would be a single ceremony in each church where groups of candidates—or converts—would be received. By the seventh century the wording of the ceremony, especially of the questions asked of each candidate, had been set in stone. There were usually seven, like the seven demons that Christ cast out of Mary Magdalene. The assumption of the ceremony—and one that continues to this day in the modern wording of the baptism ceremony—was that the candidate, be it he or she, newborn baby, child, or adult, was in the hands of Satan and hence needed to be exorcised.

Exorcism during baptism is one of the earliest traceable forms of the ceremony, but it was a commonplace ritual. None of the sinister overtones that later ages attached to exorcism then existed. It was essentially a healing process and could be as uncontroversial as genuflecting before an altar or crossing yourself in church—which in its own way is a form of exorcism. In a report published in 1976, the Church of England described this positive aspect of exorcism in the early Church as "an extension of the frontiers of Christ's kingdom and a demonstration of the power of the Resurrection to overcome evil and replace it with good."[15] Exorcism was seen as a kind of ritual purification and cleansing to be pronounced over the sick, over food, and over drink. Even the line at the end of the Lord's prayer, "Deliver Us from Evil," was regarded as a form of exorcism.

Variations on the theme of exorcism had existed in the pre-Christian world, but it was the biblical precedent of Christ's actions in casting out evil spirits and miracle cures that inspired the early Church to take up the practice with gusto. By the third century there was a separate order of exorcists.[16] Pope Cornelius (251–253) claimed that he had fifty-two exorcists under his command. Among some they were regarded as miracle workers. Their feats became the stuff of popular legend, an integral part of the great push to convince pagans to convert. Gradually, however, the dividing line between the exorcists and priests faded and the two became one. Monks in particular were called upon to lay their hands on people thought to be afflicted by demons. These holy men, or exorcists, became renowned as healers, rivals to the traditional makers of potions, and were brought in to tackle a whole range of what were often medical complaints.

The standard tools of exorcists were prayers, incense, salt, and holy oil. From the fourth century onward, however, fear of the Devil and the awareness of original sin grew in the writings of Irenaeus and Tertullian and baptism became a frontline ceremony for combating Satan. By removing the stain of Adam's sin in the Garden of Eden from the souls of new recruits to the Church, the Devil too was being renounced. After all, he was the one who had led Adam astray. Hence the practice of exsufflation, whereby the priest blew in the candidate's face, in a gesture that recalled the heroic tales of the desert fathers hissing or spitting at demons. The Teutonic Council of Leptinnes, in 743, went a stage further and demanded that candidates renounce not only the Devil but Thor, Woden, and Saxnot as well—another sign that ancient pagan beliefs were slow to die out.

Other aspects of the symbolic gestures surrounding baptism also had their origins in the renunciation of Satan. The ceremony would start with the candidate facing west, traditionally the region of darkness and death. After a threefold statement renouncing Satan, his pomps, and his works, all would then turn to the east, the place of light and resurrection. Even immersion—partial or total—in water was meant to symbolize descent into the Devil's domain and the re-emergence into the light of Christ's presence. It was only in the post-Reformation period that the baptism ceremony was rethought and Satan slowly receded in favor of a celebration of another person entering into the Christian family.

The Christianity that emerged dominant in the medieval period was altered by the battles and compromises it had endured. Theological debate around the figure of Satan slowed to a murmur after Saint Augustine in the fifth century, and theologians had said all they wanted to say by the thirteenth century. The Devil was left to the local communities where he served as a readily understandable character, a face to put to the abstract reality of evil, and a sort of mediator, a method of assimilation between pagan ideas and the Church. Satan became an essential bridge between local superstitions and the new Christianity of the missionaries. In the process his position as God's opposite and equal was strengthened.

SIX

The Crusaders' Bogeyman

> In Islam the Devil is a trivial little character,
> stupid and unaware. When the Iranians
> described America as the Devil, they didn't mean
> it was an evil country but a stupid one, the great
> trivialiser.
>
> —Karen Armstrong

In the struggle to reconcile an all-loving, all-giving, almighty creator with the existence of evil in the world, Christianity built up Satan throughout the first millennium as the crucial limiting factor on God's omnipotence. It continued publicly to insist on monism—that God is responsible for everything—but then muddied the waters by talk of a personal, incarnate Devil. Islam and Judaism, monotheistic creeds like Christianity, were more rigorous. They resisted the temptation to place any restraints on Allah's or Yahweh's power in order to preserve his goodness. Though the Devil—called variously Iblis or Shaytan—features in the *Qur'an* and in Islamic doctrine, he is a minor irritant to both Allah and humankind but nothing more. In Judaism the focus is less on a personification of evil than on the *yetser hara*, the evil inclination within each and every one.

The eternal dilemmas that gave rise to the Devil in the Christian mind—human suffering, the human capacity to go against God's wishes, natural disasters, the unexplained, and the inexplicable—are all unambiguously laid at the door of Allah in the

Qur'an, his revelation to the Prophet Muhammad, as first set down in the seventh century. They are part of Allah's will. There is no suggestion that their existence in any way diminishes Allah and no attempt, however covert or understated, to shuffle the guilt off on to a third party.

The key concept to Islam—indeed the literal meaning of the word—is surrender, surrender to whatever Allah wills. Through punishment and being put to the test, humankind shows its love of Allah. Such trials may seem incomprehensible, but Allah had his reasons that will one day become apparent. In the meantime the good Muslim will take whatever comes his or her way and have faith. The Devil of the *Qur'an* has no power to make humanity commit evil deeds. "I had no authority over you," Shaytan tells his followers (14:22), "except that I called you and you obeyed me. Therefore do not blame me but blame yourselves."[1] The Christian Devil as the external force on whose shoulders are heaped every ill in the world has no counterpart in the *Qur'an*. Shaytan and Iblis are but pale imitations with nothing more than the shadow of Satan's power. They can and do tempt humankind as part of the process of testing, but they act with Allah's knowledge and tacit consent. They pose him no threat and have no freedom of action at all.

There are many theories as to the respective roles of Iblis and Shaytan in the *Qur'an*. What is indisputable is that both refer to an unholy figure. Iblis is a fallen angel whose demise came about as a result of his pride when confronted with Adam. However, the twin facts that he fell after the creation of the world by God—rather than before as was the prevailing Christian notion—and that he would be saved strike a discordant note. Both reduce Iblis to more of a troublemaker than an intrinsic and irreconcilable source of disharmony. The world was there and good before he came to cause trouble and in the end his rebellion does not amount to much. The story of Iblis's fall is repeated seven times in the *Qur'an* with a number of adornments. Allah banishes Iblis to hell (15:43) and denies him authority over anyone. In chapter seventeen (verse 64) he responds to Iblis's threat to tempt humans. "And beguile whomsoever of them you can with your voice and collect against them your forces riding and on foot and share with them in wealth and children and hold out promises to them." Such promises are false, Allah asserts, and will be shown to be so.

Shaytan appears in several different scenarios in the *Qur'an*, each time tempting men and women to do wrong. He is rarely successful and the *Qur'an* makes plain that it is Allah's wrath, his overwhelming power, and plan for humanity rather than Shaytan's little schemes that should concern believers. "It is only the Devil [Shaytan] that causes you to fear from his friends, but do not fear them and fear me if you are believers" (3:174). Shaytan is equated at one stage with local polytheistic gods and the ritual of slitting animals' ears in sacrifice to them. "And most certainly I will lead them astray," Shaytan threatens, "and excite in them vain desires, and bid them so that they shall slit the ears of the cattle" (4:119). Just as in the Old Testament, all other gods were treated as impostors and those who followed them heretics, or worse. The concept of demonizing opponents existed from the birth of Islam, which can be explained by the hostile reception Muhammad and his messages originally received in Mecca, which led him to undertake his famous pilgrimage to Medina in 622. Such hostility meant that the *Qur'an* has a militant tone, praising those who struggle—the translation of *jihad*—in self-defense. (The concept of the *jihad* as a holy war came later.) Likewise the missionary division of the world into two zones—the *dar al-Islam*, a peaceful territory where Allah's word is law, and the *dar al-Harb*, lands where Muslims must take the word of God by whatever means possible—was developed subsequently in Islamic law.

The Satanic Verses

The popular deities of Mecca at the time of Muhammad included the cult of three goddesses, Manat, al-Lat, and al-Uzza.

Ibn al-Kalbi (d. 821), the scholar who made a study of the pre-Islamic past of Arabia in his *Book of Idols* records how "all the Arabs used to venerate her [Manat]" with pilgrimages to her shrine, gifts, sacrifice and homage by way of shaving their heads.[2] As a young man Muhammad was drawn to the cult of al-Uzza and her shrine east of Mecca.[3] The *Qur'an* is explicit in its condemnation of the worship of such female gods who enjoy a status roughly akin to angels and therefore somewhat higher up the scale than *jinn*, or spirits (43:19).

The three goddesses in particular, sometimes called the "daughters of Allah," are central to the most notorious text associated with the Devil in Islam—the so-called "satanic verses." In section fifty-three of the *Qur'an*, Muhammad is distraught that his people are so reluctant to understand the message that he is giving them from Allah. So he appeals to Allah for help and is told that the intercession of the three goddesses might assist him. However, the *Qur'an* swiftly goes on to make clear that this guidance came to Muhammad not from Allah but from elsewhere. There is no mention of "satanic verses" in the *Qur'an*: that version of events comes in the accounts of the tenth-century historian, Abu Jafar at-Tabari:

> Satan cast on his [Muhammad's] tongue, because of his inner debates and what he desired to bring to his people, the words 'These are the high-flying cranes; verily their intercession is to be hoped for.'[4]

At-Tabari continues with details of how Muhammad's fellow citizens were "delighted at the way in which he had spoken of their gods and they listened to him, while the Muslims, having complete trust in their Prophet with respect of the message which he brought from God, did not suspect him of error, illusion or mistake."[5] All went to worship together in harmony for a brief spell before Muhammad realized, according to at-Tabari, that Satan had led him into his error and expunged the offending verses from the *Qur'an*, replacing them with the explanation—

without any mention of a devil—that remains the authorized version to this day. "These are only names that you and your fathers have invented. No authority was sent down by God for them. They only follow conjecture and wish-fulfillment" (53:23). There is no suggestion that anything in the *Qur'an* is the work of Satan—a charge that remains deeply offensive to Muslims. At-Tabari's account is treated with scorn. "No authentic *hadith* scholar," wrote Professor Syed Ali Ashraf, Director-General of the Islamic Academy at Cambridge University, "has recorded this [episode] and many great Islamic scholars have rejected it as a fabrication of the Makkan unbelievers who spread the rumor in order to cast doubt into the minds of newly converted and other people about the very authenticity of all revelations which the Blessed Prophet claimed to have been brought down to him by Archangel Gabriel."[6]

These remarks were made in the wake of the controversy caused by the publication of Salman Rushdie's novel *The Satanic Verses* in 1988. Rushdie drew on his own links with Islam and the story of the goddesses, with its poles of good and evil, to create a modern-day moral tale. Yet by seemingly championing the authenticity of the "satanic verses" and hence besmirching the good name of the *Qur'an*, Rushdie brought the wrath of some extremist Muslims down on his head.[7] On a broader level, at-Tabari's account, whatever its exact historical truth, shows that like Christianity, Islam was experiencing difficulty persuading people of the benefits of a single omnipotent god and that some degree of accommodation with existing deities might have taken place—at least until Muhammad's teachings could establish a firm hold.

A Holy War

With the papacy increasingly concerned with European matters and the Eastern Church in Constantinople taking the Word to the Slav peoples, Islam spread throughout the Near and Middle

East and along the North African coast. Only at Alexandria, historically one of the great centers of Christianity, was its forward momentum checked.

When Islam crossed the Straits of Gibraltar and entered the Iberian peninsula, the leaders of Christianity became alarmed at the fate of what it grew to regard as a lost province. When Allah's foot soldiers crossed the Pyrenees in 720 and spread to the outskirts of Poitiers in the west of France, alarm turned to panic with the realization that Islam was not just another Near Eastern cult, destined to shine briefly before disappearing over the horizon. Though it was not until the age of the Crusades over 250 years later that the Church first outlined its own ambitions to spread the boundaries of "Christendom" beyond Europe and the Mediterranean basin, the Muslim incursion into the heart of Catholicism could not be tolerated. A counteroffensive was launched against the "occupation" of Spain, with Charlemagne leading his forces against the Saracens, a Greek word originally meaning "Arab," which came, in medieval Europe, to be a derogatory term for Muslim. Charlemagne's success was spasmodic—particularly since he was simultaneously fighting off Saxon attacks on his Empire in the east.

His battle cry was taken up by others and reached fever pitch with the Crusades. Many of the Crusaders who set sail for the battlefields of the Near East were of Spanish and southern French origin and had old scores to settle with Islam. They were engaged too in what was in effect Europe's first colonial push. There was a perceived shortage of land in France, and many of the Crusaders were intent on carving out estates for themselves and their descendants in the Near East. They harbored no hopes of conversion like Saint Paul and the first apostles. Rather theirs was an aggressive mission intent on carving out a new Christian state to be known as Outremer.

Pope Urban II sent the first Crusaders on their way in 1095 at the Council of Clermont, with an impassioned appeal to deliver Jerusalem from the infidel and a promise—echoing that in the *Qur'an*—of a heavenly reward for those who lost their lives in the struggle. He died just before the Holy City was taken in 1099. A second—and much less successful—crusade followed between 1147 and 1149. In 1187, Islam recaptured Jerusalem and the third crusade (1189–1192), despite the presence of Richard the Lion-Heart and assorted European royals, failed to make good the loss. The fourth crusade (1202–1204) was a bloody and shameful affair. The Crusaders never made it to Jerusalem but spent their time sacking Constantinople, asserting the hegemony of western Christendom over the Eastern Church. After such a debacle, even the papacy had the good grace to show a little contrition and the practice of sallies to the East gradually died out.

The language of the Crusades, the rhetoric that surrounded them, was that of a religious war. But this was, as Professor John Roberts has pointed out, a smoke screen. Of crusading, he writes: "Its religious impulse could still prove an ancillary aid and rationalisation for other motives, but the first four Crusades had shown the unpleasant face of greed and cupidity."[8] Whatever the politicians'—and indeed the prelates' and pontiffs'—purposes, the Crusades became a fight with the Devil and his Saracen army. As the various armies departed for Jerusalem, the leaders of the Church embarked upon a process of demonizing Islam and its adherents, which continues to this day. The Muslims were tarred by the brush of the Prince of Darkness. Muhammad was the Devil incarnate and his followers the servants of Satan. There was no toleration, no attempt to live and let live, no sense that in their shared monotheism Islam and Christianity had much common ground. Each and every aspect of the *Qur'an* that differed from the Christian credo was misrepresented as an attack on God. If Islam had not before had a violent antipathy to western Christianity, it certainly developed one now. Coexistence was out of the question. The cosmic struggle of God and Satan was to be mirrored on earth by that of Christians and Muslims.

In the cultural backdrop of the period, Satan's central role in the battles is made abundantly clear. The French in particular developed a whole genre of epic literature to accompany the Crusades, where those who stood in the way of the march of Christendom were the soldiers of Satan. One of the most popular texts of the time was the *Chanson de Roland*, dated to the beginning of the twelfth century—though recent research has shown that it may well have existed in the oral tradition, performed by traveling players, at the time of the Battle of Hastings in 1066. Part of the tradition of *chansons de geste*—epic poems of heroic and legendary deeds centered on the life and times of Charlemagne—*Roland* tells of the first Holy Roman Emperor's fight with the Saracen king Marsile in Spain. Roland, Charlemagne's nephew, is betrayed to Marsile by Ganelon, who is presented in the text as a trickster, deceiving his fellow Franks with talk of peace. Betrayal and hatred of the infidel are the dominant themes of the work.

Yet *Roland* is not an entirely black-and-white tale. Ganelon may be a traitor, but he is shown as having good qualities, notably his loyalty to Charlemagne. Marsile has fewer redeeming qualities, but in his words and in the poet's descriptions of the Saracen king there is none of the crude demonizing of other texts. There is the suggestion that human motivations are a complex mixture and that they, rather than the machination of demons, can account for evil deeds.

The change was at first subtle, disguised in the heroic tone of *Roland* and its more general vehemence toward the Saracens. Indeed, this best known of the *chansons de geste* of the period is not entirely typical and in others of the genre appear a variety of demonic characters like Agolaffe, black, twisted with a long nose, big ears, and sunken, menacing eyes, or Abisme—literally hell— and Isembart, who heads an army of horned monsters. The medieval literary tradition held that evil within could rarely be disguised behind a benign countenance. The wicked looked wicked and that tended to mean like the Devil of the popular imagination. In French art, Muslims were demonized. The fourteenth-century *Grandes Chroniques de France*—now kept in the Bibliothèque nationale in Paris—contain illustrations showing horned, fanged Saracens, part primitive man and part beast, confronting Charlemagne's troops, whose faces depict the pious determination usually associated with angels.

The association of Islam and Satan led to the villains of various plays and spectacles of the time being named after the Prophet—Mehmet or Mahoud or, in Chaucer, Makomete. It was a device that lived on in the English language in the works, for example, of Edmund Spenser (1522–1599), who in his *Faerie Queene* used the name Mahound for a heathen idol by whom wicked characters swear.

The paranoia that this atmosphere of "if you're not with us, you're with the Saracens and Satan" created left no one beyond reproach. Even the first ever French Pope, Sylvester II (ruled 999–1003), was posthumously accused of making a pact with the Devil by the English Benedictine chronicler, William of Malmesbury. A great champion of the Crusades, Malmesbury held that Sylvester's crime was to have "flown" as a young man to Spain to consort and learn magic from the Saracens. When he was later elected Pope, he used his magic skills to fashion a head that replied to all his questions. This head told him he would only die when he had said mass in Jerusalem. So he decided never to venture to the Holy Land. However, one day he said mass in a Church that he only subsequently realized was dedicated to the Holy Cross of Jerusalem. He immediately fell ill and summoned his cardinals to his deathbed, admitted his pact with Satan, and asked by way of reparation that his body be cut up alive into pieces and thrown out of the Church. The story of Sylvester's heresy was a popular one in medieval chronicles. Another writer, Sigabert, says that there was no deathbed confession and that Pope Sylvester went straight to hell to repay his debt to the Devil. Yet another version has it that throughout his pontificate he was accompanied everywhere by a black dog, traditionally a symbol of the Devil. Even the names of the three dioceses he headed—Rheims, Ravenna, and Rome—were taken as somehow satanic because they all began with *R*'s.

The truth behind these stories is instructive of the times.

Sylvester had indeed visited Spain as a youth and had excelled in the study of such novel disciplines as mathematics and astronomy, which were regarded as magic, necromancy, and therefore tantamount to heresy. Such new thinking made him a controversial figure, and later chroniclers, eager to discredit him, chose the most obvious course—link him with the demonic Saracens and thereby damn him.

Even the simplest social customs associated with Islam were demonized. One habit picked up from the Muslims by the Crusaders on their travels was that of frequent bathing. When they brought such new ways home with them, they were accused of importing satanic rites. Bathhouses in towns were dubbed temples to the Devil and—in a characteristic jump of the imagination, linking sex with evil—it was suggested they were the scene of perpetual orgies. As yet cleanliness was far removed from godliness. By another sleight of hand, Christianity tried to either disguise its own vulnerabilities or justify its actions by accusing the Saracens of doing the opposite. The brutality of the Crusaders was buried under a volley of accusations that the Muslims were brutal, that the concept of *jihad* was that of Holy War and was part of the *Qur'an*. Neither charge stands up to scrutiny. Christianity contributed to increasing Muslim brutality rather than vice versa.

The Original Infidels

The earliest victims of the Crusaders were the Jews of Metz, Mainz, Worms, Prague, and Speyer. In 1096, before setting out on their long march toward the fabled land of Outremer, the Crusaders turned on those they regarded as the Devil in their midst. The demonization of the Jews of Europe was one of the earliest, most enduring, and most pernicious examples of the Christian habit of stigmatizing as servants of the Prince of Darkness everyone who did not share their beliefs.

Spread mainly around Europe, living in the cities, the one and a half million Jews were vastly overrepresented in professions like law, medicine, and finance. In the Dark Ages, they were often among the few literate and numerate residents of most towns and because of their consequent importance, they were regularly targeted by disaffected rulers and envious fellow citizens. Though their prime motive in these attacks was greed, it was often buried and cloaked in Christian rhetoric. At times of great religious strain or enthusiasm, there was—and remains—a pre-disposition, encouraged by some clerics, to turn on those who sat outside the "normal" confines of an increasingly Church-dominated society. Anyone who was "other" was linked with the ultimate "other," Satan. The Jews were the original interlopers at the party, God's chosen people who, in Christian eyes, had rejected Jesus and crucified him. Officially, the death of Christ remained in Christianity's eyes humanity's sin, but an increasingly popular view, laying it at the door of the Jews, prevailed. Such a crime, to the medieval mind, could only have been prompted by the Devil and the Jews were taken as the servants of Satan.

As great bands of men gathered in the towns and cities of Europe to prepare for the battle ahead, they terrorized the Jews. Often the land-hungry Crusaders were men who had sold all their possessions and borrowed to fund their expedition. Their debts would be to Jewish moneylenders and in the heat of the moment, the Crusaders, about to embark—in the imagery of the age—on a holy war, demanded that such sums be written off as a mark of respect for their moral courage. When the Jews refused, they were attacked by the Crusaders, who had no difficulty finding willing helpers among the townsfolk. In Mainz alone, 1,000 were killed.

An additional factor in the Crusaders' outrage with the Jews was the fact that they were prominent in the court of the Saracen rulers of Spain. The *Qur'an* is on the whole positive in tone about the Jewish prophets, and in the Islamic Empire the perse-cution of Jews was unusual. Building on their common ground—Judaism and Islam developed parallel approaches, in spirit at least, to law, philosophy, and mysticism—Jews were given senior positions in the Muslim world. One tenth-century caliph in Cordoba in Spain took tolerance to such an extent that his city blossomed—briefly—as the cultural center of the Jewish world. The sight of the Jews working with the Muslims to keep control of Spain, Christianity's lost province, served only to demonize both races by their association. "The Christian demonising of the Jews," says Rabbi Norman Solomon, a former head of the Centre for the Study of Judaism and Jewish–Christian Relations, "goes right back to the Jewish rejection of Jesus—the old question of the Jews having killed Jesus. In that the image of the Jews as demons was made."[9]

From the second century onward what we would now call anti-Semitism gathered force as Christianity and Judaism went their separate ways. Officially tolerance was decreed but from the early centuries of the Church the popular mood was decidedly less benign. Saint John Chrysostom (c. 350–c. 407), in eight sermons delivered to the people of Antioch in 387, provided all the weapons used against the Jews by succeeding generations. They were carnal, lascivious, avaricious, accursed, and demonic. They had murdered all the prophets and then crucified Christ and worshiped the Devil. Saint Jerome (c. 340–420) used his leadership position to hammer home a similar message. On the Jewish synagogue, he was particularly outspoken. "If you call it a brothel, a den of vice, the Devil's refuge, Satan's fortress, a place to deprave the soul, an abyss of every conceivable disaster or whatever else you will, you are saying less than it deserves."[10] Such a battle cry to attack Satan's temple did not go unheeded. One of the earliest recorded incidents of Christians burning down a synagogue came in 338 at Callicnicul on the Euphrates.

Christian leaders who encouraged demonizing of the Jews, and those in their congregation who followed their lead, pointed to Jewish laws and customs that set them apart from the rest of society. Regulations covering food, the slaughter of animals to be eaten, cooking, and male circumcision all made the Jews different and prompted innumerable rumors. Jews, according to popular legend, smelled of sulfur—like the Devil—until they were baptized. This *foetor judaicus* was contrasted with the "odour of sanctity" that enveloped Christian holy men and women. It was also said that Jews, like the Devil, had horns and a tail. King Philip III of France (1223–1268) required Jews in his realm to attach a horn-shaped figure to the customary Jewish badge.

Jews were accused of worshiping Satan at secret ceremonies. They kidnapped children at his behest, the charge went, to offer them in sacrifice to him. In 1144 in Norwich, then one of the largest cities in England, a young apprentice boy called William, the son of a wealthy farmer, disappeared just before Easter. He was last seen going into a Jew's house. When his body was discovered days later in a wood outside the city, it was, according to the chronicler, Thomas of Monmouth, a monk of Norwich Priory, with his head shaved and "punctured with countless stabs." The boy's distraught mother accused local Jews of kidnapping her son and killing him in a bizarre and blasphemous ritualized reenactment of Christ's passion. Her charges were substantiated by a Christian servant working in one Jewish house who claimed to have seen the ceremony.[11] In the wave of hysteria that followed, a group of Jews were accused of the crime before an ecclesiastical court and had to be rescued by the sheriff, who placed them in Norwich Castle for safekeeping. Miracles were claimed in the name of the dead boy. The appointment of a new Bishop of Norwich, sympathetic to such claims, stoked up the fires of anti-Jewish prejudice in the city. One story that made the rounds suggested that the Jews murdered a child each and every Easter—which coincided with the feast of Passover—to use his or her blood in their special Passover bread.

William was canonized by popular acclaim as a Christ-substitute who performed miracles. Rumors abounded about bizarre Jewish rituals and blood sacrifices. Behind these Christian myths of satanic rituals among the Jews of Norwich lay a deeper anxiety. Demonization and persecution were—and still are—

often a reaction to fear or insecurity. Such fantasies about Jews as devilish child slayers show an almost oedipal fear of Christianity's parent faith Judaism, an unresolved rivalry reflected in the unhappy relationship between the two creeds.

There is an echo of William's fate in Chaucer's *Canterbury Tales*. "The Prioress's Tale" tells of a young God-fearing boy who sings hymns to the Virgin Mary in the Jewish quarter— described as full of "cursed jues" and "for foule usure and lucre of vileynye." He is then seized and murdered by the Jews. Their inspiration is "Oure first foo, the serpent Sathanas, That hath in Jues herte his waspes nest."

It was suggested that the Jews had poisoned wells and caused the Black Death, which swept Europe in the fourteenth century. In 1348 Clement VI, the fourth of the Avignon popes, tried to stem such rumors by assuring his flock that the plague was the work of the Devil. His efforts seem only to have merged the two ideas of Jews and Devil as one in the popular mind. The demonic Jew as a poisoner became a stock figure in literature and legend, culminating in Christopher Marlowe's Barabbas in *The Jew of Malta* (c. 1592).

Clement was unusual in standing out against the tide of Christian anti-Semitism. Pope Gregory IX, whose *Liber extra* was one of the first attempts to set out a basic textbook of canon law, saw fit in 1236 to condemn the *Talmud*—a Jewish commentary on scripture and its primary work of scholarship—as satanically inspired. Earlier in the same century under that keen advocate of crusades, Innocent III (1198–1216), the Fourth Lateran Council of 1215 had promulgated various anti-Jewish and anti-Muslim laws—denying them, for example, the ownership of land and restricting how they might dress—at the same time as including a forcible restatement in its first article of the Devil's role as the source of all heresy and disbelief.

The cultural backdrop of the age gives a flavor of the association between Jews and the Devil. In medieval art the standard image of the Jew—with a long, hooked nose and cloaked in black—merged with that of the Devil. One of the earliest dated sketches of a Jew, on the 1277 Forest Roll of Essex, carries the caption "Aaron, son of the Devil." In other works dating from this period Jews are shown as riding goats, at that time a symbol of lechery and the Devil's favorite animal. In the medieval plays that reenacted Christ's Passion and death, the guilt of the Jews was explicit. This pigeonholing is clear in Shakespeare's *The Merchant of Venice*, where it is remarked of Shylock "The Jew is the very Devil incarnal." Furthermore, the Jew was associated with Judas, Christ's betrayer, and Judas with the Devil. In an illumination from the German eleventh-century *Gospel Book of the Emperor Henry III*, Judas is seen at the Last Supper with the Devil, as a black imp, in his mouth.

While the demonization of the Jews was an important driving force in anti-Semitism, some have questioned whether the Devil was an essential part in this process. Christian diabology certainly brought with it a bitter harvest for the Jews, but, as Jeffrey Burton Russell writes, "if no idea of the Devil had existed, the course of anti-semitism would probably have been little different. First of all, it had as many social as religious causes. Second, the religious causes consisted of ancient barriers between Jews and Christians, each group excluding the other from its community. Without a Devil, Christians would still have excluded Jews, blamed them for the crucifixion and regarded them as sinners cut off from the mystical body of Christ, the corporation of the saved. Diabology was a handy weapon, but it was just that: a weapon, not the cause of anti-semitism."[12]

A Credo without a Devil

One of the most obvious distinguishing features between Judaism and Christianity is the former's lack of interest in the Devil. There is no Hebrew word for devil, just the more ambiguous figure of Satan in the Book of Job.

Toward the end of the first century, and especially after their defeat at the hands of their Roman overlords in 70 A.D., the Jews

moved away from the extreme political clericalism of the Sadducees in favor of a more philosophical approach in what became
known as the rabbinical age. The *Talmud* was completed in
Jerusalem around the end of the fourth century. Its scholarship
reveals an environment where the debate over good and evil
concentrated less on the image of the Devil and more on a psychological understanding of suffering in the world. Judaism
remains more concerned with the *yetser hara*—the evil inclination that is found within each one of us—than with any external
force for evil.

   According to Rabbi Norman Solomon, Judaism "lacks a
strong sense of original sin. It is not totally absent but is
nowhere near as strong as in Christianity. Things are more
evenly balanced between good and evil. With God's grace you
will overcome. It is God-centered. There is no sense of being
under the control of another sinister power."[13] Alongside this
dominant trend, however, has run a parallel but weaker tendency
to look to a Devil-like figure as the polar opposite of God. For
most of the past 2,000 years, it has been little more than a
shadow, but in the medieval age, with Judaism demonized and
attacked by Christianity and its Crusaders, a more mystical
dualist strain of Judaism made its presence felt in times of trial.

   The principal insight into Judaism at this time of wandering,
fragmentation, and persecution comes from the writings of
Moses ben Maimon, known to the modern age as Maimonides.
A scholarly Jew in Egypt in the twelfth century, his writings
reveal the dominant rationalist theology of the time, taking its
lead from the *Talmud*. Yet he also makes repeated references to a
different kind of Judaism, more popular, almost folklorish, that
believed in black-and-white magic, conjured up good and evil
spirits, and found expression in ceremonies that lasted through
the night with accompanying séances, magic potions, and the
like. It was this undercurrent that blossomed into the Kabbalah
of twelfth-century France and Spain. In the *Talmud*, the word
"kabbalah" is used in the sense of received doctrine or tradition,
oral teaching that postdates the Hebrew Scriptures. However, it

grew to encapsulate a movement that felt insight could be gleaned by direct communication with God, that certain gifted individuals had the capacity to transmit God's wishes to their fellow humanity. In this it was influenced by the Gnostics, who had made their impact on Christianity centuries earlier.

As was the case with Christian Gnosticism, there was a profusion of claims to divinely inspired insight and the Kabbalah did not really achieve any sort of organizational form until the second half of the twelfth century in Provençal France, when there was a systematic rooting out of the more fanciful flashes of wisdom and mystical trinkets. Popular among the Kabbalists, though not in any meaningful sense a part of them, was Judah Halevi (1075–1141), a Spanish mystic and lyricist whose *Poems of Zion* rejected the Jews' fate as a despised people in Europe and sought instead a direct experience of God.

Others took a greater interest in the notion of an outside force for evil. In Spanish Judaism the Kabbalah made a bible of the *Sefer-ha-Zohar* ("The Book of Splendor"), written around 1275 by Moses ben Shem Tov of Guadalajara. "The chief doctrines he puts forward," says Professor Gershom Scholem of the Hebrew University in Jerusalem, "are essentially the consummation of the development of Kabbalistic thought during the first three quarters of the thirteenth century."[14] From a whole range of Gnostic-inspired views about such subjects as the destiny of humanity, the depth of the Godhead, and the significance of sacred texts like the *Talmud* and the *Torah*—the first five books of the Hebrew Scriptures—the *Zohar* distils a highly personal and highly influential cocktail.

In particular the author takes up the idea of a "left emanation"—an ordered hierarchy of evils, the realm of Satan, which like the right emanation, the realm of light and of Yahweh, is divided into ten spheres or stages. The ten holy *Sefiroth* or spheres or numerations—often depicted as a tree—have their counterparts in ten unholy or impure ones. Between them the two sets cover all of creation, every human dilemma. The ten evil principles are unleashed, Moses of ben Shem Tov seems to suggest, when the fifth *Sefiroth, Din*, or stern judgment, breaks away from the restraining factors of the other spheres and thereby becomes evil or destructive. The *Zohar* presents a dualist view of the world, dividing it down the middle between good and evil, God and Satan. Its influence returned spasmodically in the following centuries, notably in the writings of Isaac Luria (1534–1572). Luria captured the mysticism that is at the heart of Kabbalah, its prayers, practices, hopes, and expectations. Through his influence this type of spirituality became a major Jewish enthusiasm. Only in the eighteenth and nineteenth centuries did it fall into decline with the onset of Western-style rationalism, though a mystical fringe exists to this day.[15]

Eastern Promise

The other target of the Crusaders was the Eastern Church. The Patriarch of Constantinople remained in theory the equal of the Bishop of Rome, but as the Eastern Church developed an ever closer relationship with the Byzantine Empire, cracks began to appear in Christian unity. Tension had been in the air as early as the Council of Chalcedon of 451, when the two wings differed over the interpretation of certain doctrines.

This spirit of hostility and rivalry led, when the Crusaders retook Jerusalem during their first expedition, to the expulsion of all but Latin (Western) priests. Some Eastern Orthodox clergy were tortured, while even the Maronites, in full communion with Rome, were maltreated. It was the Fourth Crusade (1202–1204), however, that saw the would-be hammers of the Muslims side with the Venetians—a political power to rival Constantinople—and with a Byzantine prince pretender. The result was the sack of Constantinople. Pope Innocent III (1198–1216) had no wish to see Constantinople so abused, its mother Church Saint Sophia desecrated, and nuns raped in his name, but he eventually accepted the outcome of the debacle—the short-lived establishment of a Latin Patriarchate in the region. It marked a turning point in East-West relations, and despite subsequent attempts to heal the breach—at the Council of Lyons in 1274 and at Florence in 1439—Rome and the Eastern Orthodox went their own ways in a spirit of hostility and mistrust. It was only with the modernization of the Catholic Church in the 1960s that such historical wounds were treated.

Long before the final break, Eastern theology had been charting its own course with a reflective and introspective brand of monasticism that left little space for the Devil. Its founder, Saint Basil (c. 330–379), stressed that God was unknowable but all-powerful. "It is by his energies that we know God. We do not assent that we come near to the essence itself, for his energies descend on us but his essence remains unapproachable."[16] Such a mystical framework was more flexible and more successful in attributing to God those malign actions that in Western Christianity became the preserve of the Devil.

In tackling evil itself, Eastern thinkers like Pseudo-Dionysius, a Syrian monk who lived around 500, preferred to write of "a lack, a deficiency, a weakness, a disproportion, an error, purposeless, unlovely, lifeless, unwise, unreasonable, imperfect, unreal, causeless, indeterminate, sterile, inert, powerless, disordered, incongruous, indefinite, dark, unsubstantial and never in itself possessed of any existence whatever."[17] But like Western Christianity, the Church in the East faced its own dualist heresies— the Paulicians, the Messalians, the Bulgarian Bogomils, and the Byzantine Bogomils. All shared a rejection of the monism of "official" religion in favor of a more dualist approach that gave the figure of the Devil a hands-on role in the creation and continuation of evil in the world.

The Bogomils were initially a passive, disorganized group, without structure, leadership, or political ambitions. They followed Bogomil—literally meaning "Beloved of God"—a self-proclaimed prophet who lived around 950. Bogomilism tapped into political currents of anti-Byzantine feeling in Bulgaria as it was swallowed up into the Empire in the early eleventh century. By the twelfth century, though its heyday had passed,

Bogomilism lingered on, beset by internal divisions, throughout the outlying areas of the Empire. The hard-line Bogomil dualists—the Order of Drugathia, Dragovitsa, or Dragovitch—and those who took a softer line—the Order of Bulgaria—could not agree on a common course and it fragmented.

The Devil was central to the Bogomils, an opposite and equal force to God. However, they brought a new twist to the by now familiar dualist story. The Devil, they said, was God's first-born, his elder son. His younger son, Christ, was much favored by their father and the Devil—or Satanael, as the Bogomils referred to him—grew jealous. He rebelled and took a third of the angels in heaven with him to earth. There he set about making a carbon copy of God's celestial creation, a second heaven for a second god. The Bogomils therefore believed that everything to do with the world, the here and now, was evil. They took this insight to extremes, rejecting all matter and thus rejecting churches, crucifixes, food, wine, the sacraments, marriage, even sex. They regarded the Temple in Jerusalem as the epicenter of a world satanic cult.

As mainstream Christianity in Constantinople struggled to put down the Bogomil heresy, it turned to the time-honored practice of demonization. Many of the same ideas that have been used to stigmatize first the early Christians, then the Jews, and then any other dissident minority, can be seen in the following description provided by Michael Constantine Psellos (1018–1078), an adviser to the imperial court and a professor of philosophy. In *On the Operation of the Demons*, his description of the Bogomils' Easter ritual, based on hearsay, echoes down the ages to today and widespread allegations of satanic abuse.

They bring together, in a house appointed for the purpose, young girls whom they have initiated into their rites. Then they extinguish the candles, so that the light shall not be witness to their abominable deeds, and throw themselves lasciviously on the girls; each one on whomever first falls into his hands, no matter whether she be his sister, his daughter or his mother. For they think that they are doing something that greatly pleases the demons by transgressing God's laws. . . . When this rite has been completed each goes home; and after waiting nine months, until the time has come for the unnatural children of such unnatural seed to be born, they come together again in the same place. Then on the third day after the birth, they tear the miserable babies from their mother's arms. They cut their tender flesh all over with sharp knives and catch the stream of blood in basins. They throw the babies, still breathing and gasping, on to the fire, to be burned to ashes. After which, they mix the ashes with the blood in the basins and so make an abominable drink, with which they secretly pollute their food and drink.[18]

Psellos was suggesting that the Bogomils' strength came because they were secretly lacing the food unsuspecting Christians would eat. Just as the Jews were accused of poisoning wells and making Passover bread with children's blood at the behest of the Devil, the Bogomils were passing on demonic possession by way of wine and bread.

The specter of a satanic cult eventually fizzled out in the East. In the West, however, contact with the Bogomils was just one of the factors that worked Europe and the Church into a frenzy about the Devil and a group of "heretics" who are known to history as the Cathars.

SEVEN

The Cathar Heresy

> Like civil government the regular routine of
> organised Christianity could easily collapse; the
> two often disintegrated together under pressure.
>
> —Paul Johnson

Around 1172 in the small town of Saint Félix-de-Caraman, near Toulouse in the south of France, a group of men and women met with Nicetas, a Bogomil bishop who had traveled from Constantinople. Their aim was to work together to spread "true" Christianity throughout the region. They did not have in mind Rome or its bishops and priests. Their credo was the dualism that regarded this world and everything to do with it—including the papacy, with its excesses of wealth and power—as the work of the Devil. This gathering was no isolated incident. From the earliest days of the Church, a parallel dualist tendency—pitting God against Satan as two equal and opposite forces—had existed alongside the official orthodoxy of monist Christianity. Called by many names down the ages, all of them linked inevitably with the Gnostics, this twelfth-century incarnation was known as the Cathar heresy.[1]

By the time of the meeting at Saint Félix-de-Caraman, four Church councils—in 1119, 1139, 1148, and 1163—had declared the Cathars to be heretics who should be persecuted in the civil courts and flung into prison. In 1179 the Third General Lateran Council reiterated the curse. But these "heretics" who traveled to greet Bishop Nicetas were unlikely conspirators. Indeed, they wouldn't have recognized the description. They saw their gathering as a Church council rather than a cabal dedicated to breaking the unity of medieval Christendom.

The participants were respectable citizens who led blameless lives. Most of them were the *perfecti*—or perfects—of the Cathar movement. They had received the *Consolamentum*, baptism in the spirit by the laying on of hands, the only true sacrament in their view and the only way to be immunized to Satan's charms. As a result they led lives of great simplicity and piety, undertaking regular *endura*—or fasts. They traveled around their region, preaching, leading by example, avoiding all meat, wine, and worldly goods because they were created by the Devil, and eschewing sexual gratification.

The word Cathar comes from the Greek *Katharos*—meaning the unpolluted or, more loosely, the pure ones. As a collective term Cathar is a word like Gnostic. It crops up in each and every account of Church history down the ages in a bewildering variety of contexts. The Cathars have been variously described as magicians, mystics, another branch of King Arthur's Knights of the Round Table, the custodians of the Holy Grail (Christ's communion cup from the Last Supper), an offshoot of the Knights Templar after they were suppressed, and much more. Their fascination and their ubiquity can be explained by the fact that they were an often ill-documented undercurrent in society, the other side of the coin to the official Church and its ally the state; an umbrella under which sheltered the disaffected, the disappointed, and those who thought there was a better way of organizing the spiritual and material world.

Central to Cathar teaching was the idea that in the beginning the perfect state of God's world was rudely disturbed when the souls of angelic beings were stolen by Sathanas—Satan—and put into bodies of men made in his own likeness. According to the favored Cathar text *Les Questions de Jean*: "And he [Satan]

imagined in order to make man for his service, and took the lime
of the earth and made man in his resemblance. And he ordered
the angel of the second heaven to enter into the body of lime;
and he took another part and made another body in the form of
a woman, and he ordered the angel of the first heaven to enter
therein. The angels cried exceedingly on seeing themselves covered in distinct forms by this mortal envelopment."[2]

The main problem, seen from Rome, was that the Cathar
theology was not just a theoretical challenge to be debated by
scholars. It was a popular movement and its teachings had practical consequences. If the world was the work of the Devil, so
were all worldly trappings including bishops' palaces, art treasures, in fact all the paraphernalia of clerical authority in confessional Europe. The Cathars therefore excited great animosity.
The Church launched what became a crusade to discredit these
"heretics" and crush them. Their name was blackened from
every pulpit and in every pronouncement. One French scholar
who lived at the time his country (as he saw it) was plagued by
the Cathars summed up the hostility they provoked by suggesting an alternative derivation for their name. In his tract
Against the heretics of my times of 1202, Alain de Lille proposed
that the word derived from the vulgar Latin word *cattus*,
meaning "cat." This, he explained, was because the Devil
appeared to the Cathars as a cat. It was clearly a popular idea: the
Bishop of Paris, Guillaume d'Auvergne, an eminent scholar,
claimed in the 1230s: "Lucifer is permitted [by God] to appear
to his worshippers and adorers in the form of a black cat or a
toad and to demand kisses from them; whether as a cat, abomi-
nably, under the tail; or as a toad, horribly, on the mouth."[3]

Both reveal the hysteria generated by the Cathars in a Europe
where there was increasingly only one religious orthodoxy.
These descriptions also demonstrate how the Cathars' view of
the world as the Devil's work was confused in the popular mind,
and turned into a rebellion against God. With more than a little
encouragement from the Church, the populace came to regard

the Cathars not as Devil shunners, but rather as Devil worshipers, embracing every conceivable—and some unthinkable—form of hedonism. Because the popular Devil had no one defined image, the Church was able repeatedly to give him new faces—those of their opponents at any given time, and in this case the Cathars.

Despite such vilification, for much of the twelfth and thirteenth century in southern France, the Cathars—or Albigensians as they were known, after their stronghold in the Languedoc region—were the official Church, with Roman Christianity the interloper. The Albigensians at various times had their own pope, bishops, and leadership structure. They touched a popular nerve that brought them such widespread popularity that not even the impassioned pleas of Saint Bernard of Clairvaux (1090–1153) and the founder of the Dominicans, Dominic Guzman (1170–1221), could bring them back to the official fold. The movement had support at all levels of society, with powerful backers like the counts of Toulouse, relatives of the French royal family and among the richest of the chiefs who took the cross in the Crusades.

The region bordered by the Alps to the east, by the Pyrenees and the Mediterranean to the south and by the Cévennes range to the north and west, containing the basins of the rivers Garonne and Rhône, was known before the advent of the French Revolution as the Province of Languedoc. This was the Cathar stronghold, a region with its own language, its own culture of troubadours and lyric poetry (both of which later inspired Dante when he wrote *Inferno*), and a fierce independence of spirit. Two of its principal towns, Carcassonne and Beziers, had only tolerated the Saracen invaders for as long as it took to assemble sufficient force to eject them. Toulouse had never fallen and at the time of the meeting in Saint Félix-de-Caraman continued to stand as the unblemished pivot of Christian influence in the face of Muslim Spain. It was a region determined to do things its own way, a crossroads of cultural currents, with Muslim influence bringing science to the local university at Montpelier, Jews tolerated to such an extent that Languedoc was once dubbed "Judea secunda," and an absence of the gloomy pessimism and superstition that had descended on much of Europe since the Dark Ages. While there were Cathars all over the continent, it was in Languedoc, focusing on the town of Albi with its fortified cathedral, that the heresy made the most lasting impression.

For many decades Rome limited itself to making blanket condemnations and sending envoys to try to coax the people back, but by the dawn of the thirteenth century the Pope could no longer turn a blind eye to such a rebellion against his authority.

The Strains of Uniformity

This demand for uniformity and centralization from Rome was a new feature of medieval Church life. The Cathar heresy was the direct result of a medieval age when Europe was entirely Christian save for a handful of Jews and an undercurrent of ancient beliefs. The papacy had reached new pinnacles of power in the centuries after Charlemagne's coronation as Holy Roman Emperor on Christmas Day, 800, and made its presence felt in every area of politics and society. Successive popes labored to impose a single code of belief and practice on the Church in a fashion that has never since been matched in its ambition. Simple formulas, lists of sacraments, of deadly sins, of virtually every feature of Christian teaching were much in evidence in this period—some for the first time—as a means of transmitting the basics of the credo from the upper echelons of the Church to the grass roots. Leo IX (1049–1054) spent four and a half of his five years on Saint Peter's throne traveling around France and Germany commanding that his orders be carried out by priests and bishops and disciplining those dissidents who dared challenge him.

The growth in this period of religious orders like the Cluniacs and the Cistercians, fiercely loyal to the Pope and to the concept of one holy Catholic and apostolic Church, accelerated this centralization and striving for uniformity. Both were active in trying to turn the people of Languedoc away from the Cathars. With Urban II (1088–1099) developing the curia (the Church's civil service), papal monarchy aiming at a single Christian position with its priests in the confessionals imposing strict discipline grew intolerant of anyone who did not toe the party line. Such discipline needed sanctions to be effective, and the Devil was the ultimate reproach. Go against us and we will brand you a heretic, a servant of Satan, and you will spend the rest of your days in hell. One has only to glance up at the facades of the Gothic cathedrals that sprang up in northern France in this period to see the omnipresence of Satan, his face dangling there in carved effigy as a warning to those who would go against their clergy.

The Devil might be a good tool for frightening the congregation and poorly educated rural priests, but many medieval monks laughed off such threats. Within the Church the strain of maintaining both great temporal and spiritual power was proving too great. Power proved its undoing. Bishops lived in opulent palaces, monks ate the finest foods, and clergy spent their days musing over political papers and conundrums. They ceased to encapsulate the spirit of the first apostles and were no longer signs of contradiction in the secular world but too often the main orchestrators of that arena.

The Cathar heresy and its saintly *perfecti* exposed this hollow core of the Church's seemingly spectacular success. They were not, of course, alone in disturbing the monotone hue of Christian Europe. Rome grew impatient too with the rise of others who demanded a return to more enduring and simple spiritual values. Peter Waldo, a Lyon merchant who in the 1170s founded a new group denying the special authority of clerics who had disgraced themselves by their worldliness, was demonized. His followers, the Waldensians of southern France and northern Italy, were driven out of the fold and later persecuted by the Inquisition as heretics for having the impertinence to suggest that there was something amiss with the Church.

The most persecuted group of all, however, were the Cathars. They were widespread, large in numbers, and sometimes well-organized as in Languedoc where they had in effect exiled Rome's representatives. The origins of Catharism are obscure. Some say it was brought back by the Crusaders who encountered the dualist Bogomils in the Byzantine Empire and their Manichaean cousins in the Near East. Others suggest that it developed as the result of missionary journeys by Bogomils up the Danube trade routes into Germany. The presence of Bishop Nicetas in 1172 would seem to endorse this theory and there are references to Bogomil heretics being burned in Cologne in 1142.

Meeting in 1163 at Tours, the French bishops heard of the spread of the Cathars in Cologne, Bonn, and Liège. The prelates described this new heresy as a form of Manicheanism, a title the Cathars themselves rejected. They protested that they had no respect for Mani but simply saw themselves as good Christians who read the Bible and put into practice its message.

The likeness to the Manichaeans and the Bogomils was, on careful examination, only superficial. All rejected the material universe as the work of the Devil, but the Cathars and Albigensians did not turn their backs on the world. They continued to live, work, and indeed prosper in society, a cancer inside the body of Christian Europe rather than an external growth that could be isolated and removed. Again unlike the Manichaeans and Bogomils, the Cathars did not deny all forms of religious ritual and ceremony but rather concentrated their attack on the bloated and corrupt ecclesiastical hierarchy.

Rome Hits Back

Wave after wave of orators of a saintly disposition were sent to the Cathar strongholds to win the Albigensians around, but again and again failed to capture their hearts and souls. Rome—and its ally the King of France—increasingly fell back on the threat of force. The turning point came in January 1208, when the papal legate, Peter of Castelnau, was attacked and murdered at Saint Gilles in Provence by the army of Raymond, Count of Toulouse. The two had repeatedly clashed in the previous months, with Raymond holding Castelnau responsible for his own excommunication. Pope Innocent III, a stickler for administrative harmony and Church unity, took this as the opportunity to use force to restore order.

A crusade was assembled and set out with two big armies under the command of Simon de Montfort. The forces were largely gathered in northern France from men—high born and low—who had been inspired in equal measure by the promise of seizing the lands of their heretical opponents and by the oratory of Cistercian priests who told them that they were going into battle with the Devil and his followers. The Crusaders stormed Beziers and captured the city, leaving 15,000 of its citizens dead. When asked by the soldiers "How shall we know who are the heretics?" Amaury, the papal legate who accompanied them, replied: "Kill them all, the Lord will know his own." Such was the "spirit" of the Albigensian crusade.

Force, however, could only achieve part of Innocent's objectives. An army of occupation would be needed unless he could break both the spirit and the soul of the Albigensians. He aimed for nothing less than grinding into dust the very seeds of heresy in the hearts and souls of the Albigensians. The first reference to the title Inquisitor had come at the Council of Tours in 1163—the same meeting where the French bishops debated the Cathar threat. The two words—Inquisition and Cathar—became fatally intertwined around the figure of the Devil. The Inquisition would wipe out the satanically inspired Cathars and restore uniformity to Christendom. The Cathars saw these representatives of Rome as yet another manifestation of the Devil's creation on earth. The Inquisitors believed there was no room for tender consciences. They tortured those accused of heresy and when they were finished dispatched them to die. Such barbarity was justified by "evidence," extracted under torture, that the Albigensians worshiped the Devil.

The grounds for ecclesiastically sanctioned murder was well established. Anyone who was against the "official" Church was by default with Satan. Saint Jerome (340–420) had argued that the Devil's allies had, by their apostasy, relinquished the right to life itself.[4] As early as 385, Priscillian, a bishop in Spain, an ascetic and a scholar who dared to question the prevailing wisdom, had been tortured and beheaded along with his followers. Though there was a lull in the intervening centuries, in 1022 at Orleans the burning of a group of prominent heretics, including a former confessor to the Queen of France, was documented. Their crime appeared to be a tendency toward mysticism. Their talk of such vague notions as "heavenly food" was jumped upon by ecclesiastical authorities, fearful of any dissent and eager to see the Devil lurking behind every misplaced word. The accused, they said, ate not heavenly food but children. A contemporary chronicler, Adhemar de Charbannes, said that the heretics met the Devil each day in the form of a black man who gave them piles of money. In gratitude they denied Christ and actively encouraged others to do the same.

The Inquisition's ready identification of the Albigensian rebels with Satan was echoed by most senior Churchmen. Peter of Vaux-de-Cernay, a Cistercian monk, wrote in his *Historia Albigensis* (c. 1213) that the Cathars were "limbs of the Antichrist, the first-born of Satan." They believed, he claimed, that no one could sin from the waist down. Such an accusation had little basis in the lives of the *perfecti*, but its eager acceptance as gospel gave the Inquisition a *carte blanche* to act with impunity. With special powers to go over the heads of local bishops and secular courts, the Inquisitors personified the Church's claim to a jurisdiction that overruled the state and individual conscience. Staffed from the outset by Dominicans and Franciscans, the work of the Inquisition was carried out by inviting neighbor to spy on neighbor. All reports to the Inquisitors were anonymous. Once charged there was no defense or appeal. Lawyers were seldom allowed and when they were it was usually to encourage the accused to admit to heresy and then repent. Those who failed to recant faced death. They were handed over to the civil authorities for their punishment. The Church had no wish actually to be seen to be killing people.

The French kings in particular welcomed the Inquisitors, despite the fact that the Church was encroaching yet further on secular jurisdiction. Charles IV (1294–1328) built the Bastille in Paris to accommodate the extra prisoners. No one, however high born, could escape its scrutiny. Hugo de Benoils, one of the most active Inquisitors in France, organized a mass burning of heretics in Toulouse in 1275. Among those who went to the stake was Angèle, Lady of Labarathe, a noblewoman of sixty-five who was accused of having sex with Satan. It was stated that she had borne a monster with a wolf's head and a serpent's tail who only ate babies.

That such tales could be believed, much less that they were the basis for judicial process, is today incredible. It shows a deep sickness in the Western psyche, something that religion and Christianity, with its talk of the Devil, exacerbated rather than healed. The paranoid atmosphere created by the Inquisition gave this negative and unhealthy current its head. No accusation was too ludicrous. The Devil had always been an instrument of control, a threat to keep the faithful in line—now the Church was extending and institutionalizing that terror. It was an unholy alliance between the princes of the Church and the figure they claimed most to hate.

Several recurring themes in the accusations can be detected, many of which drew on the picture of the Devil that had developed down the centuries. The pillars of the Satan myth were that his followers indulged in nocturnal worship of an animal-like manifestation of the Devil, followed by a bout of promiscuous sex as likely as not rounded off by human sacrifice of some description. The more blood the better. Walter Map, an otherwise eminently sane archdeacon of Oxford and a popular figure at the court of Henry II of England, wrote in his *De nugis curialium* (Courtiers' Trifles) in the 1180s of the Publicani, a Cathar sect in Germany, and their worship of Satan:

> About the first watch of the night . . . each family sits waiting in silence in each of their synagogues; and there descends by a rope which hangs in their midst a black cat of wondrous size. On sight of it they put out the lights and do not sing or distinctly repeat hymns, but hum them with closed teeth and draw near to the place where they saw their master, feeling after him and when they have found him they kiss him. The hotter the feelings the lower their aim; some go for his feet, but most for his tail and privy parts. Then as though this noisome contact unleashed their appetites, each lays hold of his neighbour and takes his fill of him or her for all he is worth. Their elders maintain indeed, and teach each new entry that perfect love consists in give and take, as brother or sister may request or require, each putting out another's fire.[5]

(The notion of such an obscene kiss was given papal backing by Gregory IX in his bull *Vox in Roma* in 1233.)

The connection between the Devil and sexual license—and the repressed sexuality of faithful Christians—was the sine qua non of the Satan myth that the Inquisition promoted. Sex was demonized. The various Church councils that condemned the Cathars as heretics were also busy legislating for priestly celibacy, breaking a tradition of married priests that went back to the first pope, Saint Peter. Thomas Aquinas (1225–1274) was writing in his *Summa Theologica* that "virginity seeks the soul's good[;] . . .

marriage seeks the body's good. . . . Without doubt the state of virginity is preferable."[6] Sex was being pushed out of the godly sphere and becoming diabolical and inhuman, the preserve of heretics like the Cathars. By persecuting them, the Church displayed its own deeper neurosis.

The great success of the Inquisition was not that it stamped out heresy—there was still an Albigensian bishop in Carcassonne in 1326—but rather that it convinced Christian Europe that hidden in their midst was a fifth column of sexually overactive Satan worshipers. Yet the Inquisition's own figures (from 1246) show the limits of its success: twenty-eight Cathars tried and found guilty in Fanjeaux, thirty in Laurac. There were tiny numbers elsewhere.[7]

Mystery Plays

The persecution of the Cathars could only have taken place in an age as pessimistic, self-doubting, and obsessed with magic and superstition as the medieval period. The pulpit and the pursuit and public prosecution of heretics were two ways to maintain the atmosphere of satanophobia. Another was through popular culture. The omnipresence of a personal, incarnate Devil can be seen in the mystery, miracle, and morality plays of the era. Written, initially at least, mainly by clerics in simple and direct language to reach the largest audience, and often performed by the priest and his choirboys, they put the Devil in every home and in every mind.

The mystery plays were generally close to the liturgy and were performed on certain set feast days—Good Friday, Corpus Christi, and so on. Later this concept was refined and whole cycles of plays were developed covering the seasons in the Church's calendar—Lent, Easter, Holy Week, and Advent. Sometimes these cycles would be performed all in one day, with the audience gathering in the streets and a succession of carts, each containing a single scene or incident, touring the town.

The most famous of these dramas is the Oberammergau Passion Play, an account of Christ's life, death, and resurrection, still staged every ten years in a Bavarian village to honor a pledge made after the Black Death passed it by in 1634.

Performed in the vernacular rather than the Latin of the mass, the mystery plays concerned themselves with Satan's fall from grace and his subsequent appearances in the Bible. The traditional Church version of events was followed slavishly. In the *Chester Mystery Cycle*, still performed in the city's cathedral close, God (Deus) places his trust in his creation the Devil (Luciffer).

> *Nowe seeinge I have formed you soe fayer*
> *and exalted you so exelente—*
> *and here I set you nexte my cheare,*
> *my love to you is soe fervente—*
> *loke you fall not in noe dispaier,*
> *Touche not my throne by non assente.*
> *All your beautie I shall appaier,*
> *and pride fall oughte in your intente.*[8]

Luciffer ignores such warnings and betrays God. After his fall he tempts Eve and then later tries—unsuccessfully—to tempt Christ in the wilderness.

> *Sythen the world first begane*
> *knewe I never such a man*
> *borne of a deadlych woman,*
> *and hee yet wembles.*
> *Amonge sinfull synne dose hee none*
> *and cleaner then ever was anyone;*
> *blotles eke of blood and bonne,*
> *and wiser then ever man was.*

Christ's descent after his crucifixion to hell, to save the souls in Satan's lair, is recounted in graphic detail.

Jesus: Open up hell-gates annone,
ye prynces of pyne everychon,
that Godes Sonne may in gonne,
and the kinge of blys.

Sathanas: Owt, alas, what ys thys?
Seghe I never so mych blys
towardes hell come, iwys,
sythen I was warden here.
My masterdome fares amys,
for yonder a stubberne fellowe ys,
right as wholye hell were his,
to reave me of my power.

The Devil was usually played straight—according to Church teaching. Gradually the plays were liberated from the Church's influence and authorship and sometimes there was a little revealing embroidery around the themes. The voice of the Devil is employed as an ironical register of the world's sins in the Towneley cycle's *Judgement*. The demon Tutivillus gives life and drama to the piece with a roll call of his allies, the sinners whose deeds are leading to their eternal damnation:

All harlotts and horres
And bawdys that procures,
To bryng thaym to lures
    Welcom to my see!
Ye lurdanes and lyars, mychers and thefes,
Flytors and flyars, that all men reprefes,
Spolars, extorcyonars—Welcome, my lefes!
Fals Jurars and usarars, to symony that clevys
    To tell:
Hasardars and dysars,
Fals dedys forgars,
Slanderars, back-bytars!
    All unto hell![9]

This lurid and all-embracing picture of the Devil's disciples inevitably led to its own form of dualism. God and the Devil fought out a battle on almost equal terms, despite God's ultimate and assured triumph. By contrast, the morality plays tended to be more sophisticated, moving away from biblical stories and applying the teaching of Christianity to everyday tales. If mystery plays shadowed the liturgy, morality plays ran parallel to the sermons. They explored themes of good and evil, with good always triumphant, and usually featured an individual, torn between these poles, who took on the role of Everyman.

Liberation from the Church's heavy hand had another lasting effect on medieval theater—it allowed a splash of comedy. Fear prompted humor, which in its turn contributed to a downplaying of the Devil. The process was gradual and at first strictly reverent. The Devil was made to appear a fool when he was humiliated by a saint only as a crude device for stressing the saint's—and by association God's—power. Comic figures were introduced in cameo roles to give the play more entertainment value. One example was the foolish merchants at whose shop the two Marys stop to buy spices and anointing oils on their way to visit Jesus' body in the tomb on Easter Sunday. Another was the license given to the shepherds at the manger in Christmas plays to ham up their parts, which led in its turn to stock comic characters like Mak the Sheepstealer in the *Chester Mystery Cycle*. Whatever the intention, the debunking of Satan onstage proved a counterpoint to much of the propaganda of the medieval age. At a time when the Devil was painted as such a terrifying, omnipresent threat, audiences found some escape from their fears by seeing their enemy made to look foolish.

It is perhaps a sign that the Church's ambition to influence every aspect of Christians' lives could never be realized. In the often ruthless pursuit of that goal the medieval Church used Satan as the ultimate reproach. If you ate too much, you were succumbing to the Devil-like deadly sin of gluttony. If you enjoyed sex, you may well have been possessed by a demon. If you stepped out of line on any question of dogma, you were a heretic in the pay of Satan. By making the Devil look foolish and impotent, the medieval theater was staging its own rebellion against the heavy hand of ecclesiastical authority. It is no surprise then that the attitude of priests and bishops to such spectacles was not always supportive and that there were times when performers and prelates were at odds. Far from buttressing Church power, Satan onstage was becoming part of a rebellion against that authority.

One other aspect of the mystery plays is intriguing. The art historian Luther Link has argued that the costumes used for the Devil in such performances had great influence over artists and the composite picture of Satan in the popular psyche. In trying to convey the impression that the Devil was half-beast, actors would wrap up in animal skins. Link suggests that this may account for a trend in this period for artists to depict Satan as covered with hair. He writes: "Medieval costumes for the Devil of the mystery plays are behind the Devil's representations as early as the Winchester Psalter of 1150. . . . The popular pictorial image of the Devil is an excellent example of Mikhail Bakhtin's insight that the culture of the elite has its counterpoint in popular culture."[10]

A Theological Exit

One of the most enduring legacies of the Albigensian heresy to Western Christianity was the Fourth Lateran Council. It set down—briefly and tersely—what remains the Church's most definitive doctrinal statement about the Devil. Though a feature of the everyday life of the Church for 2,000 years, the Devil has seldom featured in those landmark documents that define dogma.

The Fourth Lateran Council met in November 1215 at the instigation of Innocent III and condemned heresy in the strongest terms. It gave its approval to the methods of the Inquisition and, inevitably when covering such ground, felt it necessary to make some reference to Satan. However, what was said merely echoed the declarations of the Council of Braga in 563, the last occasion on which the subject had been broached in terms of doctrine. Dualism was rejected out of hand. It was decreed that the Devil had never been independent of God but rather had been created by him as a good angel.

The looming presence of the Devil can, however, be detected in some of the Council's other pronouncements. It decreed that communion wafers and holy oil must be kept under lock and key in churches. The tabernacle became a regular landmark. The impetus behind this was the fear that Satan, or more likely one of his human army of heretics or witches, would snatch the eucharist and desecrate it at one of the nocturnal orgies they were rumored to frequent.

It is striking that despite all the debate in the Church over the Devil in these centuries, official doctrine changed very little from the sixth century through to the Fourth Lateran Council and beyond. The final redefinition of any length of the Devil's powers came at the Council of Trent in 1546, and even then it was a question of fine tuning. What held good at Braga can still be seen in contemporary Church documents. The *Catechism of the Catholic Church*, launched by Pope John Paul II in English in 1994, differs very little in substance in its references to the Devil to documents produced 1,500 years earlier.

Yet if the rule-book seemed set in stone, theologians continued to debate Satan with almost as much energy and diversity as the artists depicted him, the heretics believed in him, and the faithful feared him. The intellectual backdrop to the Fourth Lateran Council and indeed the whole Cathar epoch was the scholastic movement. This theological approach dominated the intellectual life of western Europe from the eleventh to the fourteenth century and its hold was firm over the centers of learning, the cathedral and monastic schools, and the Church-run universities.

An intellectual and erudite movement, scholasticism tried to apply logic to the fundamental questions about human existence and so provide a watertight intellectual and rational case for the Christian position. There was a right answer and a wrong answer for every issue and through scripture and logic—mutually incompatible as they may now seem to some twentieth-century philosophers—that answer could be arrived at. It was a black-and-white equation—truth and error, orthodoxy and heresy, good and evil, God and the Devil.

Credited as the founder of scholasticism, Anselm of Bec, Archbishop of Canterbury from 1093, wrote between 1085 and 1090 a whole tract on Satan entitled *Fall of the Devil*. He attempted to look at evil in the world in a logical way, at its origins in the figure of Lucifer, and at his responsibility for introducing evil into what would otherwise have been a perfect universe.[11] Though he accepted God's right to punish humankind out of love and a passion for justice, Anselm vehemently denied that the Devil had any right to carry out that punishment. He was not therefore God's instrument, but someone acting out of personal malice. Anselm rejected any suggestion that the Devil had any rights over man—then an orthodox view—and argued instead that the focus should be on God and man's debt to his creator. Implicitly, Anselm was arguing Satan out of a job.

This formula was taken up by the greatest of the scholastics, Thomas Aquinas who, after Augustine, is perhaps the most enduring influence on Christian doctrine. Best remembered for his *Summa Theologica*, in his treatise *De malo* (On evil), Aquinas outlined four categories of evil: absolute evil, an unfettered, unchallengeable principle of evil that he dismissed as an abstraction; metaphysical evil, that humans are somehow imperfect in relation to God, which Aquinas again dismissed on the grounds that that was the way God had planned it; the evil of privation, that humans might lack a vital skill like sight or hearing or taste; and the evil of sin. The first three were linked to God the creator and only in the last was the Devil given more than a passive role in tempting humankind.

Despite this relegation of Satan, Aquinas went on to create an elaborate cosmology that gave the Devil a place and a role. In trying to integrate the Devil in his God-centered schemes, Aquinas resorted to ever more complex solutions and close and detailed arguments. "The ingenious solutions of the scholastics to the ancient questions of diabology were far too ingenious," writes the American scholar Jeffrey Burton Russell.[12]

Whether or not it was their intention, the scholastics moved the theological debate away from the Devil. Yet their disagreements made little impact at a popular level. Paradoxically decline in one area was matched by growth in another. This was a troubled and uncertain period which—as in similar eras—prompted a deep devotional swell of superstition. Believers carried around countless talismans and amulets to ward off the Devil. Anselm's sophism made little impact on those who placed their trust in the Agnus Dei, a small wax cake made originally out of the wax of the altar candles, embossed with an image of the lamb of God and blessed by the Pope. Not only was this reputed to keep Satan at bay, it could also provide protection against what many in this unscientific age took to be manifestations of his power—illness, violent death, drowning, and thunder and lightning. In the last named case, the Agnus Dei kept at Saint Alban's Abbey in England proved remarkably ineffective. A bolt of lightning destroyed the whole building in the thirteenth century.

A measure of the continuing popular interest in those who bore witness to a personal and incarnate Devil—as opposed to a theological abstraction—can still be glimpsed in the Roman convent of Santa Francesca Romana (1384–1440), who was kept awake night after night by visions of hell. The story of her struggle spread around the city and was recorded in many devotional texts. The walls of her convent were decorated in garish style by the artist Antoniazzo Romano (1435–1517) to record her torment. In one scene, three demons appeared to the saint—one in the form of a lion, another as a dragon, and the third a serpent. In another she is physically assailed by an evil spirit who beats her with the bodies of dead snakes, leaving her bruised when she wakes the next morning. Later it is taws from a bull's tail that are used to torture her into joining Satan's army, then she is pushed on top of a corpse full of worms. Further on demons come to tear up her devotional books and finally she has to invoke Saint Paul to fight off a seven-headed snake.

While such murals are today regarded as an artistic treasure, they are a reminder of the powers ascribed to the Devil in the popular imagination. The divide between people and theologians over the Devil, significant as it was becoming in this period, was but a prelude to the gulf that opened up in the fifteenth century, the age of the witch craze.

EIGHT

Hocus-Pocus and the Witch Craze

> The truth is that acceptable evidence for the literal reality of ritual devil-worship, whether in England or on the Continent, is extremely scanty. The few modern attempts to get behind the assertions of the demonologist and the fictitious "confessions" extracted by torture in response to a fixed set of interrogatories, suggest that even on the Continent ritual devil-worship was probably a myth.
>
> —Sir Keith Thomas, *Religion and the Decline of Magic*

The zenith of the Devil's malign influence over this world came with the witch craze that gripped Europe from the fifteenth to the seventeenth centuries. There has been heated debate in scholarly circles over the last fifty years about the true nature of what both the Catholic and Protestant Churches presented at the time as an organized continent-wide conspiracy of witches, in league with Satan and plotting to undermine Christianity. Many eminent academics are now convinced that it was one of the greatest hoaxes of history.[1]

Hocus-pocus or not, what is incontrovertible is that up to 100,000 people were burned at the stake. The most damning "evidence" that was presented against them in courts from Spain to Germany, England to New England was the suggestion that they had made a pact with the Devil. Satan's name was on everyone's lips and witches were his handmaidens.

The span of the witch craze coincided with a period when Catholic Europe was experiencing unprecedented political, social, and religious strains. The ruling dynasties were almost constantly at war—with the Hapsburgs and Valois seemingly eternally at odds. Charles V, elected Holy Roman Emperor in 1519 and a ruler whose lands stretched from the Hapsburg inheritance in Germany to Spain, Sicily, and even to the Spanish dominions in the Americas, fought four wars in twenty years with his Valois rival Francis I of France. After Charles's death his Empire crumbled, leaving a vacuum. Attempts by later Hapsburgs to enforce their control over the whole of Germany led to the Thirty Years War (1618–1648). By then the impact of the Protestant reformers, led by Martin Luther, had been felt, with religion setting neighbor against neighbor and dividing the princes of the Empire between those who maintained their allegiance to the Pope and those who went with Luther.

In England too religion caused upheaval with Henry VIII's break with Rome and the subsequent persecutions—of Protestants under Mary I and of Catholics under Elizabeth. Accompanying this political instability, there was economic disruption and inflation. It was a moment of trauma throughout Europe that touched every level of society. What had been taken for granted—the power of the papacy and of the Emperor and even the ultimate triumph of Christianity—was under threat, and the status quo of the early medieval period was shattered. People looked for a scapegoat and found the Devil.

Since the great missionary drive into northern Europe under Gregory, the Church had tolerated a certain level of surviving traditional beliefs. It had adapted some of them to its own saints and seasons and occasionally indulged in magic. One Bishop of Barcelona, horrified by the theft of some Church silver in 1628, put a curse on the land and crops in his diocese and saw them ruined.[2] The cult of the Virgin Mary in the later Middle Ages, and the various "cures" associated with shrines dedicated to her, is a potent reminder to this day that the Church has always endorsed its own forms of magic and superstition. To argue that witches and healers were doing something sinister and unnatural, while maintaining that priests and monks who attempted healing by laying their hands on the sick were acting in imitation of Christ was an ambivalent position to say the least.

In this turbulent period, the Church seized the opportunity to eradicate traditional beliefs. There had long been persecutions and demonization of witches and healers. Witch-dunking was reported in seventh-century Russia. A *Canon Episcopi* of 906 deemed witches to be "certain abandoned women, perverted by the Devil, seduced by illusion and phantasms of demons [who] believe and openly profess that in the dead of night they ride upon certain beasts with Diana . . . fly over vast tracts of the country and obey her commands." Priests, the *Canon* insists, "should preach with all insistence to people that they may know this to be every way false."[3] However, all the evidence points to the fact that this instruction was only patchily implemented.

The political, religious, and social crisis of the fifteenth and sixteenth centuries gave new impetus to long-standing Christian intolerance of anything that was different or "other." The irony of the Church's latest crusade against heresy was that by paying so much attention to the link between the Devil and witches, clerics risked spreading the beliefs and fostering the practices that they were trying so hard to repress. It was only when the Church began to talk less of witches that they faded into insignificance.

A Reformation that Brought No Change

Witches were burned at the stake long before Martin Luther was born, but there is a clear correlation between the periods of greatest persecution and the intensity of the Catholic-Protestant struggle. The witch craze was part of the Reformation battleground. The early years of the sixteenth century were comparatively peaceful ones until Luther's break with Rome intensified the activities of the Inquisition. Then there was another spell of calm before religious rivalry in Germany unleashed the Thirty

Years War in 1618 and another frenzy of torture, public accusation, and burning.

Though both sides were vocal in identifying witchcraft with their opponents' beliefs, in practice they both embroidered on the common themes of pre-Reformation diabology to promote Satan to the apex of his powers. Catholics and Protestants alike were convinced that he was organizing a fifth column in their midst at the same time as commanding their enemy's army.

The Reformation is often reduced in the shorthand of popular history to a protest against the excesses of the Roman Church, with the witch craze alongside the sale of indulgences among the principal grievances. Many of the new "Protestants," however, placed the Devil in the dock just as much as their separated brethren. Indeed their reliance on scripture and their gloomy worldview made them if anything even more acutely aware of Satan's looming presence. Lucifer featured just as often in the writings of Luther, Calvin, and Zwingli as in anything penned by Augustine or Aquinas.

Martin Luther (1483–1546), an Augustinian monk, intensified his campaign to reform Christianity in October 1517 when he nailed his 95 Articles on the door of the Church in Wittenberg. Three years later he was excommunicated, but not before he had attracted an enormous groundswell of support from his fellow Germans and from some of the most influential rulers in the region who also resented Rome's overbearing authority and were tired of the corruption of its practices and officials. Luther's rebellion was practical and political rather than doctrinal. The heart of the Protestant Reformation was a dispute over religious authority that grew out of the very conditions and abuses that had fostered earlier uprisings of heresy among, for example, the Cathars.

Luther's theology of the Devil was traditional. He recounted his personal struggle with Satan in such graphic terms as to recall the trials and tribulations of the Desert Fathers as they battled with the temptations put before them by the Evil One in the wilderness. The evidence of this titanic struggle is examined each day by the visitors who troop around Wartburg Castle in Saxony to examine the blot of ink on the wall left after he threw a whole pot at the Devil's head.

Luther was a product of his time. He was convinced from an early age that he had been singled out by Satan. In his first year of training with the Augustinians, he wrote that he was aware of the Devil in the silence and solitude of the monastery. He would spend up to six hours a day in the confessional seeking the strength to fight off Lucifer's attacks. The fear of being alone was one that remained with him throughout his life. "Eve got into trouble when she walked in the Garden alone," he later wrote. "I have my worst temptations when I am alone."[4] The concept of *anfechtung* is central to Luther's preoccupation with the Devil. There is no satisfactory translation from the German, but it covers both powerlessness before God and the Devil. "Early this morning," Luther recalls in his *Tischreden*, "when I awoke the fiend came and began disputing with me. 'Thou art a great sinner,' said he. I replied 'Canst you not tell me something new, Satan?' " Such torment is a recurring theme in his accounts of daily life. At Coburg the Devil appeared to Luther as a serpent and then in the form of a star. At Wartburg Castle, at the height of his dispute with Rome when his future hung in the balance, he saw the Devil pelting nuts at the ceiling and rolling casks down the stairs. He equated his own self-doubt with openness to Satan. "Now is the time," he wrote to his confidant Spalatin, "to pray with our might against Satan. He is plotting an attack on Germany and I fear God will permit him because I am so indolent in prayer."

On another occasion, Satan caused Luther to be surrounded by an unpleasant odor. This scatological theme was seen again in Luther's belief that the Devil resided in his bowels. Luther suffered for most of his adult life from chronic constipation and developed a theory that his own strained and tortuous bowel movements were a way of forcing Satan and all that was bad out of his body, an unusual form of personal exorcism. "But if that is not enough for you, you Devil," he once wrote, "I have also shit and pissed. Wipe your mouth on that and take a hearty bite."

Conventional in his obsession with the Devil, Luther did embark on some tinkering with the prevailing Christian notions about Satan. His conviction that God's omnipotence could in no way be compromised—even by such accepted notions as free will—led him to fashion a belief in predestination. According to this doctrine, humans have no power to achieve their own salvation. They are either one of the elect who will enjoy God's favor in perpetuity, or they are destined for the Devil to whom God gives authority over the wicked. Their actions on earth, whether good or bad, are therefore irrelevant. Any other approach, Luther argued, would be to deny God's full majesty.

Predestination left the Devil in a somewhat ambiguous position. By taking the souls that God rejected, he was almost an equal and opposite power to him. Yet by having no real power, save that which God gave him, he was rendered impotent, a nuisance akin to the Shaytan of Islam.

Luther differed most obviously from Catholicism over exorcism. Though he once exorcised his student, Johann Schlaginhaufen, Luther grew to abhor the whole ritual of exorcism. "To be occupied with God's work helps against the world, the flesh and the Devil and all bad thoughts. This is the true holy water with which to exorcise the Devil." With his suspicion of clerical attempts to come between God and his people, Luther disliked anything that hinted at ecclesiastical magic. He also preferred to take his lead from scripture rather than tradition when it came to the formulation of teaching. And though some saw Jesus' miracles as exorcisms, the Bible, Luther held, was unequivocal in its opposition to necromancy and ritualized magic. It was a lead that other Protestant Churches would later take up. In England, the Second Edwardian Prayer Book abandoned the use of the words of exorcism in the baptism ceremony. Luther did make a distinction between faith and superstition. His tales of battles with the Devil were not, to his own mind at least, an incitement to further hellish fears but rather a message of hope. "When the Devil harasses us," he wrote, "then we know ourselves to be in good shape." The Devil was a way of strengthening rather than frightening humankind.

Luther was one of the most prolific religious writers ever. His volumes of theology, personal reflection, sermons, and homilies reached a mass market. The use of new printing technology to produce cheap and popular pamphlets was one of the key factors in his success and meant that his message was widely disseminated. His obsession with the Devil was not confined to the written and spoken word—he could turn his hand to music. "Music drives away the Devil and makes people gay," he once said. His personal doctor recalled that on one occasion he found Luther in deep despair and it was only singing that brought him back to good humor. One of Luther's most famous hymns gives a succinct summary of his diabology:

> *A Mighty Fortress is our God*
> *A good weapon and defence;*
> *He helps us in every need*
> *That befalls us.*
> *The old, evil enemy*
> *Is determined to get us;*
> *He makes his cruel plans*
> *With great might and cruel cunning;*
> *Nothing on earth is like him . . .*
> *But if the whole world were full of devils*
> *Eager to swallow us,*
> *We would not fear,*
> *For we should still be saved.*
> *The prince of this world,*
> *No matter how fierce he claims to be,*
> *Can do us no harm;*
> *His power is under judgment;*
> *One little word can fell him.*

Luther also contributed to building up further the character of Satan in popular culture with volume after volume of *Teufels-bucher* or "Devil's Books." In the period 1545–1600, they told in simple and easily accessible terms of individual demons who visited such sinful afflictions on their victims as love of dressing up, of food, of party-going, of dancing. The *Teufelsbucher* came in many formats—poetry, drama, letters—but their premise remained the same, that the Devil was behind all the vices of the world. It was a return to the style of an earlier age and left little room for the playful, even comic, demons seen in some of the medieval mystery plays. In a troubled epoch, Satan was not to be taken lightly.

The Torturers' Textbook

With Satan as much a feature of Protestantism as of Catholicism, his name was traded as an insult by the two sides as they struggled for the soul of Europe. Luther wrote of Rome as "pos-sessed by Satan and the throne of the Antichrist" while Catholic exorcists reported that the devils they drove out of alleged witches named the Protestant leader as their ally. In Germany in particular there was a flourishing trade in cartoons showing the Devil whispering his instructions in Luther's ear.

Luther's many writings on the Devil were matched on the Catholic side by one of the most widely read books of the age, the *Malleus Maleficarum*, sometimes called "The Hammer of the Witches." Though it was used by both Catholics and Protestants in their common pursuit of witches and Devil worshipers in their midst, it is best remembered as the textbook and *vade mecum* of Rome's Inquisition. Published in 1486 before Luther's split, there were sixteen separate German editions before 1700 and eleven in French. Its popularity can be ascribed to the confident assertion of its authors—Heinrich Kramer, Dean of Cologne University, and Jacob Sprenger, Dominican Inquisitor-General in Germany—that all ill-fortune, medical, physical, or natural,

could be explained away by witches acting in unholy communion with the Devil.

The *Malleus*⁵ redirected the gaze of the Inquisition from the
Cathars to a new group of heretics, those who performed the
traditional rites and ritual magic that had long been a part of
the landscape of Europe. Part and parcel of that tradition were
those with magic powers of healing, sometimes called witches
and warlocks. The origins of their craft—spells or *maleficium*, as
they were known—is unclear. Some describe them as part of the
pagan rites of the pre-Christian era, others trace them back to
Zoroaster. Whatever the derivation of their knowledge, witches
were one of the many sources of solace for the population in
times of sickness and ill-fortune, a rival that Christianity could no
longer even grudgingly tolerate. Witches and warlocks provided
an easy target for the Church, intent on rallying the faithful with
a bout of demonization.

Prior to the publication of the *Malleus*, no single written set
of instructions for the Inquisition had existed. Individual popes
had given a lead. In 1317, for instance, Pope John XXII (1316–
1324), an able administrator but a pontiff with a paranoia that
heretical clerics within the Church were trying to undermine
him, had Bishop Hughes Gerard of Cahors in France arrested for
trying to kill him by poison and *maleficium*. The Pope himself
interrogated the accused seven times before he was handed over
to the Inquisition. Some of the suggestions in the *Malleus*—for
instance, that sorcerers fashioned dolls of their enemies and
jabbed them with pins—predate the book itself (and went on
later to feature in voodoo ceremonies). Pierre Recordi, a
Carmelite taken by the Inquisition in Carcassonne in 1329, was
accused of making wax puppets from a concoction that contained his own saliva and the blood of toads. He offered these
creations to Satan if he could be granted possession of certain
women in his area. The Inquisition claimed he would place the
doll on the doorstep of those he had targeted and then demand
that either they let him have his wicked way or risk being
attacked by a demon.

Pope Paul II's decision in 1468 to allow the use of torture to extract confessions in cases of *crimen exceptum* allowed the witch craze, orchestrated by the Inquisition, to gather momentum. Innocent VIII's bull *Summis desiderantes affectibus* in 1484 ordered that witches be treated with the utmost severity. It is significant that the dire measures this document envisaged applied only to Germany, then the center of unrest in continental Europe. Two years later came the *Malleus*. Many of the worst features of the witch craze are actively promoted in its pages. It is never questioned that witches are working with Satan. Indeed the *Malleus* has tough words for those who doubted the reality of witchcraft: "Those who say that there is no witchcraft in the world, but only in the imagination of men who, through their ignorance of hidden causes, which no man yet understands, ascribe certain natural effects to witchcraft, as though they were effected not by hidden causes but by devils working either in themselves or in conjunction with witches."

When confronted with someone accused of witchcraft, the *Malleus* recommends on its opening pages, the first thing to do is to present them with the charge. "Mind that witches generally deny the question," it adds without a hunt of impartiality. "For witchcraft," it continues, "is high treason against God's majesty. And so they [the accused] are to be put to torture to make them confess. Any person, whatever his rank or position, upon such an accusation may be put to torture. And he who is found guilty, even if he confess his crime, let him be racked, let him suffer all other tortures prescribed by law in order that he may be punished in proportion to his offence."

The *Malleus* emphasized what became another of the distinguishing features of this collective madness—namely, that the witch was an intermediary between the Devil and humankind, just as the priest stood between God and his people. Where previous—and indeed subsequent—generations of Christians believed themselves to be under attack by the Devil himself, in this late medieval era it was the witch who posed the greatest threat. "And if it be asked whether the Devil is more apt to injure men and creatures by himself than through a witch," intones the *Malleus*, "it can be said that there is no comparison between the two cases. For he is infinitely more apt to do harm through the agency of witches. First because he thus gives greater offence to God by usurping to himself a creature dedicated to him. Secondly, because when God is offended, he allows him the more power of injuring men. And thirdly, for his own gain, which he places in the perdition of souls." By setting up this symmetry of competing trios—God, priest, and people opposed to Devil, witch, and people—the *Malleus* exposed the de facto dualism that existed within charges made by the Inquisition. Yet the official line of the Church remained that God was omnipotent and that the Devil was ultimately under his control.

Keen to name names in its accusations of widespread Devil worship, the *Malleus* pointed a finger at women, animals, and the weather as particularly prone to Satan's control. Continuing the antiwoman current prevalent in Christianity since the time of Augustine, the *Malleus* presented the attraction that men felt for the opposite sex as evidence that women were by their very nature channels of the Devil. As ever it was Eve who had let down her kind. "Though the Devil tempted Eve to sin, yet Eve seduced Adam."

Anyone who then accepted the *Malleus*'s diabology would look first at the women in their community for signs of possession. In the 1630s at Alvebrode near Hanover, a blind and lame widow called Steingrob attracted the attention of the Inquisitors. Her son had asthma and one daughter had died of consumption. According to the widow's fellow villagers her other daughter was the fount of all the family's misfortune and therefore a witch. Hectored by their accusations and fearful of the attentions of the Inquisition, the poor woman tried to drown herself but was rescued. She was fortunate in that she fell into the hands not of a priest but of a wise physician who treated her mental disturbance and with whose help she made a full recovery.

On both animals and the weather, the *Malleus* stood in the mainstream of a tradition dating back to pre-Christian times.

Wild animals and the storms that ruined crops and prosperity had long been associated with evil spirits. The *Malleus* reinforced its picture of the Devil at work with the authority of Aquinas: "Saint Thomas, in his *Commentary on Job,* says as follows: 'It must be confessed that, with God's permission, the devils can disturb the air, raise up winds and make the fire fall from heaven. For although in the matter of taking various shapes, corporeal nature is not at the command of any angel, either good or bad, but only at that of God the Creator, yet, in the matter of local motion, corporeal nature has to obey the spiritual nature. . . . But winds and rain and other similar disturbances of air can be caused by mere movement of vapours released from the earth or the water; therefore the natural powers of devils is sufficient to cause such things.' So says Saint Thomas."

There were those—especially in intellectual circles—who doubted the wisdom of the *Malleus* and suspected the witch craze as tapping an unsavory vein in humankind. Montaigne (1533–1592), the French essayist, wrote of the excesses of the Inquisition: "After all, it is rating one's conjectures at a very high price to roast a man alive on the strength of them."

In the heart of the Church there were voices raised in protest, even among the fanatically loyal Jesuits. Founded in the sixteenth century by Saint Ignatius Loyola, this quasimilitary order was in the vanguard of the Counter-Reformation, especially in Spain. In his *Spiritual Exercises,* the handbook of Jesuits to this day, Ignatius described the Devil variously as "a military chief," "a false lover," and, as a "woman, inasmuch as he is weak in spite of himself, but strong in will; for as it is in the nature of a woman, quarrelling with a man, to lose courage, and to take flight when he shows himself undaunted. . . ." The founder's personal obsession with demons can be seen by one of the wall paintings that line the rooms where he lived in central Rome. Ignatius is portrayed, dressed in his distinctive black robe, walking among the poor and afflicted, casting out the small, winged, and horned black imps that had caused their sickness.

In Germany, the Jesuit Friedrich Spee von Langenfeld (1591–1635) had very different views. He recorded his distaste for the whole Inquisitorial exercise in *Cautio criminalis*, in 1631. At first it was unsigned—presumably for fear of what the rest of the Order would make of such apostasy—but later generations identified von Langenfeld as the author. He wrote of how he had prepared 200 people found guilty of witchcraft and heresy for death and how the experience turned his hair gray because he believed them all to be innocent:

> Even if an attorney were allowed to the prisoner, the former would from the outset be suspected himself, as a patron and protector of witches, so that all mouths are shut and all pens are blunted, and one can neither speak nor write. . . . I swear solemnly that of the many persons whom I have accompanied to the stake, there was not one who could be said to have been duly convicted; and two other pastors made me the same confession from their experience. Treat the heads of the Church, the judges, myself, in the same way as those unfortunate ones, make us undergo the same tortures, and you will convict us all as wizards.[6]

The Archbishop of Mayence also risked his life by going public with his opposition to the witch hunt. Pope Gregory IX (1227–1241) gave the arch-Inquisitor, Conrad of Marburg, a free hand to root out heresy in Germany.[7] His frequent recourse to ordeal by water, thumbscrews, the rack, and devices such as the Iron Virgin, a coffin in which a suspect was enclosed and then run through with knives, horrified leading Churchmen. In 1233, the Archbishop appealed to the Pope to stop Conrad:

> Whoever fell into his hands had only the choice between a ready confession for the sake of saving his life and a denial

whereupon he was speedily burnt. Every false witness was accepted, but no just defence granted—not even to people of prominence. The person arraigned had to confess that he was a heretic, that he had touched a toad, that he had kissed a pale man, or some monster. Many Catholics suffered themselves to be burnt rather than confess to such vicious crimes of which they were not guilty. The weak ones, in order to save their lives, lied about themselves and other people, especially about such prominent ones whose names were suggested to them by Conrad. Thus brothers accused their brothers, wives their husbands, servants their masters. Many gave money to the clergy for good advice as to how to protect themselves and the greatest confusion originated.[8]

Gregory's reaction to this epistle is not recorded, but he rushed to canonize Conrad after his murder in 1233 by a group of nobles similarly outraged at his activities.

Voices such as the Archbishop of Mayence were crying in the wind. The Church's official line was that the troubles of the late medieval world could all be laid at the Devil's and witches' doors. Many decent God-fearing people went along with this suggestion, even if they suspected the neighbor being hauled up before the Inquisition was innocent. Fear of the Inquisition, fear of being tainted by association with those accused, and, sometimes, a wish to see their neighbor put down were just as likely to prompt public acceptance of the witch craze as any deep conviction that the Devil was about to triumph over the world. In the hysteria of late medieval Europe, anyone who was your enemy must be supping with Satan. Anyone who stepped out of line, even by being sick, came under suspicion. Those who had harmlessly gone about traditional rites and magic became like the Jews under Hitler, the capitalists under Stalin, the intellectuals under the Khmer Rouge. They were regarded as the agents of a foreign power, unpatriotic at best and traitors at worst, enemies of the people who had made a pact with Satan.

Hieronymus Bosch (c. 1450–1516) gives perhaps the most grotesque depiction of such a pact in *Garden of Earthly Delights*, now in Madrid's Prado Museum. Bosch continued the medieval tradition of portraying the Devil not as a person but as a grotesque animal—in this case a pig. His acolyte is a toad, while a helmeted demon, wearing as a seal an amputated foot, holds an inkwell before their victim. Bosch does more than simply show the Devil as a beast for the pig is wearing a nun's veil, implying that Satan can take possession of even the most outwardly virtuous person. And the pig is only the most obvious source of evil in *Garden of Earthly Delights*. Nearby stands the haunting Treeman, a head joined to what looks like a broken eggshell, supported by two tree trunks.

The concept of a pact with the Devil had been floating around in the Christian canon for many centuries. One of the earliest manifestations concerned Saint Basil (c. 330–379), Bishop of Caesarea. A lowly born Christian slave fell in love with the daughter of a senator and in his desperation to woo her he turned to a sorcerer. The sorcerer enlisted the assistance of the Devil, but only after the slave went at dead of night to a pagan tomb to renounce his baptism and deny Christ and gave a written undertaking of fidelity to Satan. Saint Basil intervened to save the poor man from himself. By the power of his prayer he wrested the pledge from the Devil and, tearing it to shreds before an assembled and admiring throng, freed the slave from the clutches of hell.

In the late medieval era pacts with the Devil were linked with a sense of Christian society breaking down and its norms being subverted. Myths put forward by the Inquisition included the charge that there were men and women who were having sex with the Devil or one of his demons. The theory of incubi—copulating male demons—and succubi—rarer cases of demons dressed up as women to trick men—came direct from Genesis and the wanton daughters of men, but the Inquisitors took it over as their own.

The common depiction of the Devil as an animal or part-animal gives a clue as to the popular appeal of this idea. Animals according to the strict Christian sexual code and Thomas Aquinas in particular[9] have uncontrollable sexual urges that distinguish them from humans. Since he is part-animal, the Devil attempts to exert his power through his own sexual amorality. Augustine, the ultimate sexual pessimist, had no doubt that feckless women could be seduced by male demons. He based his conviction on the fact that in imperial Rome stories of women making love with celestial creatures were taken as gospel. Augustine's spin on the legend was to point out that the creatures were actually demons.

The Inquisitors

The Inquisition became central to the witch craze. It had perfected its methods on the Cathars and the Waldensians; now it had another group to target with a religious fervor as ruthless as it was misplaced. The alleged witches offered a new kind of challenge. It was doubtless no comfort to them as they were stretched on torture racks that the Cathars and Waldensians at least belonged to a clearly defined group. There was some substance to the charge of rebellion leveled against them, if not to the accusations of satanic worship, orgies, and human sacrifices. In the witch-hunt, however, all the evidence points to the fact that there was no revolt. Some of those pursued by the Inquisition undoubtedly practiced traditional rites and magic. King James I of England (in his *Daemonologie* of 1597) estimated that as many as one in twenty of his subjects had skills with magic potions and remedies.

Many of those caught up in this craze, however, were hapless individuals who fell into the hands of the Inquisition in pitiful circumstances. Today they would be referred to psychiatrists or social services on account of their needs. Then, they were burned at the stake, accused of making a pact with the Devil. It is important to distinguish between the stereotype of a witch, fashioned in the pulpit and in various pious writings, and the majority of the men and women who died at the stake. Witches in the popular mind—and later in children's fairy tales—were old, isolated women who preyed on youngsters and traveled by broomstick to gather with their peers at nocturnal sabbats (adapted from the Jewish word at a time when the connection between Jews and witches was taken as read), where they exchanged spells and indulged in strange and sordid ceremonies, kissing the Devil's private parts and celebrating a pastiche of the Christian mass.

The lives of those who burned at the stake were very different. They were women like Appolonia Meyer, a simple soul who worked as a domestic servant in the German town of Friedberg in 1686. She fell pregnant by one of the men who worked in the same house as her. The man instantly dumped her, leaving her with the then terrible prospect of single motherhood. When her baby was due she went off to the hills behind Friedberg, gave birth, and strangled her child, leaving it under a tree. She believed she would avoid disgrace, keep her job, and a roof over her head. She may even have entertained a secret hope of being able to tempt her lover to take her back and marry her. The emotional and psychological strain took their toll on Appolonia. Tortured by guilt at her crime of infanticide, she grew deluded as to the fate of her child and went to see a Franciscan priest. She asked him for a baptismal certificate; he reported her to the Inquisition. By the time it had finished with her, Appolonia had admitted that she had killed her child after making a pact with the Devil. She would provide him with a newborn infant to satisfy his well-known lust for young flesh and she would be able to marry her lover. "The Evil Spirit," it was recorded, "left her no peace. It was only a moment. The Devil touched it [the child] as if he were a midwife. It happened quite quickly that the child came out. She strangled it immediately with the hand, and she felt no pain in the delivery. She left it lying quite naked, uncovered and unburied. . . . The Devil did not go with her, but remained staying by the child, and she did not look back." Appolonia was burned as a witch.[10]

Appolonia had committed a crime but she was not a witch. Like many, some would say the vast majority, of victims of the witch craze, she was simply caught up in its net. Hysteria gave an excuse to punish those like her for breaking society's norms, by dressing up her crime as part of a demonic conspiracy. Society would be purged of its "undesirables." The witch-hunt also offered a useful way of dishing your enemies in local or dynastic squabbles. In his 1937 classic, *Witchcraft: Oracles and Magic among the Azande*, E. E. Evans-Pritchard summed up this tendency succinctly: "Sufferers from misfortune seek for witches among their enemies."[11] One of the best known of such victims was the so-called "Angel of Augsburg," Agnes Bernauer, the daughter of a humble barber who made the mistake of falling in love with the heir of the Duke of Bavaria. Young Prince Albrecht returned her affection and for many years they lived together while his father turned a blind eye to such an unsuitable liaison. In time, however, Duke Ernst became worried about the succession, and arranged a match for his eldest son with a woman of a suitable pedigree. Albrecht's heart was not flexible to dynastic concerns, and he refused his father and instead married his angel. They set up home in a castle at Straubing under the protection of Albrecht's kindly uncle.

Duke Ernst was not to be easily thwarted. He waited his time until Albrecht went away leaving his bride unprotected. The Duke had her seized, imprisoned, and denounced as a witch. The Inquisition did his bidding in double-quick time and when Albrecht returned from his trip it was to learn that his love had been thrown off a bridge and drowned. This particular tool of the Inquisition was a popular spectator sport since it was believed that witches were able to float because they had rejected the waters of their Christian baptism. Indeed, when Agnes briefly rose to the surface after plunging into the water, the crowd took the Inquisition at its word. An executioner hurried downstream to hook Agnes's long golden hair in his pole and push her under the water until she was dead. On hearing the news, Albrecht declared war on his father and they remained at odds for many years before the son relented, made peace, and married a suitable woman who bore him ten children. He never forgot his angel, though, and built a highly ornate and much visited shrine to her at the castle where they had lived.[12]

The Devils of Loudon

Father Urban Grandier's ordeal at the hands of the Inquisition drew crowds to the French town of Loudon from as far afield as England. One of the most celebrated victims of the witch craze, his well-documented sufferings have intrigued writers like Aldous Huxley (1894–1963), author of *Brave New World*,[13] dramatist John Whiting, and director Ken Russell whose 1971 film, *The Devils*, complete with Derek Jarman sets, spared nothing of the sexual excess allegedly inspired by Satan.

In the early years of the seventeenth century, Urban Grandier took up the post of curé of Saint Peter's Church in the French town of Loudon, in the bishopric of Poitiers. A clever, worldly, but vain man, he soon earned himself a reputation among his fellow priests as having ideas above his station. They thought him overly grand in manner and self-importance. Most of all they resented his popularity as a preacher, particularly with the ladies of the town. For years they suffered their insufferable colleague in silence until the Inquisition gave them a chance of revenge.

Their animosities were brought into the open by the revelation that Grandier was offering more than spiritual comfort to some of Loudon's most eligible young women. The local clergy denounced him to the bishop and Grandier was hauled up before the episcopal court where he fought a series of battles to save his post and his reputation. Just when success was in sight a new accusation surfaced. The Mother Superior of Loudon's Ursuline convent, Sister Jeanne des Anges, claimed that the curé had seduced her and several of her nuns. Furthermore, she added, he had converted them to witchcraft and taught them to worship the Devil. The Mother Superior was well known locally for her tendency to make up stories. A dwarf and ill-educated, she was certainly not Grandier's type. But, in the prevailing atmosphere of the witch craze and driven on by their own envy, the curé's accusers did not hesitate to overlook such factors. The Inquisition was called in and they extracted a terrible revenge on Grandier.

In the person of Father Jean-Joseph Surin, the Inquisition began by ordering public exorcisms of Sister Jeanne and her nuns. John Maitland, later the Duke of Lauderdale, had enjoyed a strict religious upbringing and was, until he set foot in Loudon, convinced of the possibility of demonic possession. What he witnessed there changed his mind: "When I had seen exorcizing enough of three or four of them [the nuns] in the chapel, and could hear nothing but wanton wenches singing bawdy songs in French, I began to suspect a *fourbé*." Further exorcisms of the nuns in the parish church did little to alter his initial impression.

I saw a great many people gazing at a wench pretty well taught to play tricks, yet nothing so much as I have seen twenty tumblers or rope dancers do. Back I came to the nuns' chapel where I saw the Jesuits still hard at work, at several altars, and one poor Capuchin, who was an object of pity, for he was possessed by a melancholy fancy that devils were running about his head and was constantly applying relics. I saw the Mother Superior exorcised, and saw the hand on which they would have made me believe the names Jesus, Maria, Joseph were written by miracle (but it was apparent to me that it was done with aquafortis); then my patience was quite spent and I went to a Jesuit and told him my mind fully.

"Bereaved of sense and reason," another observer reported, Sister Jeanne rolled on the floor. The spectators were delighted, especially when she showed her legs. Finally, after many "violences, vexations, howlings and grindings of teeth, two of which at the back of the mouth were broken," the Devil obeyed the order to leave his victim in peace. The extent to which the nun, for much of her life overlooked and dismissed on account of her looks and intellectual limitations, enjoyed being the center of attention cannot be judged, but a clue can be gleaned from the fact that she subsequently published an autobiography and toured France to talk up her experiences.

While Sister Jeanne was drawing the crowds, Grandier had been arrested and imprisoned in an attic. The windows and all other openings to the outside world had been bricked up to stop the Devil escaping from him and polluting the rest of the population of Loudon. As the Inquisitors began their torture, powerful enemies lined up against Grandier. The Bishop of Poitiers sent a message to the townsfolk instructing them to inform the Inquisition of any evidence they had against their curé. They need fear no comeback, he stressed. Among the many tortures that Grandier suffered in an attempt to make him confess to being the Devil's disciple was repeated poking with a long sharp needle. Part of the myth built up around the Devil and the notion of possession was that those in his pay often had some physical mark to denote their association. A third nipple, today regarded by the world of medicine as an eccentricity of birth, was during the witch craze taken to be the sign of Satan. Undeterred by finding that Grandier had no such abnormality, the Inquisitors, briefed by the Mother Superior—and through her, they believed, the Devil himself as he was exorcised from her twisted body—scoured Grandier's flesh with the needle looking for weak spots. Sister Jeanne had reported that as part of the curé's pact with the Devil he had been given areas on his body where he could feel no pain—presumably so as to be able to resist the efforts of the Inquisition. She identified these as on his back, his shoulders, and on each testicle. However, when the torturers got to work, they discovered that quite contrary to the nun's advice, Grandier suffered a great deal of pain when probed. But still it was not enough to make him confess. The Inquisition, however, worked on the basis that the accused was guilty. If a confession could be extracted so much the better, but the absence of one presented no obstacle. It took the civil court little time to find him guilty and sentence him to death for diabolical activities.

The Inquisitors had his broken body drenched in sulfur, to make it burn faster, and paraded him around town, stopping first outside his church and then outside the convent, still trying to make him repent. Finally, they brought him before 6,000 people who had gathered in the main square to watch him be burned alive. As a final twist in this sorry tale, the usual standby of strangling the accused before the flames got to him had to be abandoned because someone had made off with the rope. The Inquisitors said it was the Devil. Others pointed to a Capuchin who bore a particular grudge against the curé.

English Restraint

When the witch craze reached the shores of Protestant England, its impact was less terrible than on the Continent. There was no locally produced copy of the *Malleus* until modern times. Those who doubted the whole conspiracy theory were more vocal and influential. In 1584, Reginald Scot refuted the idea of a diabolic compact in his celebrated *Discoverie of Witchcraft*, which remains to this day a standard text for those who regard the witch craze as one of the great hoaxes of history. You might just as well "beleeve that the moone is made of greene cheese," wrote Scot. If witches could cast successful spells, why "should they not live in all worldlie honor and felicitie? whereas contrariwise they leade their lives in all obloquie, miserie and beggerie, and in fine come to the gallowes."

There were, however, some ready in times of social and political upheaval, to see the Devil's hand at work. Sir Edward Coke, leading lawyer of the late Elizabethan and Jacobean age, defined a witch as "a person who hath conference with the Devil, to consult with him or to do some act." Under the statute of 1603

tougher laws were enacted prescribing the death penalty for dabbling in spells and *maleficium*, both of which were seen as "conference with the Devil." The act was repealed in 1735. In the
interim the evidence from prosecutions, writes Professor Sir
Keith Thomas, "suggests that in England witchcraft was prosecuted primarily as an antisocial crime rather than as heresy"[14]—
more a question of causing damage to other people and their
property than Devil worship.

George Gifford, an Essex cleric writing in 1587, gives a surprisingly unbiased account on witch-hunting during the reign of
Queen Elizabeth I, showing how the traditional spells and magic
of rural England became a crime against God:

> Some woman doth fal out bitterly with her neighbour;
> there followeth some great hurt. . . . There is a suspicion
> conceived. Within fewe yeares after shee is in some
> iarre with an other. Hee is also plagued. This is noted of
> all. Great fame is spread of the matter. Mother W is a
> witch. She hath bewitched goodman B. Two hogges died
> strangely; or else he is taken lame. Wel, Mother W doeth
> begin to bee very odious and terrible unto many. Her
> neighbours, dare say nothing but yet in their heartes they
> wish shee were hanged. Shortly after an other falleth sicke
> and doth pine, hee can have no stomacke unto his meate,
> nor hee can not sleepe. The neighbours come to visit him.
> Well neighbour, sayth one, do ye not suspect some
> naughty dealing: did yee never anger Mother W? Truly
> neighbour, sayth hee, I have not liked the woman a long
> tyme. I can not tell how I should displease her, unless it
> were this other day, my wife prayed her, and so did I that
> shee would keepe her hennes out of my garden. Wee spake
> her as fayre as wee could for our lives. I think verely shee
> hath bewitched me. Every body sayth now that Mother W
> is a witch in deede, and hath bewitched the goodman E.
> Hee cannot eate his meate. It is out of all doubt; for there

were [those] which saw a weasil runne from her house-ward into his yard even a little before hee fell sicke. The sicke man dieth, and taketh it upon his death that hee is bewitched; then is Mother W apprehended and sent to prison, shee is arrayned and condemned.[15]

As on the Continent, the majority of those accused of witch-craft were misfits, inadequate, and marginalized. But the witch craze claimed some well-born victims too. Lady Alice Kyteler, said to be the richest woman in Kilkenny, in Ireland, was accused by her bishop, Richard de Ledrede of Ossory, in a celebrated case of making potions and healing ointments out of dead bodies and of having sex with the Devil in various incarnations, namely, a black shaggy dog, a cat, or a black man. Lady Alice escaped trial by going to England, but her maid, Petronilla, was burned as a witch in November 1324.[16] Although Lady Alice appears to have been an unconventional woman for her era, the charges laid against her had more to do with jealousy, greed, and revenge than with any heresy. She had seen off three husbands and her fourth was in poor health. Her children by her previous marriages and her present husband's relations decided that such a chain of events could not simply be put down to misfortune and accused her of poisoning her partners. Behind the charges lay their ambition to get their hands on her very considerable fortune and their jealousy of her favorite child, William Outlawe, whom she had named as her heir.

Though the English were restrained in their pursuit of witches, outlawing burning and resorting only in extremis to hanging, their Scottish neighbors showed no such inhibition. It was the practice, as in Germany, for the whole town to celebrate the burning of a witch with a public banquet. Among those who fell victim to this mass hysteria was an ancestor of the Queen Mother, Janet Douglas, Lady Glamis, who perished at the stake in 1537. She was found guilty of trying to assassinate King James V of Scotland by poison and magic. There are grounds for seeing Lady Glamis as the victim of a political intrigue, punished on trumped-up charges. Her ghost is still said to haunt Glamis Castle, the family seat.

It was of course fear of the Devil that contributed to widespread acceptance of the charges of witchcraft. The post-Reformation Church in England was just as assiduous as its Catholic rival at contributing to hysteria about Satan. The Elizabethan Communion Service warns sinners to stay away from the altar "lest after taking of that holy sacrament the Devil enter into you as he entered unto Judas, and fill you full of all iniquities and bring you to destruction both of body and soul."

The Devil was a looming presence in the Elizabethan and Jacobean world. As E. M. W. Tillyard puts it in *The Elizabethan World Picture*: "However widely biblical history was presented in medieval drama and sermon, even though many Protestants may have had the gospels by heart, the part of Christianity that was paramount was not the life of Christ but the orthodox scheme of the revolt of the bad angels, the creation, the temptation and fall of man, the incarnation, the atonement, the regeneration through Christ.[17] The perennial questions of good and evil, of the cycles of hope and despair, of optimism and pessimism, figured large, with the Devil very much a part of the scheme of life.

A European Export

Although the witch craze lost some of its vehemence in crossing the Channel to England, it managed to remain virulent as it traversed the Atlantic and infected the free soil of Puritan New England. Its last and most terrible outbreak took place in the village of Salem in Essex County, Massachusetts, where in 1692 the local pastor, the Reverend Samuel Parris, accused a series of local women of being witches.[18]

It all began with three young girls dabbling with fortune-telling, part of traditional magic. Their experiments might have gone unnoticed had not one been the daughter and another the niece of Reverend Parris. With a fervor and hysteria born of his extreme Puritan Protestantism and mirroring the excesses of continental Europe, he immediately took to his pulpit to denounce the witchcraft that was polluting his congregation. Satan was always at hand, he warned. When the girls' behavior became increasingly erratic—eleven-year-old Abigail Williams was reputed to be able to pick up burning logs without flinching—a witch craze was born.

Under pressure, the girls named three local women as responsible for bewitching them. Two denied the charges but a third confessed. Titubu, a West Indian slave who worked for the Parrises, said she had made a pact with the Devil and he was "a thing all over hairy, all the face hairy and a long nose." Her husband was persuaded to testify against her and the charges stuck. The reign of terror that gripped New England targeted 150 people, many of whom had been associated with Reverend Parris's predecessor, the Reverend George Burroughs, who was popularly reputed to be a wizard. Nineteen women were hanged as witches and one man pressed to death as a wizard. Two others died in prison. When Sarah Good stood on the scaffold on July 19, 1692, she turned to the hangman and cried out: "I am no more a witch than you are a wizard, and if you take away my life, God will give you blood to drink."

History recalls that Salem was the scene of many strange goings-on in this period. When one Bridget Bishop, accused of witchcraft, was escorted into the Salem Town courthouse, she was said to have turned her "evil eye" on the roof of the meeting house, which immediately collapsed. In the twentieth century, such reports could be investigated by structural engineers, but in seventeenth-century Salem it was instantly named as the work of the Devil and his wenches. This extreme reaction might be attributed to the climate created by the joyless and remarkably intolerant Puritans. It might equally be ascribed to a response to a new wildness that was full of danger and primeval fear. But quite why this God-fearing community got so worked up remains a mystery. The nineteenth-century historian Charles

Upham gave perhaps the most plausible explanation: "The people . . . had a few years before been thrown into dismay by the loss of their charter, and from that time, kept in a feverish state of anxiety regarding their future political destinies. In addition to this, the whole sea-coast was exposed to danger: ruthless pirates were continually prowling along the shores. Commerce was nearly extinguished, and great losses had been experienced by men in business. A recent expedition against Canada had exposed the colonies to the vengeance of France."[19] This would reflect the political and social upheavals on the Continent that gave rise to the witch craze.

Whatever the causes, Salem remains associated with witchcraft. A son of Salem and a descendant of one of the judges involved in the witch-trials, the novelist Nathaniel Hawthorne (1804–1864) had his own ideas about what prompted the outbreak—Puritan sexual repression and the unkindness that comes with it—as he reveals in his most celebrated novel, *The Scarlet Letter.* Hawthorne provides a vivid and memorable picture in *Young Goodman Brown* of otherwise God-fearing townsfolk gathering at dead of night in the forest to celebrate the sabbat.

Among them, quivering to-and-fro, between gloom and splendour, appeared faces that would be seen, next day, at the council board of the province, and others which, Sabbath after Sabbath, looked devoutly heavenward, and benignantly over the crowded pews from the holiest pulpits in the land. . . . And with the final peal of that dreadful anthem, there came a sound, as if the roaring wind, the rushing streams, the howling beasts, and every other voice of the unconverted wilderness, were mingling and according with the voice of guilty man, in homage to the prince of all. The four blazing pines threw up a loftier flame and obscurely discovered shapes and visages of horror on the smoke-wreaths, above the impious assembly. At the same moment, the fire on the rock shot redly forth and formed a glowing arch above its base, where now appeared a figure. With reverence be it spoken, the figure bore no slight similitude, both in garb and manner, to some grave divine of the New England churches.

The witch craze was finally extinguished in Salem through the determination and wise counsels of some of New England's leading citizens. Its demise coincided with the end of the European hysteria. The Church was squaring up to new threats. The scientific revolution, the Enlightenment, the philosophizing of the materialists like Hobbes all chipped away at the base of superstition that had sustained the Inquisition. Theologians moved on to address these new challenges and while the doctrine of *nullus diabolos, nullus redemptor*—no Devil, no God— was regularly trotted out, the Devil ceased to be a central figure in the debates and doctrine of either Catholic or Protestant Churches. But they had created a monster they could not control and Satan continued to crop up in every avenue of life and culture as a menace, a mischief, and a metaphor for evil.

NINE

Rebel Rebel—a Literary Interlude

> The reason Milton wrote in fetters when he
> wrote of angels and God, and at liberty when of
> devils and hell, is because he was a true poet and
> of the Devil's party without knowing it.
>
> —William Blake, *The Marriage of Heaven and Hell*

In the late seventeenth and early eighteenth century the witch craze melted away almost as quickly as it had appeared. The Inquisition carried on its work in Spain until the first quarter of the nineteenth century but there it had always been more concerned with Moors and Jews than witchcraft. The Spanish Inquisition claimed its final victims in 1826—a Jew who was burned at the stake and a Quaker schoolteacher who was hanged. His crime had been to introduce the "Protestant" hymn "Praise be to God" instead of "Ave Maria" into morning assembly.

Throughout the rest of Europe a growing realization among both clergy and laity that the witch craze had gotten out of hand sidelined the Inquisition. The lead in turning the tide against the Inquisition came from the elite and trickled down to the masses. The governing classes had been alarmed when the Inquisition began to turn its attention on them and had responded by giving their support to those thinkers and writers who loudly proclaimed that the whole witch craze was a hoax. They pressed their governments to draw a line between what were legitimate concerns of clerics and what were not.

For the most part the ancient traditions and beliefs that survived the torturers' rack took many decades, even centuries, to reassert their presence. Yet for a small and often privileged minority they retained their attraction and the removal of the threat of persecution produced renewed interest. In France, Madame de Montespan, Louis XIV's mistress, was advised by a sorceress, Catherine Deshayes, and took part in "black masses" with L'Abbé Guibourg. Montespan would drape herself naked across an altar and drink potions to make herself more attractive to the King. When news of these bizarre—and in Montespan's case desperate—rites reached Louis, he had her banished from the court. Her two assistants were executed in 1680, but their patron survived.

Montespan's fascination with pagan practices was mirrored by that of the highborn young men who—in pursuit of sexual freedom and adventure—joined ostensibly "satanic" hellfire clubs in various European capitals in the early years of the eighteenth century. The most famous of all met at Medmenham Abbey on the banks of the River Thames at West Wycombe, and was presided over by the Chancellor of the Exchequer, Sir Francis Dashwood. Religious ceremonies were parodied, with Dashwood in a monk's robe and a general air of debauchery—rather than evil—pervading events.

The climate in Europe was changing. Christianity's grip on the hearts, minds, and souls of the Continent was weakening. The Reformation saw a renewal of Christendom that broke Rome's authority but it must not overshadow the other reformation that was already in progress when Luther nailed his 95 Articles to the church door. Starting in Italy in the fourteenth century, the Renaissance rejected the Church's control of the intellect and liberated humanity to think freely once again, to explore the potential of the here and now rather than concentrate all efforts on saving souls in the next world. It was not an anti-Christian movement, though its effect was to debunk the claims of the Church to authority over every area of life. The majority of Renaissance thinkers were decidedly moral and godly in their outlook. Their determination to consider afresh how to make the most of this world and how to understand the universe was not tempered by any fears of reducing God. Rather they saw such questioning as fundamental to a clearer understanding of God and his plan. This was to be glimpsed, they held, not through a veil of superstition and prejudice but through the medium of the developing field of science, of mathematics, and of astrology.

Ecclesiastical hostility was unsurprisingly enormous and during the Counter-Reformation the Renaissance was all but extinguished. However, its spirit lived on, triumphant as the age of piety, relics, and fear was swept away at the end of the seventeenth century. The Enlightenment was dawning—humankind need no longer feel at odds with its environment, clinging to life only with God's protection. Events that had once been seen as dictated by the whim of spirits, or as the fallout from the cosmic battle of God and the Devil, were increasingly re-evaluated in the light of scientific knowledge. The imaginary became real, the unknown no longer a threat but a challenge. In the process, the Devil went into a decline, still feared by many but seen increasingly as a relic.

Renaissance men were still theologians, and some exerted enormous influence. Desiderius Erasmus's (1466–1536) reach extended far beyond the seminaries and brought debate about the Devil to a wider audience. He and other Christian humanist thinkers did not deny Satan's existence but relegated him to what they considered a more fitting station, the ranks of the also-rans. Erasmus suggested that the Devil was best seen as simply a metaphor for the vice and evil tendencies in human hearts. "Consider as the Devil," he wrote in *Enchiridion christianum*, "anything that deters us from Christ and his teaching."[1]

Later materialists including Thomas Hobbes (1588–1679), René Descartes (1596–1650), and John Locke (1632–1704) added more nails to the Devil's coffin when they rejected the whole notion of incorporeal substances. Descartes defended Christianity but insisted that the spiritual and material worlds were separate. Therefore, he argued, the Devil exists in the spiritual world insofar as he features in scriptural revelation, but has no power to interfere with the material world of nature.[2] There were no demons, according to Hobbes in *Leviathan*. In "Of the Kingdome of Darkness" he writes: "for we erre, not knowing the Scriptures . . . by introducing the Daemonology of the Heathen Poets, that is to say, their fabulous Doctrine concerning Demons, which are but Idols or Phantasms of the braine, without any reall nature of their own, distinct from humane fancy; such as are dead mens Ghosts, and Fairies, and other matter of old Wives tales."

Such philosophical developments were fueled by the pace of scientific discovery. Nicolaus Copernicus (1473–1543), who in *Revolutions of the Celestial Orbs* put the sun, not the earth, at the center of the solar system, and Giordano Bruno (1548–1600), who wrote of the sun as the symbol of the living principle that gives life to the earth, felt the full force of the Church's disapproval. Bruno, once a Dominican, was burned at the stake by the Inquisition as an "impenitent heretic." Galilei Galileo (1564–1642) was another whose passion for science and discovery cost him dear. But though the Church could persecute individuals, it could not keep the lid on questions they were asking, nor the answers they were suggesting. They all pointed to the potential for scientific and rational explanations to many of the phenomena hitherto blamed on Satan.

The dramatist Ben Jonson provides in *The Devil Is an Ass* a vivid description of the seventeenth-century mind, torn between a credulity that belonged to an earlier age and a skepticism that was as yet unconfirmed; between faith in magic and the supernatural and a brimming confidence in the potential of applied science to unlock the mysteries of the universe. One of the central characters of the play, Fitzdottrel, a dabbler in magic, longs to meet the Devil because he wants to find hidden treasures. Yet at the same time as he is—symbolically—looking back to the beliefs of a previous era, he also places his trust in the skills of financial advisers who promise to pay him enormous sums of money and get him a dukedom. Unable to decide between the religious and the secular he is warned by his spouse about false spirits and replies:

> *Spirits! O no such thing, wife; wit, mere wit.*
> *This man defies the Devil and all his works.*
> *He does't be engine and devices, he!*
> *He has his winged ploughs that go with sails,*
> *Will plough you forty acres at once! and mills*
> *Will spout you water ten miles off*

The Renaissance had little time for the Devil as an incarnate being or as a source for disquiet and the mysteries of the world. It did not reject him but tried instead to recast him and his role. In *The Devil Is an Ass*, Jonson used a Satan figure to expose the follies of mankind. Pug, a minor devil, visits Jacobean London for the day and is appalled by what he sees. "Talk of the university?" he queries. "Hell is a grammar school to this."

The landscape of the Jacobean tragedy was in general a grizzly and often grotesque one, with evil triumphing over good. John Webster's *The Duchess of Malfi* (1614) contrasts the saintly widowed Duchess and her two scheming evil brothers, Ferdinand, who has designs on her, and the Cardinal, who is corrupt and greedy. The broader image of a society poisoned by a combination of the Church and the aristocracy is a constant theme. In Webster's *The White Devil* (1608), as in *The Duchess of Malfi*, the wicked deeds of the characters are ascribed not to an external figure of Satan but to the evil inclination within the human makeup.

The greatest dramatist of the age, William Shakespeare, (1564–1616), says very little about the Devil. He includes references to the Devil—"the prince of darkness is a gentleman"[3]—but he was disinclined to tackle the question of evil per se. In Shakespeare's plays, evil is addressed as a factor in social and political disorder: The characters who kill kings and subvert the political hierarchy are those who are most readily associated with evil. These schemers, usually in some way misfits, include Edmund, the bastard son in *King Lear*, the hunchback Richard III, and Iago in *Othello*.

The *Oxford Illustrated History of English Literature* has no hesitation in deeming Iago "the sheerly satanic in man, bound by the acute malevolence that is his nature to wreck and destroy."[4] Yet the streak of evil that Iago displays has no particular origin and there is only the vaguest impression that he is possessed. When he is pressed as to why he has poisoned Othello's mind against his bride Desdemona, and precipitated both their deaths, he offers a whole variety of explanations but fails to convince with any and ultimately refuses to answer:[5]

> *Othello: Will you, I pray, demand that demi-devil*
> *Why he hath thus ensnar'd my soul and body?*
> *Iago: Demand me nothing: what you know, you know:*
> *From this time forth I never will speak word*[6]

Accused of being a devil, Iago does share with Satan the hallmarks of the trickster—clever, cunning, playful, full of energy, fleet of foot and mind, able to persuade his victims to act against their own best interests. But the suggestion in *Othello* is that some people are simply born evil, that it is part of the human condition.

In *Macbeth*, a different line is pursued in regard to evil. Lady Macbeth is more taken over by evil, a victim of it, than by nature evil. The whole play is pervaded by a strong sense of looming and threatening evil, with the three witches in the first act setting the tone amid thunder and lightning and later in the third act planting the idea of kingship in Macbeth's head. Overtaken by guilt and remorse after her schemes to murder Duncan have borne fruit, Lady Macbeth is unable to sleep. She describes the evil that she has done as if it is something that has infected

her: "Out, damned spot! Out I say! One: two: why then 'tis
time to do't. Hell is murky! Fie, my lord, fie! A soldier and
afeared?"[7]

Both Lady Macbeth and Iago can be fitted into a broader,
classical approach in Shakespeare in regard to evil. The Bard does
not blame the Devil, but rather fate. The evil person is set in the
context of his fate, has no free will to affect the situation, and
therefore is not wholly responsible for his actions. As in the
Greek tragedies, they are part of a bigger scheme as Gloucester
acknowledges in *King Lear*:

> *As flies to wanton boys, we are to the gods:*
> *They kill us for their sport*[8]

More traditional representations were still a part of the popular Protestant England culture—notably in John Bunyan's *The
Pilgrim's Progress* (1678). This celebrated work, composed
partly while Bunyan was in Bedford Jail because of his preaching
in public, features a Devil-like creature, Apollyon who torments
Christian.

> *Now the monster was hideous to behold, he was*
> *cloathed with scales like a Fish (and they are his pride)*
> *he had Wings like a Dragon, feet like a Bear, and out of*
> *his belly came Fire and Smoke, and his mouth was as*
> *the mouth of a Lion. When he was come up to*
> *Christian, he beheld him with a disdainful*
> *countenance, and thus began to question with him.*

In the course of this exchange, Apollyon tries to convince
Christian to turn his back on God, the "King of Princes." When
he refuses Apollyon flies into a rage, shouting, "I am an Enemy
to this Prince: I hate his Person, his Laws and People: I am
come out on purpose to withstand thee." Apollyon then rains
darts down on Christian for half a day, intent on killing him. As
Apollyon moves in for the kill, God comes to Christian's rescue,
gives him new strength, and helps him fight off his attacker, who
flaps his dragon's wings and flies off.

Bunyan stands foursquare in the Christian tradition in his representation of the Devil, the face of evil. That picture of the half-man, half-beast, dark, sinister, and cunning, continued to resound in the popular mind. But other writers—influenced by the Renaissance—took an altogether different approach. Two in particular—Dante Alighieri (1265–1321) and John Milton (1608–1674)—produced some of the most compelling and enduring images of Satan and his lair, hell.

Dante's Devil

For the last fifteen years of his life, after his political ambitions in his native Florence had been crushed at the hands of the ultra-Catholic party, Dante wrote his *Comedy*, a three-part epic journey in best Greek tradition through hell, purgatory, and paradise. It is a comedy not in the sense that we use the word today—though the cycle does have an uplifting ending. Dante once explained the origin of the title as originating from the words *comus oda*, or rustic song.

One of the characteristics of Renaissance literature—harking back to ancient Greece and its poets, in preference to the piety and superstition of medieval mystery plays—is immediately apparent in *Comedy*. The narrator is accompanied throughout by Virgil, whose verse style influenced Dante enormously. *Comedy* reflects the Renaissance's scientific curiosity in its concern with the physical structure of the cosmos, but its interest is not simply an attempt to fashion a plan of the universe. Dante had a moral purpose, to reconcile the ethical world with the physical world around him. Again, in typical Renaissance mode, rather than follow in the footsteps of earlier generations and start with Christianity and then make the world fit in with that view—including blaming everything unpleasant on the Devil—Dante chose to take what he believed to be the reality of the universe and shape an ethical code that reflected and celebrated it.[9]

The world of Dante's *Comedy*—called *Divine* by its admirers, whose appellation has stuck—is made up of a series of concentric spheres with the earth at the center, moving outward to the planets, the sun, the stars, and then heaven. In the center of the earth is hell, again a series of layers with the degree of privation building up at every stage. The narrator journeys in *Inferno* through the many layers of hell, meeting individuals whose vices have landed them there and seeing at every stage humanity's sinfulness and rejection of God.

The picture of the underworld is borrowed from the Greek and Christian traditions but amplified in its terrifying and gruesome dimensions by the poet's imagination. Upper Hell, nearest to the earth's surface, is entered by a vestibule crowned with the doom-laden words "Abandon every hope, all you who enter." This leads first to limbo where virtuous non-Christians like the poets Homer, Horace, Ovid, and Lucan live in only mild discomfort, shut off from God's redeeming light. The travelers proceed on to a circle—or layer—populated by the lustful (famous lovers like Helen of Troy and Cleopatra), the gluttonous, hoarders, spendthrifts, the angry, and the slothful. These categories broadly follow the seven deady sins, codified in the Christian world by Pope Gregory the Great in the sixth century.

The travelers experience an unhappy crossing of the River Styx, one of the distinguishing physical features of the Greek underworld, before landing at the infernal City of Dis where howling figures like the Furies, again from Greek mythology, threaten them from the gates. All the time hastening on past each obstacle, yet knowing there is only worse to come, the narrator and Virgil arrive at the layer of violence—the treacherous River Phlegethon, the plains of burning sand and the terrifying and eerie "Wood of Suicides":

> *no green leaves, but rather black in colour,*
> *no smooth branches, but twisted and entangled,*
> *no fruit but thorns of poison bloomed instead*
> (CANTO XIII:4–6)

> *around me wails of grief were echoing,*
> *and I saw no one there to make those sounds:*
> (CANTO XIII:22–23)[10]

The narrator is rooted to the spot as he watches two black dogs tearing a wench limb from limb, but is urged on by Virgil to the great barrier and waterfall where they plunge over the edge while harassed by a mighty monster. At the base they find yet more sinners—this time guilty of fraud and malice, and containing a fair number of deceased popes. Finally, the two end their trek and reach the core of hell where they glimpse the figure of Lucifer:

> *The king of the vast kingdom of all grief*
> *stuck out with half his chest above the ice;*
> *my height is closer to the height of giants*
>
> *than theirs is to the length of his great arms;*
> *consider now how large all of him was:*
> *this body in proportion to his arms.*
>
> *If once he was as fair as now he's foul*
> *and dared to raise his brows against his Maker,*
> *it is fitting that all grief should spring from him*
>
> *Oh, how amazed I was when I looked up*
> *and saw a head—one head wearing three faces*
> *One was in front (and that was a bright red)*
>
> *the other two attached themselves to this one*
> *just above the middle of each shoulder,*
> *and at the crown all three were joined in one.*
>
> *The right face was a blend of white and yellow,*
> *the left the colour of those people's skin*
> *who live along the river Nile's descent.*

Beneath each face two mighty wings stretched out,
the size you might expect of this huge bird
(I never saw a ship with larger sails):

not feathered wings but rather like the ones
a bat would have. He flapped them constantly,
keeping three winds continuously in motion

to lock Cocytus eternally in ice.
He wept from his six eyes, and down three chins
were dripping tears all mixed with bloody slaver.
(CANTO XXXIV:28–54)

He is chewing in each of his jaws a notorious sinner—Judas Iscariot and Brutus and Cassius, conspirators against Caesar. The two travelers climb down Satan's hairy, immobilized body until they reach his thigh, where in a dramatic moment, they turn their gaze upward to the stars, to the heavens, and are liberated from the Inferno.

Though much of *Inferno* embellishes traditional images of hell and damnation, Dante's Devil is not a conventional one for his age. For one thing Lucifer is offstage for virtually the whole progress, only appearing at the very end. This stands in marked contrast to the omnipresent Satan of the medieval pulpits. When he is finally reached, he can scarcely be compared with the sly, cunning, devious driving force behind the witch craze. Dante's Lucifer is a spent volcano, a tragic, empty, foolish, helpless character, encased in ice, weeping.

Though he gives the Devil a physical presence, Dante's description turns the Devil into a metaphor for nothingness, a void, a cold, empty place. Missing too from Dante's *Inferno* is any mention of demons. The tortures that the travelers see as they descend through hell are not carried out by winged, horned imps, but by impersonal, abstract forces. The prisoners of hell—including Pope Boniface VIII (1294–1303), Dante's political enemy—are shown to have brought sorrows on their own head.

The metaphor is carried further. Dante's narrator is, in a conventional sense, well understood and practiced by the medieval theater, Everyman. Yet in *Inferno*, with its final scene of resurrection, the parallels are less with humanity's experience than with Christ's descent after the crucifixion. The reader is invited to get inside his psyche and see as he would have seen not only the tormented souls in hell, but by association the sinfulness of the world. This first hint of psychological realism was a theme taken up with gusto by Milton in his portrait of Satan.

Though it was Dante's intention to emphasize the positive— "to remove those living in this life from their state of misery and lead them to the state of felicity" as he wrote at the time— his positioning of Hell at the center of the cosmos gives the Devil a dominating role; putting heaven at the furthest periphery increases the impression. The physical arrangements of *Comedy*, however, should not be confused for its moral message. In simple terms Dante's view on good and evil was that man, when filled with God, will rise to heaven, but when weighed down by stupidity and sin will go to hell. The tendency to do good outweighs the tendency toward sinfulness. God is at the center of Dante's moral cosmos, a world in which there are no boundaries. The Devil, despite his physical presence, is nowhere.

Milton the Kingmaker

Dante's lasting contribution has been to create an image of hell in all its labyrinthine horrors that remains with us to this day. John Milton's psychological portrait of the Devil has had the most profound impact on succeeding generations. His view eclipsed all previous images, turning them on their heads and fashioning in their place a picture so compelling and credible that it remains the standard account of Satan, and the yardstick by which all other impressions must be judged.

Born in 1608 into a Protestant family, Milton was a child prodigy who traveled continental Europe as a young man, meeting some of the leading figures of the Renaissance including Galileo who is mentioned in *Paradise Lost*. He became a propagandist for the Commonwealth and Oliver Cromwell, principally in his Latin pamphlet *Defensio Secunda* (1654). The collapse of this brief interlude in Britain's monarchical tradition hit him particularly hard and with the Restoration in 1660, he found himself in prison. Released through the good offices of friends, he dedicated much of his later years to writing *Paradise Lost*, which was first published in 1667, and the much shorter *Paradise Regained*, which appeared in 1671. He died in 1674.[11]

The two works pivot on Christ's life and death. *Paradise Lost* looks back to the sins that he redeemed by his sacrifice, and *Paradise Regained* points forward to the gifts that will come to humankind as a result of that sacrifice. The theology of *Paradise Lost* is not exceptional. It follows the traditional account of an almighty bust up in heaven, Satan's fall, his temptation of Adam and Eve, their abuse of the gift of free will, the original sin, and Christ's passion. What is extraordinary is Milton's poetry, his portrayal of Satan for the first time as a rounded, credible, at times sympathetic and always seductive figure. Gone were the cardboard cutout monsters of yore. Psychological realism dominates the text, carrying the reader along with Adam and Eve as they are tempted, making their fall understandable.

Most revolutionary of all is that the Devil, the original rebel, is at first glance the hero of *Paradise Lost*. Despite all the baggage of distrust and suspicion that any reader carries with him or her on picking up the book, Milton manages to make Satan magnificent. He has no cloven hoof, no outward sign of inward evil—save the lines on his face, scarred by lightning. The horned enchanter, the creature who inhabits Luther's bowels and eats his excrement, the jester, the bandleader of rabbles of old women chanting spells over a cauldron in the woods is transformed. Like Dante, Milton looked back to ancient Greece for inspiration and his Satan is a classical hero. He takes on—in God—a previously unchallenged opponent; he is defeated, and as a consequence is condemned to a horrific realm outside the world of his opponent. Yet he is transformed into an awesome but magnetic giant "of mighty Stature" (I:222), passionate and energetic, courageous—in the first speech he delivers from hell— even in the face of defeat.

> *What though the field be lost?*
> *All is not lost; the unconquerable Will,*
> *And study of revenge, immortal hate,*
> *And courage never to submit or yield:*
> *And what is else not to be overcome?*
> *That Glory never shall his wrath or might*
> *Extort from me.*
>
> (I:105–111)[12]

Simultaneously, Milton debunks his hero. In a maneuver all too familiar to media-watchers today, he builds Satan up in the eyes of his readership only then to start undermining him. Milton's Satan is ugly. He smells. There is a hint that he commits incest with his daughter, Sin. Indeed, he is both the partner and the begetter of Sin. And behind his swagger, his theatricality, and his fine and clever words, there is something sinister and untrustworthy.

> *So spake the false dissembler unperceiv'd;*
> *For neither Man nor Angel can discern*
> *Hypocrisy, the only evil that walks*
> *Invisible, except to God alone,*
> *By his permissive will, through Heav'n and Earth*
>
> (III:681–685)

There is a fatal flaw buried within this outwardly impressive Satan. Wrath, so often a motivating force in epic heroes—Achilles in the *Iliad* or the raging, vengeful Turnus in the *Aeneid*—is overlaid in Milton's Satan with hatred:

> *he above the rest*
> *In shape and gesture proudly eminent*
> *Stood like a Tow'r; his form had not yet lost*
> *All her Original brightness, nor appear'd*
> *Less than Arch Angel ruin'd and th'excess*
> *Of glory obscured: As when the Sun new-ris'n*
> *Looks through the Horizontal misty Air*
> *Shorn of his Beams, or from behind the Moon*
> *In dim Eclipse disastrous twilight sheds*
> *On half the Nations, and with fear of change*
> *Perplexes Monarchs. Darken'd so, yet shone*
> *Above them all th' Arch Angel: but his face*
> *Deep scars of Thunder had intrencht, and care*
> *Sat on his faded cheek, but under Brows*
> *Of dauntless courage and considerable Pride*
> *Waiting revenge*
>
> (I:589–604)

Milton's genius goes further than simply showing Satan as a flawed, menacing character. He explains why Satan has become as he is, what it is that has happened to him that makes him thus, and engages our sympathy, if not our trust. Satan becomes a kind of whiskey priest, a disappointed man, a washed-up idealist turned cynical, expelled from the main arena and now sitting on the sidelines doing his damnedest to ruin things. Milton exploits to the full the tragedy and the pathos of this position—the untamed, doomed rebel:

> *round he throws his baleful eyes*
> *That witness'd huge affliction and dismay*
> *Mixt with obdurate pride and steadfast hate*
>
> (I:56–58)

When he first glimpses the wonder of Eden, from his vantage point on Mount Niphates, Satan is full of contradictions and yearnings:

> *O Sun, to tell thee how I hate thy beams*
> *That bring to my remembrance from what state*
> *I fell, how glorious once above thy Sphere;*
> *Till pride and worse Ambition threw me down*
> *Warring in Heav'n with Heav'n's matchless King*
>
> (IV:37–41)

Even the initial impression of heroism is dispelled, for Satan in *Paradise Lost* is nothing but a marshal hero, able to guide his force of demons to wreak chaos, cunning enough to convince Adam's beloved Eve to eat the forbidden fruit. But, the authorial voice makes clear, that is not the same as, nor ultimately a match for, moral supremacy and Satan's courage is contrasted with Christ's. Christ is truly heroic because he has a purpose, to save souls. Satan's bravery is self-serving and futile. In the midst of his marshaling there is an undertow of malevolence—as in a passage that Milton scholars, including Christopher Ricks, have likened to a description of a twentieth-century fascist rally:

> *He through the armed Files*
> *Darts his experienc't eye, and soon traverse*
> *The whole Battalion views; their order due,*
> *Their visages and stature as of Gods,*
> *Their number last he sums. And now his heart*
> *Distends with pride, and hardening in his strength*
> *Glories . . .*
>
> (I:567–573)

As C. S. Lewis once remarked, Milton gradually reduces Satan from a bright angel to a peeping, prying, lying thing that ends as a writhing snake.[13]

Milton's approach is understandable in the light of the peren-
nially irreconcilable facts surrounding the Devil—God's omnipotence and Satan's existence. How can there be a Devil—or in a
metaphorical sense more appropriate to Milton's age, how can
there be evil—when God is almighty, all-knowing, and all-
loving? Milton's Satan gives voice to the attraction in the human
heart for evil, its weakness, its temptability. His Satan also shows
the hollowness of those claims, but sets them against a God who
to many is often distant and occasionally incomprehensible.

Though at the very outset of the epic Milton states his intention to "assert Eternal Providence / And justify the ways of God
to men" (I:25–26), the God of *Paradise Lost* is at times inconsis-
tent, human, even spiteful.[14] He sends his angels on pointless
journeys, and exudes an air of unconcern, that he can outwit
everyone if only he could summon up the energy. Though there
is a clear contrast between the hell of Books One and Two and
the heaven of Book Three, for much of the poem, God looks on
in an existential kind of fashion as humanity suffers for his
amusement. This stance results from Milton's overriding concern with the doctrine of free will. He rejected the Protestant
obsession with predestination. In *Paradise Lost*, God may have
foreknowledge of humanity's fall, but it is in no sense predeter-
mined. It is brought about by the exercise of free will, distancing
God from evil in the world. In this scheme Satan fills the
vacuum, a tool of God more than a threat, an exploiter of a void
rather than a challenge to God's omnipotence, which is never
in doubt throughout *Paradise Lost*. Satan will always lose
because God—described as "heav'n's perpetual King"—holds all
the cards.

The story of the Garden of Eden is dealt with in less than four
chapters in the Book of Genesis, yet it became a key event in
explaining the existence of evil in the world and Christ's death
and resurrection, not to mention the role of the Devil. Milton
imposed three-dimensional characters with recognizably human
motivations on to the episode. He was blind when he wrote
Paradise Lost, and it has been suggested that he was re-creating

the world he had lost with his sight as well as the world of Eden that humanity had lost because of Adam and Eve's original sin. Milton's attitude here was ambiguous, springing from one of the central paradoxes in *Paradise Lost*—that the fall was a good thing. Milton presents the Devil, on one level, as God's tool, seen when Satan puts humankind in a position to choose good over evil by precipitating the fall. True goodness is defined by its opposition to evil and contrasted with the "cloistered virtue" of Adam and Eve living a good life before the Devil gave them an alternative. In *Paradise Lost*, the adversary who puts false goodness to the test takes on the character of The Adversary.

Nine of the twelve books are set in the Garden of Eden. Milton transformed the role of the serpent, identified as Satan in disguise, into a con man with a clever way with words. While Adam's motivation is presented as straightforward—his love for Eve—her encounter with Satan in Book Nine, when he finally persuades her to eat the forbidden fruit, is a more complex and symbolic account of human temptation. At first Satan is transfixed by Eve's beauty:

> *That space the Evil one abstracted stood*
> *From his own evil, and for the time remain'd*
> *Stupidly good, of enmity disarm'd.*
> *Of guile, of hate, of envy, of revenge.*
> (IX:463–465)

Eve is so taken aback to hear a serpent talking that she is flattered by his praise and seduced by his arguments. The image of Satan whispering in her ear is one much used when trying to convey the notion of temptation.

> *Squat like a Toad, close at the ear of Eve;*
> *Assaying by his Devilish art to reach*
> *The Organs of her Fancy*
> (IV:800–801)

The serpent tells her that God has forbidden the fruit of the Tree of Knowledge because he wants to keep her ignorant. If the fruit is bad, God created it and therefore he must be bad. There is a sense that from the moment she listens to the serpent, Eve is sinning. The reader sins with her in being tempted by Satan. As she reaches and eats the fruit, the reader too bites into its flesh.

Shakespeare brought the Devil into the human psyche; Milton put the diabolical in the human psyche into the Devil. In capturing the public imagination, giving form to their fears, making Satan a real temptation, Milton broke new ground. He shaped what had previously been a slice of the Bible into a rollicking good story, full of theatricality, climactic moments, tragedy, and recognizable humanity. The controversy that his new-look Satan provoked with ecclesiastical authorities and even with his fellow writers only heightened his reputation and the impact of *Paradise Lost*.

Down but Not Quite Out

By a strange irony, just as Milton produced the most impressive, credible, seductive, and memorable portrait of the Devil in the Christian tradition, Satan was increasingly dismissed as an incarnate reality in urban and intellectual circles. Only among the slavishly God-fearing and rural communities did the Devil still cut a terrifying figure. *Paradise Lost* may have slowed this process of decline; it may even have reversed it temporarily. After its lavish fourth edition in 1688, illustrated by John Baptist de Medina, it began to prompt extensive debate and commentary among other writers and poets. However, it did not rescue the Devil from the retirement home of theology, nor did it prove particularly effective in countering ridicule of the Christian Devil in enlightened circles in the eighteenth century.

Voltaire (1694–1778), who was part of much of the new thinking of that age, dismissed *Paradise Lost* as "a disgusting fantasy." As science and reason vanquished superstition and magic, Voltaire and his fellow *philosophes* attacked the Church's hold over European society and government, a process that the Reformation and the Renaissance had begun. Descartes and Hobbes had drawn a sharp distinction between the spiritual and material worlds, while still stressing that both were of equal worth. The eighteenth-century Enlightenment took the argument one step further. Voltaire was prepared to accept that God created the world—flicked a switch and set the whole celestial machine in motion—but thereafter it was a matter for humankind. Though educated by the Jesuits, he would have no truck with ecclesiastical hierarchy and Christianity in general. *"Ecrasez l'infame"*— crush the infamy—he used to write of the Church at the end of his letters.

Voltaire's contempt for the prevailing Christian school of thought known as Optimism—that God created the world good, had a plan, and humanity must simply have faith and stick with it—is obvious in his writing, and is seen most powerfully in his wittiest novel, *Candide* (1759), pointedly subtitled *Optimism.* The young Candide travels Europe with his tutor, Doctor Pangloss, a confirmed Optimist who holds that they live in the best of all worlds, that the bad in some lives is balanced by the good in others to make a level playing field. Even after Pangloss has been hanged, dissected, and flogged at the bench of a Turkish galley, he still maintains that God's world is good and that the evil that has befallen him is balanced out by others' fortunes. Though the young Candide observes such absurdities with hope still alight in his heart, the author's position comes through most powerfully in the character of Martin—cynical, forever disillusioning Candide. At the very end of this entertaining odyssey, Martin and Candide agree on what seems to be Voltaire's pessimistic philosophy. "Let us work without arguing; that's the only way to make life bearable."

Though the Optimists and the *philosophes* were at daggers drawn, they did agree on one matter. Neither had much time for an incarnate Devil. Voltaire saw Satan as an absurd device used by a power-crazy Church to impose its superstitious beliefs and hence its will on people. The Optimists considered the Devil a distraction from the business of setting natural evil against natural good.

Two beliefs unite the various characters known to history as the *philosophes*, first a determination to shape a popular movement and second a disdain for the Church. They rejected its beliefs as intellectually flawed and as socially manipulative. They regarded organized religion as one of the causes of evil. They argued that every traditional dogma of Christianity might be refuted if not in accord with natural reason. Even as a metaphor for evil, the Devil was redundant. In this atmosphere of rejecting everything to do with Satan, some Enlightenment men took matters a stage further. One person forever associated with the satanic is Donatien Alphonse François, Marquis de Sade (1740–1814) who gave his name to sadism. Not only did he refute the Devil, but God too. He argued that good and evil were unnecessary encumbrances; everyone should do whatever took their pleasure. In trying to imagine what that would be, de Sade, with heavy irony, made what popularly has been the Devil's program his own—sexual license and amorality.

No survey, however brief, of the Devil's role in the eighteenth century can ignore Johann Wolfgang von Goethe (1749–1832) and his *Faust* dramas. The Faust legend—the tale of a traveling magician who in return for knowledge sells his soul to the Devil via the spirit of Mephistopheles (literally, the not-light-loving-one)—had first reached a wide audience thanks to Luther. His follower Melancthon put the Protestant reformer's account of this folklorish story into book form in 1540. Johann Spiess then took up the theme in his 1587 *Historia von Dr. Johann Faustus*, known popularly as the "Faustbook" and translated and distributed across Europe.

Goethe, however, gave the story a new edge in keeping with the age of the Enlightenment. His Mephistopheles, like Milton's Satan, draws on sources other than the Christian tradition.

Goethe despised Church organization. During the sixty years he spent writing his *Faust*, he flitted from one denomination to another, ending up an atheist. He always vehemently denied the existence of the Devil.

In Mephistopheles there is the cynical twist of Martin in *Candide*, the ironic commentator on society, overlaid with much menace. As a character he is as much a dispassionate observer as an active Devil, a spokesman for anti-Christianity as much as a metaphor for the less attractive side of life. There are moments when Goethe's Mephistopheles comes close to the Satan of the Book of Job. In the Prologue, he is very much a part of the court of heaven, involved in heated exchanges with God. "I have never hated you," God tells him. "Of all the spirits who deny me, I blame the rogue the least. The activity of humans all too quickly slackens into laziness, so I give them a companion to push them and work on them and act as Devil" (Prologue 337–343). Once on earth, Mephistopheles is a liar, a trickster, someone who can cause disorder and suffering. He also has the capacity to change form at will, starting off, in another traditional image of the Evil One, as a black dog when he first appears in Faust's study.

The genius of Goethe's *Faust* lies in its subversion of the legend. In a scene in the Witch's Kitchen, Mephistopheles, far from being the sinister tempter, stands back and casts his critical eye on himself, observing his own emasculation. His horns and his tail have gone. All that remains of his traditional armor is his cloven hoof, but even then disguised in shoes. Goethe appears to be charting the Devil's own decline in the age of Enlightenment. Satan can no longer be picked out from a crowd: Evil is more subtle, more pernicious, and on the part of Mephistopheles less single-minded, more complex and unsure in its motivations.

This *Faust*—which was later illustrated by the French nineteenth-century Romantic artist Eugène Delacroix—beggars any single or simple interpretation. Its power to question, to reverse, and to subvert is seen in its climax when, despite all of Mephistopheles' efforts, Faust is saved. Even when he was tempted by the deadly sin of lust, he turned it into love. At the end of his life he is consigned not to hell, as prearranged, but is carried by boyish angels into heaven. Mephistopheles is left powerless on the sidelines, idly considering whether it would be worth buggering the youthful attendants.

A Romantic Indian Summer

The French Revolution changed Europe forever. It swept away the established political and legal order and with it Christendom. It was Napoleon who abandoned the Holy Roman Empire, after the Revolution separated Church and State. Any ambitions the Churches had of absolute political power were at an end. As well as changing forms of government in Europe, the Industrial Revolution was replacing the old hierarchy—the *ancien régime*—with a commercial elite who valued God as a tool of capitalism. Urbanization gathered speed, and the old patterns of the countryside, traditionally the home of a more authoritarian and unquestioning form of Christianity, came under threat.

As people moved from villages to towns, they abandoned their old habits, the ancient fears of devils and spirits and the Christian Devil, and turned to new political ideologies that sought to make sense of their new misery, the often terrible conditions in which they lived and worked. Blaming it all on Satan was one alternative, but the pull of Marxism, for example, proved stronger. The Church authorities and the old order were perplexed by what was afoot. They took comfort in seeing the Devil's hand in the changes. They were not alone in demonizing those who would put them down—some revolutionaries took their cue from Milton and saw the Devil as a symbol of rebellion against the Church and the *ancien régime*. Both sides, in effect, reduced Satan to a symbol—accelerating a process that had been in train for centuries. But at the end of the eighteenth century the Devil, in the hands of the Romantics, became a potent and positive symbol, liberated from any biblical or ecclesiastical restraints, used at whim as a cultural and social metaphor. In the process Milton's creation was twisted and distorted.

Romanticism scarcely merits being classified as an intellectual movement, as its theological credentials are scant. It was an expression of rebellion—by writers and artists against both traditional Christian morality and science. It was riddled with contradictions, among which was its penchant for the symbols, the mystery, and the overblown language of good and evil that was part of Christianity. Many Romantics, though, were fervently anti-Christian with little or no time for the Church. The engraver, artist, and poet William Blake (1757–1827) was as dismissive of God as he was laudatory of the Devil. "God," Blake wrote, "is in the lowest as well as in the highest causes." An avid reader, Blake is often described as casting his mind back to the earlier thoughts of Gnostics and the view that the world was fundamentally evil. To Blake the process of industrialization was not a blessing but an evil, and he used traditional Christian language in one of the most famous references to the Devil—the "dark satanic mills" of his hymn "Jerusalem"—to describe the factories and burdened workers that he observed while staying at Felpham.

When addressing the question of evil in the world, however, Blake did not seek to push it off on the Devil, but rather located it—in his epic poem "Jerusalem"—firmly in the human psyche.

> *It is the reasoning power,*
> *An abstract objecting power that negatives everything.*
> *This is the spectre of man, the holy reasoning power,*
> *And in its holiness is closed the Abomination of Desolation*

Again in his "Everlasting Gospel," God says to Christ:

> *If thou humblest thyself, thou humblest Me.*
> *Thou also dwellest in ternity.*

Thou art a man. God is no more.
Thine own humanity learn to adore;
For that is my spirit of life

Blake reiterates the point in his "Songs of Innocence and Experience" (1789–1794):

Cruelty has a Human Heart,
And Jealousy a Human Face;
Terror the Human Form Divine,
And Secrecy the Human Dress

Such a view allowed no absolutes, no poles of good and evil in God and the Devil. In Blake's 1808 pen and watercolor "Satan Watching Adam and Eve," the Devil is intertwined with the serpent, in traditional and Miltonesque tradition, but is a beautiful cherub, his wings and curls framing a tragically contorted face. The ambiguity is seen to greater effect in his "Christ Tempted by Satan to Turn the Stones into Bread" (1816–1818), where the Devil appears not as a monster or even a sinister presence, but as a kindly elderly man, a character more usually associated with depictions of God himself. The positioning of the two figures suggests ambiguity—Christ and Satan look as if they are performing a strange dance together, each mirroring and complementing the other's movements.

In the works of perhaps the most celebrated Romantic, the poet Lord Byron (1788–1824), the same note of ambiguity is present. In "Cain: A Mystery" (1821), Byron portrays Lucifer as a complex character, lauding him for his support of Cain in his battle with tyranny, yet also showing him standing apart from and even enjoying human suffering. When Lucifer and Cain debate the role of the serpent in the Garden of Eden, the Devil claims that humankind's suffering comes from within:

Cain: But the thing had a demon?
Lucifer: He but woke one

In those he spake to with his forky tongue.
I tell thee that the serpent was no more
Than a mere serpent: ask the cherubim
Who guard the tempting tree. When thousand ages
Have roll'd o'er your dead ashes, and your seed's,
The seed of the then world may thus array
Their earliest fault in the fable, and attribute
To me a shape I scorn, as I scorn all
That bows to him, who made things but to bend
Before his sullen, sole eternity;
But we, who see the truth, must speak it. Thy
Fond parents listen'd to a creeping thing.
And fell.

What distinguishes Lucifer from Jehovah—or God—in the poem is his coldness, distance, and lack of love. While Jehovah can be cruel and insensitive to Cain, it is Lucifer who brings ill-fortune to the world by his refusal to integrate himself with Jehovah.

Percy Bysshe Shelley (1792–1822), like Byron a vocal opponent of organized religion, did not believe in the Devil and could be brutal in his analysis of how Satan had come about:

Like panic-stricken slaves in the presence of a jealous and suspicious despot, they [the Christians] have tortured themselves ever to devise any flattering sophism by which they might appease him [God] by the most contradictory praises, endeavouring to reconcile omnipotence and benevolence and equity in the Author of an Universe where evil and good are inextricably entangled, and where the most admirable tendencies to happiness and preservation are forever baffled by misery and decay. The Christians, therefore, invented or adopted the Devil to extricate them from this difficulty.

(*Essay on the Devil and Devils*, 1819–1820)

Shelley respected the need for a satanic figure to act as a symbol for evil. At the same time and with typical Romantic ambivalence, he saw the Devil as a rebel and thereby as a symbol for anyone who wished to overthrow the established order. In *Defense of Poesy*, he wrote:

Nothing can exceed the energy and magnificence of the character of Satan as expressed in *Paradise Lost*. It is a mistake to suppose that he could ever have been intended for the popular personification of evil. . . . Milton's Devil as a moral being is far superior to his God as One who perseveres in some purpose which he has conceived to be excellent in spite of adversity and torture is to One who in the cold security of his undoubted triumph inflicts the most horrible revenge upon his enemy. . . . Milton . . . alleged no superiority of moral virtue to his God over his Devil.

The Devil became the Romantics' hero—or antihero. He inspired a whole host of writers to produce outlaws with a heart, sublime criminals. Goethe's friend Johann Schiller (1759–1805) in *The Robbers* (1781) portrays the central character of Karl Moor as an evil genius who pays homage to Milton's *Paradise Lost* as he goes about stealing.[15]

The Romantic fascination with the Devil in the nineteenth century spread beyond England. François-Auguste-René de Chateaubriand (1768–1848), regarded by many as the founder of French Romanticism, was an ardent admirer of *Paradise Lost*, but he took an entirely different line from Byron or Shelley. In *Le Génie du christianisme* (1802), Chateaubriand argued that Milton's Satan, while a towering and magnificent figure, was a villain who wished to overthrow the status quo. The author, a deeply conservative figure, rejected any notion of heroism and indeed set a tone that was markedly less revolutionary than its English equivalent.

One of Chateaubriand's disciples, Victor Hugo (1802–

1885), walked in Milton's footsteps with a trilogy of long narrative poems, *La Légende des siècles,* which—in *La Fin de Satan,* published posthumously in 1886—portrayed the Devil as a compelling, wicked, but somehow sympathetic figure. Like Milton, Hugo found in Satan's actions the seeds of his own destruction.

The Devil was undoubtedly showing signs of ageing at the end of the nineteenth century. His physical existence was increasingly discredited and even in his role as a metaphor for evil many considered him overused. Newer, more abstract and philosophical and political explanations for the ills of the world were inexorably gaining ground at the dawn of the twentieth century. Yet, though retirement beckoned, the Devil could still count on his natural constituency. Poets, artists, and writers may have dismissed him in favor of other solutions to eternal dilemmas, but in the popular psyche in times of trial, his scapegoat status was undiminished.

PART THREE

TOO SOON FOR AN OBITUARY

The Devil is not to be regarded as a mere
mythological personification of evil in the world;
the existence of the Devil cannot be denied.
—Karl Rahner

TEN

Dead and Buried?

> To admire Satan . . . is to give one's vote not
> only for a world of misery but also a world of lies
> and propaganda, of wishful thinking, of
> incessant autobiography. Yet the choice is
> possible. Hardly a day passes without some slight
> movement towards it in each one of us.
>
> —C. S. Lewis

Talk of the Devil had become distinctly unfashionable in the mainstream Christian churches in the twentieth century. There is the odd mention here, a passing reference there, but the figure who once rivaled God as the name on every cleric's lips has now passed into a strange limbo.

It is not that the Devil has been dropped from the credo. He is there lurking in the background, with polite though brief references to him in all the A–Z's of belief. Church leaders don't like mentioning him for fear of sounding medieval, superstitious, out of touch, or—sin of sins—unworldly. His status is now roughly akin to that of the disreputable relative with a dark past whose family cannot quite disown him for fear of somehow compromising themselves, but about whom they remain tight-lipped to all but the most persistent inquirers.

The *Catechism of the Catholic Church*, published in 1993 and heralded as an accessible collection of all fundamental doctrines,[1] makes no more than cursory mentions to Satan—as the Miltonesque "seductive voice" who lured Adam and Eve (article

391), and as a dangerous force but ultimately insignificant when compared to God. The official monist line of an almighty, omnipotent creator is unswervingly maintained. Article 395 states that:

> Satan's power is not infinite. He is only a creature, powerful from the fact that he is pure spirit, but always a creature. He can impede but not stop the building of God's kingdom. Although Satan may act in the world out of hatred for God and His Kingdom in Christ Jesus, and although his action may cause grave injuries—directly of a spiritual nature and indirectly even of a physical nature—for every person and all society, God's providence allows his activity. It is a great mystery that providence, which directs human and cosmic history with gentle power, should permit diabolical activity, but "we know that all things work together for good for those who love God."

The Polish philosopher Professor Leslek Kolakowski, now a Fellow at All Souls College in Oxford and a neutral though merciless observer of the Church's discomfiture on the question of Satan's survival, summed up the dilemma in a celebrated piece entitled "A Shorthand Report of a Metaphysical Press Conference given by the Devil in Warsaw on December 20, 1963." "The Devil," Kolakowski wrote playing the part of Satan,

> is falling into oblivion. So be it. Sometimes I visit churches to hear the sermons. I listen attentively with perfect composure, trying not to smile. It is becoming more and more unusual for any preacher—even a poor village priest—to mention me: in the pulpit, in the confessional, anywhere. The man is ashamed to do it, simply ashamed. Why people might say, "Dear me, a fossil. He still believes in fairytales."[2]

It is tempting to see the great watershed in the Catholic Church's attitude as the reforming and modernizing Second Vatican Council (1962–1965). After all, it took a new stance on virtually everything else in Catholicism and candidly admitted past mistakes and exaggerations in an unprecedented manner. Most superstitions were, at an official level, jettisoned. The new, streamlined Devil is there in the sixteen principal documents of the Council, but there are just four mentions, all of them standard rehearsals of his role in the Garden of Eden in bringing sin into the world.[3]

The true timing of the decision to put the Devil in mothballs is harder to pin down. At the end of the nineteenth century, the Devil was functioning at the heart of Catholicism in many of his traditional guises. In Pope Leo XIII's 1884 encyclical *Humanum Genus*, the Devil is employed to demonize the Catholic Church's opponents. Though the butt of Leo's scapegoating were Freemasons, the Salvation Army, Baptists, and Buddhists—all save the last relatively recent rivals of Catholicism—the Pope's language was such that he could just as easily have been living three hundred years earlier and talking of witches. All his targets were "societies in the kingdom of Satan," Leo raged. The Masons in particular provoked his wrath. "In our days . . . those who follow the Evil One seem to conspire and strive all together under the guidance and with the help of that society of men spread all over and solidly established, which they call Free Masons."[4]

A familiar pattern can be seen here. There was a serious side to the accusations against the Freemasons. The Church saw, especially in continental masonry with its thirty-three stages of initiation, something self-avowedly sinister and at least superficially satanic. Many of the rituals had echoes of the occult and ancient magic. The Vatican also disliked the links it saw between these continental Masons and organized crime, especially the Mafia in Italy. However, the vast majority of Freemasons then and now had nothing to do with the thirty-three degrees and were harmless bourgeoisie indulging in schoolboyish rituals and dressing up, at the same time as making a few good business contacts.[5] The three degrees of initiation undertaken by these Masons are no more harmful or satanic than donning whites to play cricket.

Yet the papacy reflected the popular prejudice that even these "social" Masons constituted a secret society, a body with its own codes, something that the majority did not understand and hence targets of the collective fantasy that fueled the paranoia about witches. Any secret group with its own practices must be doing things that the rest of society forbids, indulging in the sort of acts that many secretly dream of but which they know are out-of-bounds—orgies, black magic, and nocturnal sacrifices. Leo added the extra ingredient by giving the Church's blessing. He condemned the Masons and linked their name to Satan. Their perverse status was assured and no amount of good works or openness—today they hold come-and-see days and tell anyone who asks their secrets—has subsequently managed to dispel that image. The Catholic Church and the Church of England continue to demonize Masons as opponents of Christianity.

Similar rhetoric, albeit phrased with a little more thought to his audience's expectations and a more tender conscience for the belief of others, can be seen in a talk Pope Paul VI gave in November 1972, a decade after the opening of the Second Vatican Council. "What are the greatest needs of the Church today?" he asked. "Do not let our answer surprise you as being oversimple or even superstitious and unreal: one of the greatest needs is defence from that evil which is called the Devil. . . . We find it [evil] in the kingdom of nature where so many manifestations seem to us to indicate a disorder."[6] Evil, he went on, "is not merely a lack of something, but an effective agent, a living spiritual being, perverted and perverting. A terrible reality, mysterious and frightening. . . . It is contrary to the teaching of the Bible and the Church to refuse to recognise the existence of such a reality, or to regard it as a principle in itself which does not draw its origins from God like every other creature; or to explain it as a pseudo-reality, a conceptual and fanciful personification of the unknown causes of our misfortune."

The Devil could not be ignored. He could not be put into storage with other embarrassing reminders of an earlier and more superstitious age. "This question of the Devil and the influence he can exert on individual persons as well as on communities, whole societies or events, is a very important chapter of Catholic doctrine which is given little attention today, though it should be studied again." Again sounding like a medieval pontiff, Paul asserted: "We can assume his sinister action where denial of God becomes radical, subtle and absurd, where hypocritical and blatant lies assert themselves against evident truth, where love is extinguished by cold, cruel selfishness, where the name of Christ is employed with wilful and rebellious hatred, where the spirit of the gospel is watered down and denied, where despair has the last word."[7]

It was an unusual speech for a Pope who on many matters took a mildly progressive line.[8] Unable simply to ignore the Devil, Paul felt that this skeleton in the cupboard of the modern Church needed talking about. Much of his address was quietly philosophical in nature. Evil, as much as its personification in Satan, was Paul's theme, as indeed it had been in a previous and more debated offering of June 29 of the same year to mark the ninth anniversary of his election. There too Paul had returned to the imagery of an earlier age: "Through some cracks in the temple of God, the smoke of Satan has entered."

John Paul II is renowned for speaking his mind uncompromisingly and unswervingly. A man with the popular touch, fond of resonant, powerful, occasionally doom-laden images, he is a doctrinal traditionalist. Yet he is rarely heard to utter Satan's name and has only made glancing references to him. In a 1988 Angelus talk, he spoke of how Christ "with his victory over the Evil One brought about the Kingdom."[9] Less obviously but more substantively, in the summer of 1986 at a general audience, John Paul reaffirmed the teaching of the last major Church document to dwell on the Devil, the Fourth Lateran Council of

1215. The Devil and other demons, he said, "were created good by God but have become evil by their own will." He took a textbook approach to original sin. "As a result of the sin of our first parents, this fallen angel has acquired dominion over man to a certain extent."[10]

The Exorcist

The Devil tends to bring out the paradoxical side in those who sit on the throne of Saint Peter. John Paul indicated in the same August address that the idea of demonic possession still has a place—albeit much circumscribed—in the canon. "The church does not lightly support the tendency to attribute many things to the direct action of the Devil; but in principle it cannot be denied that Satan can go to this extreme manifestation of his superiority in his will to harm and to lead to evil." The ministry of exorcism illustrates the Devil's continuing though understated place in the Catholic credo. The Church maintains a network of diocesan exorcists, but unlike previous ages does so discreetly. In many parts of the world—especially western Europe and North America—it is distinctly reluctant even to reveal the name of the (usually) single priest in each diocese detailed to deal with such matters. Only the bishop will know. Their names are not listed in the diocesan directory.

John Paul's remarks were little noticed at the time, but take on a greater significance when seen in conjunction with details published in France in 1993 of the Polish pontiff carrying out an exorcism, the first pope in modern times to do so. In *My Six Popes*, a memoir by the former Prefect of the Pontifical Household, Cardinal Jacques Martin, it is revealed that on March 27, 1982, John Paul II exorcised a young woman. No further details have been supplied by the Vatican. This was not John Paul's only brush with the thorny subject of exorcism. In May 1994, he fell while getting out of the bath in the papal apartments and had to postpone a trip to Sicily. The official diocesan exorcist of Catania on the island said that during an exorcism "a demon said that if I were to cast it out of the body it had possessed, it would see to it that the Pope would be unable to visit Catania as planned."[11] The official response was predictable. Archbishop Luigi Bommarito of Catania told reporters that the priest in question "seemed a little excitable." He added: "We have to be very careful about things of this kind."[12] That is the general tone of the contemporary Catholic Church. Exorcism happens, but the men at the top give the impression they wished it didn't. Then, we discover they're doing it themselves. Certainly exorcism is regarded as a last resort. Once hostile to psychiatry, Catholicism now prefers to refer those who claim to be possessed to medical experts. Yet, as with the Devil, it is not willing to abandon the rite of exorcism.

It is very difficult to persuade Catholic exorcists to talk about their work. Father Gabriele Amorth, the principal exorcist of the diocese of Rome, is an exception. A burly, pugnacious man whose bulldog face is deeply lined, he works from an anonymous Church administration building on the outskirts of Rome. His room is stark and low-key, just one crucifix on the wall and a second on the table. Father Amorth is not shy about his ministry, and can quote verbatim, as if for comfort, the rare addresses on the theme by Paul VI and John Paul II. He clearly regards them as a charter for his continuing work. "It was very necessary to reconfirm in our own times the existence of the Devil which has been put in doubt by a culture of humanism, rationalism and materialism. The Church has never had a doubt that the Devil exists. Our language may be more discreet today, but the idea remains the same."[13]

Father Amorth claims to have carried out 50,000 exorcisms, but adds that Rome is an unusual place. "There is more here. This is because it is the centre of the Church, the most attacked place. Jesus Christ was attacked by Satan and the centre of Jesus's Church suffers in the same way." However, of the 50,000 people who had come to see him, Father Amorth considers that only eighty-four were genuine cases of possession (a figure borne

out by other estimates such as the one in 500 quoted at a conference for the leaders of Christian healing centers). He says:

> It is very important to be helped by a psychiatrist because
> in some cases diagnosis can be very difficult. It is vital too
> to distinguish two causes: for most people it is an illness of
> the psyche which can be cured by psychiatry—though
> some of these doctors give people too much medicine,
> intoxicate them and make them cretins. And then there
> are the others, the small numbers of real possessions. In
> these most serious cases, often they were outwardly
> normal people, going about their lives in a normal way.
> They didn't know about their possession. But there would
> be crises every day, times when they couldn't function,
> when they would go out of control.

When he undertakes an exorcism, always with someone medically trained present, he says there are various telltale signs. The
person can become unnaturally strong or speak in foreign lan-
guages of which they have no knowledge, or reveal facts about
others present in the room which are secret. "One girl of fifteen," he recalls, "threw off six men who were holding her
down, her strength was so enormous." Others in his experience have been paralyzed. One person vomited nails during the
exorcism, another fragments of glass, a third pieces of radio
equipment.

The priest sees four main reasons for possession: first, that
"there are people who have been casting spells, doing bad things
through the Devil, like the witches who made a pact with Satan.
They deliver themselves to Satan"; second, that those possessed
have been dabbling with black magic, however innocently; third,
that they have fallen in with a satanic sect; and finally, that they
have somehow been singled out by God to suffer and be put to
the test like the desert fathers. There is a remarkably familiar ring
to these categories—the Catholic Church's thinking about possession and the Devil has changed very little since the thirteenth

century. The Devil is now rarely spoken of and exorcism ever less often resorted to. Under a cloak of secrecy, there can be little debate and progress.

However odd Father Amorth's experiences sound to twentieth-century ears, however unusual his personal demeanor and his language, he is a priest in good standing with his bishop. His actions are officially sanctioned. The Vatican too has its own exorcist in Monsignor Corrado Balducci, an articulate and persuasive middle-aged man whose office abounds with sinister reminders of years spent in missionary work. He believes that it is not so much the leadership of the Catholic Church that has gone quiet on the Devil, but theologians and teachers who have made him unspeakable. "In the 1960s a new theological lobby was born that said that the Devil did not exist. But God told us that the Devil exists. How can we deny this?"[14]

Monsignor Balducci distinguishes in his work between what he calls ordinary demonology—"run of the mill stuff," and extraordinary demonology—personal infestation and possession. Many of those who approach him claiming the latter are "psychiatric cases," Monsignor Balducci accepts. "But diabolic possession is different. The psychiatric cases are conscious of their problem. With possession, people don't realise because the Devil takes over the body not the soul. They believe they are fine, but their actions give them away."

Out of the Mainstream

Mainstream Anglicans have no time for Satan. David Jenkins was a controversial Bishop of Durham—the fourth most important see in the Church of England—between 1984 and 1994, but, by and large, he spoke for his communion's theological establishment. On a BBC radio debate in December 1993, he remarked: "If evil is the question, the Devil is not necessarily the answer. We ask the right questions but are satisfied with the wrong answers." The Devil, Bishop Jenkins continued, was one of the canon of Christian myths, powerful on the imagination, historically significant, more than just a fairy tale. Myths get at a truth that is beyond reason, he stressed, but they must seem to be real to serve any purpose, to be understandable, and the Devil no longer seems real.[15]

Those in touch with the numerically strong Evangelical wing of the Anglican communion, with its strong Protestant concentration on the Bible and its charismatic style of worship, would dispute Dr. Jenkins's premise for writing Satan's obituary. Some continue to indulge in old-fashioned demonization of anyone they disagree with. At the 1988 Lambeth Conference, the once-a-decade gathering of the worldwide Anglican communion, Bishop Willie Pwaisho of Malaita, in Melanesia, made a robust intervention in the debate on women priests. "If women for the episcopate and women for the priesthood has [sic] come as a result of women's liberation, then I think it is satanic."[16] Nearer to home, Bishop Graham Dow, one of the suffragan (assistant) bishops in London, has established quite a reputation for his willingness to talk of the contemporary role of devils and demons. Bishop Dow has published two tracts on the theme— *Those Tiresome Intruders* and *The Case for the Existence of Demons*—both anecdotal and highly personal, but speaking for a constituency with Anglicanism.[17] He writes: "When the Christian Church is learning again to welcome the Holy Spirit's power as a vibrant reality in daily experience, so also we are becoming more open to the possibility that evil spirits are also a part of the way things are. In short, we are regaining our confidence in spiritual power as a reality." A note of the sort of dualism that made the early Church fathers despair is here. If there is a good spirit, there must be an evil spirit too—equal and opposite forces. The Bishop also writes of his experience of picking up an evil spirit that made him choke while taking communion. He is unguarded in his description of exorcism as "normally a routine and unspectacular ministry to take its place alongside prayer for healing, confession, counselling, medical and psychiatric help, each form of knowledge making its contribution to the healing process."

The Anglican communion has approached exorcism with a good deal more openness than Catholicism. A report by the Bishop of Exeter for the Church of England in the 1970s, for instance, was compiled by a commission, including Catholic representatives and a consultant psychiatrist, and later published.[18] It acknowledged that there was a positive aspect to exorcism, or deliverance as it preferred to call it, as "an extension of the frontiers of Christ's kingdom and a demonstration of the power of the Resurrection to overcome evil and replace it with good." While seemingly defending the Devil against those who deem him an irrelevance—for instance by emphasizing that the New Testament is explicit in teaching of "a personal origin of evil"— the report concludes by debunking him, albeit gently and confusedly. Christ was a man of his time, it points out, and he used language and images that those around him would understand. If his flock believed that illnesses and infirmity were caused by possession by evil spirits, he did not disillusion them but showed a "spirit of accommodation." The suggestion is that had Christ lived in a more medically advanced age, he might not have spoken about demons at all.

The report stresses that Christ's real purpose was to identify evil in the world. Just because the Devil is no longer a widely accepted metaphor in our times, it says, the existence of evil cannot be overlooked. "Evil, a distortion of right orderliness, proceeds from created, intelligent wills, whether human or demonic. . . . Thus humans may accept demonic temptations, while black magicians sometimes attempt (perhaps with success) to obtain demonic aid." The language here becomes ambiguous, attempting to placate the evangelicals with their penchant for talk of the Devil, but also to alert a wider audience to the need to address evil. The report is less than clear when it turns to exorcism. It endorses the exorcism of places. "Demonic interference . . . is common on desecrated sites such as ruined sanctuaries, as well as in connection with seances." But with people, it is markedly less emphatic. "It cannot be overstressed that, as it is usually understood, this concept of demonic possession is

extremely dubious." Those who fear they are possessed are rec-
ommended to see a doctor, to redouble their efforts to live a
Christian life, and only as a last resort to seek out a priest. Even
then the traditional theatrical methods of exorcism are rejected
in favor of two hours "seated in a deep armchair" and the combined efforts of a priest and doctor.

Canon Dominic Walker is one of those charged with putting
the report into effect. From his vicarage on a main thoroughfare
in the Regency seaside town of Brighton, he coordinates the
work of the Christian Exorcism Study Group and tries to diffuse
some of the hysteria that the word "exorcism" can provoke.
"Psychiatrists sometimes diagnose people as having possession
syndrome. There are people who don't respond to drugs or
benefit from psychotherapy and who may show extreme symptoms such as speaking in a known foreign language of which
they have no knowledge. Whilst this might be explained in terms
of the Jungian understanding of the collective unconscious, the
person may also be instantly cured by the rite of exorcism. Sometimes prayers of exorcism can have a placebo effect upon people
in a state of mental anguish and on the rare occasions when psychiatrists are baffled, it restores those who are deemed to be psy-
chiatrically ill to normal health."[19] Canon Walker believes that
some clerics can create possession in the minds of those who
turn to them. "It does worry me when some conservative Evangelicals or conservative Catholics take on an exorcism case and
find exactly what they are looking for! It is certainly possible to
question someone who believes in demons and possession in
such a way that priest and sufferer are using the same kind of language. I have seen people do this [so] that the sufferer responds
in a way that he or she believes is expected of him or her by the
exorcist. The exorcist may even plant the idea of 'possession and
exorcism behaviour' into the mind of the sufferer and through
this projection and hysterical reaction, the desired symptoms are
presented."

Such a view has been endorsed by eminent scientists. In his
1957 textbook on brainwashing and religious conversion, *Battle*

for the Mind, Professor William Sargant examined the effect that traumas—such as taking part in a war—can have on the mind. Emotional crises, he suggested, can bring on a hysterical state, leaving the individual open to suggestion by determined and dogmatic "healers," and thereby convinced that they may be possessed. Possession, for Sargant, a man of strong religious beliefs, was a psychological, not a spiritual state. Yet like many of his Catholic counterparts, Canon Walker cautions against writing off the whole exorcism ministry. There has been a tiny percentage of his referrals whom he is convinced have been in the grip of something evil, if not possessed. One such was in Fiji where the woman said to be possessed slid round the room like a snake. "The force of evil I have encountered on those occasions is more than the sum of human sin, there is cosmic evil."

The Protestant churches vary enormously in their contemporary approach to the Devil. Methodism has never, from its very inception at the start of the eighteenth century, had much time for exorcism. Luther was unusual among the Protestant reformers in upholding this Catholic ritual. Methodism in Wesley's time had a strong sense of the Devil tempting humanity away from the path of righteousness; today though its catechisms make references to evil and sin, there are none at all to the Devil. He has been dropped from the credo.

One of the distinguishing features of Methodism was its break from authoritarian and hierarchical structures. In this century the tendency for individual Christians to fashion their own beliefs about the Devil in the vacuum created by lack of leadership is exacerbated in local Methodist churches. Ministers and congregations can make up their own minds without any great central restraint. Especially in rural areas—where the tendency is to see the Devil in nature's cycles and surprises—you stand a good chance of hearing the Devil referred to whatever the silence of the official catechism.

Methodism in North America and Europe is a broad alliance, ranging from left-leaning liberals working to a social agenda determined by Christ's example in the New Testament, to fundamentalists who insist that references to the Devil in the Bible be taken at face value. In America, the Good News Movement founded in 1967 by Charles Keysor, a minister from Illinois, has exerted substantial influence on the United Methodist Church through its newsletter *Good News*. This backs an agenda that is theologically conservative but that favors the sort of demonization of all things modern or different that medieval popes made their own.

In Britain the diversity of belief within contemporary Methodism can be seen in a 1976 working group report of the Faith and Order Committee, which, while stating that demonic possession was "improbable" and recommending recourse to a doctor, did not explicitly rule it out "in totally exceptional cases." The report had been prompted by the involvement of Methodists in an exorcism that went tragically wrong in the autumn of 1974. A charismatic Christian who had assisted at a previous exorcism had become convinced that the demons driven out on that occasion had infested him. He approached a group in Barnsley, in the north of England, which was jointly run by an Anglican vicar and a Methodist minister. At first they counseled him to see a doctor, but when he persisted they ended up spending the whole night with him in the church's vestry, trying to exorcise him. The next morning, though they believed that their task was not complete, the two ministers left to take services. The man went home to his wife, became convinced that she was the Devil, and bit out her tongue. She bled to death. The case made national headlines and the coroner called several expert witnesses on exorcism. No charges were pressed against those in the church group, and the man was treated by doctors for a mental condition.

The Church of Scotland, in 1976, concluded that "such a ceremonial as exorcism does more harm than good by its existence within the practice of the church. We believe that it effects nothing that cannot be accomplished by the expeditious use of medical skills and pastoral skills." While there are those within the Baptist Union who would subscribe to such views, there is also a sizable group who believe in an external and incarnate Devil. The Baptists, if anything, have an even looser central structure than the Methodists, making generalizations dangerous. In broad terms, those touched by the charismatic movement tend to favor the traditional image of the Devil and indulge in a ministry of exorcism.

The divisions are seen most clearly in the United States where the biggest Baptist group is the fifteen million-strong Southern Baptist Convention, the largest Protestant denomination in America. This is split between moderates and conservative Bible-literalists who see the Devil at every turn. In the 1960s and 1970s the moderates were in the ascendancy, suggesting that every word of the Bible did not have to be taken at face value. Progressively through the 1980s, the conservative wing grew in strength with its uncompromising fundamentalist line and talk of the Devil.

The Fundamentalist Fringe

One of the most famous products of a Southern Baptist upbringing is the global evangelist, Billy Graham. His message reaches an audience of hundreds of millions through satellite television, worldwide tours, and publications like *Weekly World News*. Its headlines and content emphasize the Devil's physical omnipresence. "Satan's Skull Found in New Mexico," one banner boasts. "Satan's Face in Hurricane Andrew," states another.

"When I hear people doubt the existence of the Devil, I shudder," the Reverend Graham told his followers in a typical article.[20] "The Devil is real and that he is wielding unholy power and influence, there can be no doubt. Switch on your radio and television if you feel you need concrete evidence. Scan your newspaper. How else do you explain the acts of hatred and violence that are all too common? Could hearts filled with God's love deliver such acts of destruction? Would sane, thinking men and women behave in this way if they were not in the grip of evil? . . . Some people consider the Devil as a joke—a laughable cartoon character because in the Middle Ages he was portrayed as a buffoon with pointed horns, a long evil tail, and a pitchfork. In reality Satan is a resourceful, highly intelligent powerful spirit."

This is the traditional line of mainstream Christianity, which has been abandoned in recent times, leaving the field to maverick figures. The size of the following that Graham attracts can, in part at least, be put down to the attraction such a message holds. The mainstream churches talk of evil in an abstract way and encourage a personal sense of sin, but Billy Graham and those of his ilk are ready with an easy answer to all the world's problems—the Devil. Blame it on someone or something outside, concentrate your efforts on fighting the Evil One and the world will be a better place.

Such an approach has been gaining ground in Britain with Bible fundamentalists from the house church movement gaining new members at the expense of the mainstream churches. At a conference of the evangelical Dawn 2000 group in Birmingham in February 1992, one of the speakers, Peter Wagner, warned his audience to check their bags when they returned from overseas travel. There was a real danger, he warned, of picking up a foreign demon and then bringing it back into this country, especially if you had visited a temple or pagan shrine.[21]

The idea of external forces of evil in the form of devils and demons continues to be attractive. It absolves those who take it on board from a direct sense of responsibility for anything that goes wrong. Mainstream churches make the link between individual actions like overconsumption in the West and violent pillage of the natural world. The fundamentalists offer an altogether more traditional message. It's the Devil. Jeanette Winterson, in her award-winning novel *Oranges Are Not the Only Fruit*, paints a memorable picture of a small evangelical Protestant church, the Glory Crusade and its obsession with Satan.[22]

Such a phenomenon can also be witnessed in many of the

religious sects that appeared overnight in the 1970s and 1980s. One of the most enduring, the Moonies, has even gone so far as to develop its own variation on the traditional theme of the Devil. Central to the credo of the Unification Church—to give it its chosen name—is the Divine Principle. This includes a new approach to the Old and New Testaments and makes an emotional and ultimately sexual link between the Archangel Lucifer and Eve. Their bonding is on a spiritual plain, so that when Eve enjoys conjugal rights with Adam, she passes on original sin, like a sexually transmitted disease. There is no mention of the apple. The fall in the Moonies' plan creates a satanic trio of the Devil, Adam, and Eve—all false prophets and battling against the true trinity. When Cain kills Abel, the personification of bad murders the personification of good. According to the Moonies' founder, "this meant that the satanic side had struck God's side, God's efforts to separate good and evil in Adam's family had been frustrated and the side of goodness lost."

This attachment to the Devil also flourishes on the fringes of mainstream Islam. The *Qur'an* may portray Shaytan as a joker, a minor irritant, but there are still Muslims who have faith in exorcism. On the troubled Gaza Strip, devout Muslims have recourse to the talents of the exorcist Sheikh Siyad El Tartar if they want to get rid of demons or *jinns.* The sheikh's principal tool is a container of saline solution. He cuts a hole in it, puts it to his lips, and spits verses of the *Qur'an* into it. Thus dissolved the holy verses are attached to the arm of the possessed person and pass into his or her body, forcing the *jinn* to flee—allegedly through the big toe, the only place, according to the sheikh, where a spirit can leave the body without injuring itself.[23] Women are alleged to be more at risk than men. They are regarded in Muslim culture as weaker physically and in their beliefs, and, rather like the incubi of medieval Christianity, Muslims hold that *jinns* fall in love with women and take up residence in their bodies. Once there they prevent their hosts from becoming pregnant by kicking their husbands' sperm out of their wombs.

The sheikh's methods are mild in comparison with some.

Occasionally, fundamentalist Muslims use sticks to beat demons out of a possessed person's body. The belief is that the "patient" feels no pain, only the demon, but in November 1994 a Muslim woman was jailed at the Old Bailey in London for killing a young girl after beating her with sticks to drive out a demon.

Much more common in Christianity—though frowned on by the Catholic authorities—are the activities of unlicensed exorcists, priests who set themselves up without official sanction. The most famous of these is Archbishop Emmanuel Milingo, the exiled Catholic Archbishop of Lusaka. He was recalled to Rome by the Vatican in 1983 to a desk job in the curia overseeing tourism after causing alarm among missionary priests in his African homeland by his habit of combining Catholic ritual with the exorcism of evil spirits in a fashion more usually associated with traditional African pagan religions. Milingo can be seen as following in the tradition of those like Saint Augustine of Canterbury in the early Church, attempting coexistence and accommodation with local beliefs as a way of allowing Christianity to take root, before embarking on a full frontal attack on the pagan cults. Where Augustine was lauded by Pope Gregory the Great, Milingo was hauled over the coals by John Paul II.

The intention behind the Vatican's action was that Milingo would disappear without a trace amid the Roman bureaucracy. Instead, his reputation has grown and grown. A cottage industry now surrounds him, with tapes and books and large-scale "healing events," not unlike those organized by Billy Graham.[24] Milingo is explicit in his talk of the Devil and in his criticism of those in power in the Catholic Church for downplaying the threat: "We are now in the last days of Satan's reign, and he is working overtime through his agents to complete the takeover of the world," he has written. "His agents . . . have penetrated to the very heart of Christ's Church . . . to lull Christians, especially priests, into believing that the Devil and his demons don't exist. Satan plays with priests like toys when they don't believe in him."

Most senior figures publicly treat Milingo as a loose cannon,

but privately confirm their acute embarrassment both at his out-
bursts and his continuing popularity. Each time Milingo is
ordered to move house by the Vatican, the crowds follow him,
trekking to more and more obscure suburbs of Rome. Most
recently, Archbishop Milingo took over the basement of the
Domus Mariae, the House of Mary, a large, impersonal Church-
owned office block on the Via Aurelia, two miles from the
Vatican. People queue to see him from four o'clock in the
morning. They go in in batches for blessing and healing. Most
have illnesses that the doctors have failed to cure; some don't
even bother with science. They put their faith in Archbishop
Milingo to cast out the devils that are causing a whole range of
ailments, including colds, flus, depressions, and cancers. Milingo
fulfills a need that has been overlooked by the Church authorities for too long and shows that there are Christians who still
place their trust in superstition and magic as well as in Jesus.
Magic and superstition exerted such a grip in medieval times
because they answered a basic human need. Science, enlightenment, and secularism have much diminished that need, but it
still lingers on, as the crowds at the Domus Mariae show.

The Church authorities are perhaps being a little hypocritical
in disowning Milingo's "magic" when at the same time they promote such causes as the cult of the Shroud of Turin, and the
special properties ascribed to some Marian shrines and their
waters. There is an annual ceremony performed by the Cardinal
Archbishop of Naples with great panache on the altar of his
baroque cathedral when the blood of the city's patron Saint
Gennaro is said to liquify. The dried blood, held in two
ampullae, becomes liquid for no reason that science can find.
When it fails to do so at the appointed time—as it did in 1980—
disaster is predicted for the city. The ceremony is part of a continuing intertwining of primitive superstitions and mainstream
beliefs in Naples, a city where successive natural disasters have
resulted in something of a cult of death. The earthquake in 1980
claimed 5,000 lives.

Unsurprisingly, age-old traditions continue in Naples at the end of the twentieth century parallel to more familiar Christian beliefs, with ecclesiastical suppliers selling talismans to ward off the Evil One alongside cassocks and albs. The Neopolitans remain vaguely pagan in their devotion to a multiplicity of deities that have been collected, often uneasily, under Christianity's umbrella. There is, for example, a cult of veneration of the bones of plague victims at the Cimitero della Fontanella, a cave where the superstitious come to consult the spirit world and in particular a skull known as *capitano*, reputedly able to predict lucky lottery numbers to the faithful.

A similar and residual attachment to Devil-like evil spirits is seen in many cultures all around the world. In Africa, Milingo's home continent, belief in God coexists with faith in traditional malignant deities. In 1994 some one hundred people, mainly elderly women, were burned alive in the remote Northern Transvaal region of South Africa. Most were accused of being witches and of causing lightning strikes on villages. Many were set on fire in their homes after a witch doctor had pointed an accusatory finger at them. The young did the burning and the old were their victims. Seth Ntai, the Minister for Safety and Security, makes clear that witch burnings have been a part of life in the Northern Transvaal for centuries, but he admits that the current upturn is linked with political upheaval in South Africa, with marked increases in 1990 when Nelson Mandela was freed and in 1994 at the time of the first elections. "In 1990 the youth were saying that because Mandela was free, we had to do away with all evil things and kill the witches. And last year, they were saying that the old government must be buried with its witches and [erroneously] that Mandela had said that witches must be killed."[25]

Perhaps the best-known example of traditional magic and Christianity intertwining is voodoo, in Haiti and in the Bayou of the United States. The early slaves brought to the Caribbean were not allowed their own gods and idols, so they appropriated Christian saints into syncretic cults. As a result in voodoo today, statues of Patrick, the great Irish missionary saint usually portrayed by Christianity holding a scepter and stamping on a snake, are seen as representations of Damballah-wedo, the great serpent spirit. Saint James, with his horse and sword, has become the warrior spirit Ogu.

This mishmash of beliefs, with sinister overtones, continues to thrive. New Orleans is dotted with voodoo shops selling black beads alongside statues of Our Lady. The Churches, after centuries of futile attempts to kill off such cults, have today adopted a more passive disdain. While still warning of the dangers involved, they in practice turn a blind eye. It is a policy that sits happily with the apparent indifference of the main denominations to Satan. Issues that once excited theologians and sent innocent men and women to the stake are brushed aside as no more than relics of a superstitious age. What talk there is of the Devil is carried on in carefully chosen terms that make what was once terrifying sound bland.

Christianity that begat the Devil has not, however, killed off its creation. He continues to thrive on the margins, in exorcism rituals, among the mavericks of the Vatican and Islam, and in the fundamentalist theology of the born-again movement. He retains a place in the popular soul of Christianity, the catchall character to blame for actions too terrible to ascribe to a loving God and too frightening to put down to dark urges in the human psyche.

ELEVEN

The Underbelly of Society

> Tis now the very witching time of night
> When Churchyards yawn and hell itself breathes out
> Contagion to this world.
> Now could I drink hot blood
>
> —William Shakespeare, *Hamlet*

In September 1991, Procter & Gamble, the multinational responsible for such household names as Ariel and Pampers, announced that it was changing its logo. The man-in-the-moon face and thirteen stars that had for many years been a distinctive feature on the packaging of its products was being redesigned. The company had bowed to pressure to rethink a trademark that some took to be a satanic symbol. When looked at from a certain angle, a group of dogged protesters suggested, it looked like 666, the mark of the Devil first mentioned in the Book of Revelation. Procter & Gamble's announcement came just four months after the British Driver and Vehicle Licensing Centre, which allocates license plates to cars, confirmed that the configuration 666 would not be used again.

For a society where the Devil is usually presented as a historical irrelevance, both decisions are hard to account for. Why did Procter & Gamble go to the expense of changing their trademark? To silence a fringe of evangelical Christians? To a degree, but they were also playing up to a much broader consumer group—those who, while formally dismissing Satan, continue in their irrational moments to steer clear of anything that hints at powers of darkness. Why take a risk, however remote, by buying Ariel when there are at least half a dozen alternatives on the supermarket shelf?

Superstition lives on in an epoch that theoretically considers the Devil redundant. For many, that superstition amounts to nothing more than simple gestures whose origins are buried back in the mists of history and folklore—not booking into room 13 in a hotel, not walking under a ladder, and so on. Yet the Devil, whatever the Churches' reticence on the subject, is endemic in a Western culture that continues to set store by superstition and traditional practices. Popular game shows on television about moral choices turn readily to the pantomime figure of Satan—in red, with a tail and horns—as a symbol for wrongdoing,[1] while advertising commercials, with their finger on the popular pulse, frequently employ the Devil. One insurance company promotes its wares by showing a small, horned monster with a pitchfork tripping up those foolish enough to decline fully comprehensive coverage. The makers of a wickedly good fountain pen promote it with a sultry model whose close-cropped hair rises into two peaks. And in an altogether more sophisticated play on traditional demonic iconography, Pirelli the tire manufacturer shows a treacherous road surface as the snake of the Garden of Eden.

Whatever his fate in the Churches, Satan's place in popular culture seems secure. In a post-Christian age he continues to function as a metaphor for evil. Indeed, though they would blanch at the suggestion, the Churches have been so successful in imprinting the face of the Devil on what Jungians might call our collective unconscious that he has latterly found a second career outside the world of religion.

Even the law is apt to pay the Devil a respect that the Churches only grant grudgingly, behind the closed doors, in the presence of exorcists. In Denver, Colorado, in October 1994, a U.S. federal judge ruled that an inmate serving ten years for kidnapping must be allowed to perform satanic rituals in his cell. Robert James Howard had argued that satanism was a legitimate religion and as such demanded the respect afforded by the First Amendment. Judge Edward Nottingham felt moved to agree. "We ought to give the Devil his due," he wrote in his judgment.[2]

The judge's comments are but one of many examples that the Devil's demise has been much exaggerated. In the most august debating chambers, reported sightings are relayed. In June 1993, the brother of the Princess of Wales, Earl Spencer, used his maiden speech in the House of Lords to tell of satanic goings-on in Harlestone Woods, close to his ancestral home at Althorp.[3] These and other stories that continue to crop up about Satan and his secret army are little changed from the charges leveled against witches, Cathars, Gnostics, and any number of medieval heretics. If there is a set picture of the Devil in our minds, then there is also a standard list of his activities. The fantasy of a subversive society within society that condemned thousands of witches and wizards lives on.

Labeling something satanic can be a way of expressing distrust or disgust. Pedophiles or pornographers, for instance, are often deemed demonic when there is no evidence they have any interest in Satan. It is a word that sums up contempt. Equally the tag "satanic" is readily applied to marginalized, misunderstood, but often harmless groups—the sort of misfits who in a previous age would have been caught up in the witch craze. Such nomenclature can become a self-fulfilling prophecy. Those alienated by society can turn their anger against those whom they perceive as having pushed them to one side by indulging in the most antisocial form of behavior they can think of—Devil worship. It is easy enough to pick up the rudimentaries.

In a 1990 textbook designed to help chief police officers throughout America deal with occult groups, author William Edward Lee Dubois identifies the most common group of satanists as those who take on the name as a way of dealing with their own problems. Typical "self-styled satanists," he writes, are unpopular, marginalized, male high school students whose "concepts of how to worship come from a variety of sources including books, videos, heavy-metal songs and general population assumptions about satanic worship."[4] Dabbling in satanism can be either a cry for help or a cry of rebellion. Youngsters in particular adopt these gestures with the specific purpose of being caught so that their grievances can be acknowledged. In the process, the age-old fantasy that the Devil is eating away at the core of society is perpetuated.

Modern-Day Dualists

The most persistent talk of the Devil has come in the context of self-styled cults and churches, or New Religious Movements as they are reverently termed. Sometimes they are avowedly Christian churches, often led by a self-styled prophet, that get so obsessed with the Devil that their rituals take on a bizarre and disturbing hue.

There is a strong temptation among such cults to develop a siege mentality, to see the whole world against them—as indeed it usually is—and to ascribe such opposition to the Devil rather than to any rational factor. An echo of the Gnostics' rejection of the world as evil can be heard. Professor Eileen Barker of the London School of Economics, a sociologist of religion and one of the foremost authorities on new religious movements, believes that "there are undoubtedly situations in which members [of such organizations] have become 'burnt out' or seriously affected in one way or another . . . [S]trongly held hell-fire-and-damnation beliefs in evil forces or satanic possession can result in states of uncontrollable terror or overwhelming feelings of guilt. In extreme cases, these can contribute to people losing control and possibly harming themselves and others."[5]

The deaths at Waco of members of the Branch Davidian Sect under David Koresh, or 900 followers of the People's Temple in Guyana who took cyanide at the behest of Jim Jones in 1978, immediately come to mind. Most recently, in October 1994, there were the deaths of forty-eight members of the Order of the Solar Temple in two Swiss villages. This cult had a particular obsession with the Devil and the associated figure of the Antichrist. One month before the final mass suicide, a British woman, Nicky Dutoit, was killed by the cult near its Montreal headquarters because they believed she had given birth to the Antichrist.

Such groups maintained, in theory at least, a primary belief in God. Others dispense with God and choose instead to worship the Devil. Here two distinct trends can be seen. First, there are disconnected groups of occultists who employ Satan as a cover for their own sexual sadomasochistic, clandestine, psychopathic, and illegal activities. These tend to be isolated and only come to light when an incident alerts the authorities. Second, there are the public groups that take satanism as a religion and attempt to articulate theologies.

Into the first category falls the case of Ilenia Politano, which made world headlines in 1994. Her parents, Laura, twenty-one, and Michele, a twenty-three-year-old plumber, came from Polistena in Calabria in the rural south of Italy where, like Naples, ancient rites and rituals have been annexed, but not wholly tamed, by Christianity. Though Polistena itself is a relatively developed town, Ilenia's parents came from country stock and lived in an apartment on the ragged outskirts of the town. They had long been convinced that the house was possessed and that demons had caused the death of Laura's father the previous year. They had decided—after consulting a local spiritualist—to have Ilenia as a way of ridding the house of its evil atmosphere. Soon after Ilenia's birth, they became convinced that far from delivering them and their home, their daughter was possessed. At first it was nothing more than her constant crying and a look in her eyes. They tried bathing her in water from the Marian shrine at Lourdes, but she howled. Superstition combined with distorted religious beliefs to convince the family that they had to attempt an exorcism. They summoned the baby's uncle Vincenzo Fortini, who had been on the fringes of a Devil worshiping sect in his hometown of Castelli Romani near Rome, a noted center of black magic. The men of the family stripped to their underwear and tried to exorcise Ilenia; the women looked on as the two-month-old died. Doctors who examined her body found that she had bled from her mouth and her bottom and been violently and repeatedly shaken. When police raided the house they found a crucifix, a plastic statue of the Madonna filled with holy water, sand, salt, magic symbols, and photocopies of exorcism rites taken from various occultist books.

Myra Crawford, a thirty-year-old black woman from Louisiana, was blinded in March 1994—allegedly by a demon—while driving on Interstate 20. She and her two sisters who were with her claim that she was attacked by an evil spirit who plucked out her eyes. Police are at a loss to know what happened, but have discovered that the three sisters had come into contact with black hoodoo, a rural variant of voodoo. David Otto, a professor of religion at Centenary College in Shreveport, believes that hoodoo is still widespread in rural parts of the South, often running in tandem with Christianity and turned to when people feel ill or unwell.[6] Myra Crawford had been suffering from headaches and had consulted a hoodoo doctor who told her she was possessed. "You're a rural black, you are surrounded by a culture of white people that hate you and keep you impoverished," Professor Otto said of the case. "In that setting, hope may be hard to find and so would any sense of power. Hoodoo becomes a supplement to Christian faith that one needs in order to find that power and authority—and that hope."

In rural Norway there have been a series of deaths connected with satanism that have involved both ancient pagan rites and modern music. Heavy metal music—characterized by loud electric guitars and relentless rhythms—has long borrowed the symbols of satanism to appeal to a sense of rebellion and rejection of conventional mores in its mainly adolescent fans. It has dabbled with the occult, and the lyrics of songs by heavy metal stars including Judas Priest and Motorhead display a fascination with death. Evangelical Christians have grown fond of detecting "satanic messages" in heavy metal, sometimes allegedly when records are played in reverse. In 1990, however, Judas Priest were cleared of provoking the suicide of two of the band's fans by using subliminal messages in their music. Expert opinion was produced to show that if people are predisposed to violence or extreme behavior, music may help them along the way, but it does not in itself cause the actions. The verdict confirmed what many have long held—namely, that the antics of heavy metal performers, clad in black, throwing crucifixes to the ground, are nothing more sinister than immature black humor. In Norway, however, an offshoot of heavy metal known as "black metal," with a message of violence against Christianity, has taken a more threatening turn.

Groups like Darkthrone recorded songs whose lyrics—when they could be deciphered over screams and white noise—mixed the explicitly satanic with references to Scandinavia's pagan past, "Sextons hiding in fear" and a "new god" who will bring "Something to burn," as in "A Blaze in the Northern Sky."[7]

While such sentiments were confined to the recording studios and concert halls, they were merely disturbing. When fans and artists started to act out these fantasies, the police became involved. First Dead, a singer with the black metal group Mayhem, killed himself. Then Count Grishnackh, lead singer of Burzum, stabbed to death Mayhem's star and founder, Euronymous. In May 1994 he was sentenced to twenty-one years in prison. Fans took their idols at their word and indulged in an orgy of church-burning. In 1992, six churches went up in flames—mainly in out-of-town areas and small communities. Count Grishnackh had been arrested and questioned about the arsons but released for lack of evidence. It was soon after that he murdered Euronymous. In 1994, fourteen churches were targeted and thirteen people prosecuted for arson. In court they claimed that Norway was a pagan country and that Christianity had to be driven out.[8]

Common to all these cases is the inversion of norms, the rejection of "normal" behavior by people on the edge. For the most part they acted as individuals and in no way can be seen as part of a satanic network. Yet throughout Western society, there are groups whose raison d'être is the worship of the Devil.

The Satanists

Most satanists believe themselves to be in a polemical relationship with Christianity. Whatever Christianity does, uses, and preaches, they do, use, and preach the opposite. Where Christianity speaks of light and of Jesus as a bringer of that light, the satanists see only darkness and tend to operate under cloak of night. Their rituals are a travesty of Christian ceremonies, with inverted crucifixes and the Judeo-Christian symbol of the pentagram turned on its head.

Some more articulate satanists dispute such a linear relationship with Christianity. They claim to be the heirs of the early pagans whose traditions were subsumed by Christianity. Their use of symbols may predate Church use, but in practice the argument is impossible to sustain, especially on the basis of what goes on at satanic rituals. The driving force behind many satanic cults may in part be a yearning for a pagan past, but it is overlaid and distorted by a paranoid hatred of the Church and all it stands for.

Far from being able to trace a line of descent back to pagan times, the current crop of satanist groups would be hard-pressed to go back much beyond the late 1960s. The use of mind-expanding drugs, an easy-come, easy-go attitude to sex, and the search for alternative lifestyles that characterized that swinging period provided fertile ground for satanic ideas. Rebellion against society's norms has a tendency to lead to talk of the Devil. In the late 1960s, this was overlaid by a renewed interest in Eastern mysticism and by an ethos that dismissed the tried and trusted and encouraged shopping around in exotic backwaters for personal satisfaction. Something similar can be detected in the 1980s trend to New Ageism, though its roots can be traced more obviously back to paganism.

There is very little sign of cooperation among the explicitly satanic groups in the United Kingdom. Most, like the Order of the Black Chalice, are obsessively secretive—especially when it comes to calculating the extent of their membership. An avowedly antisocial force, they eschew any wider organization or attempt to explain themselves, though a controversial occult bookshop in Leeds, the Sorcerers' Apprentice, acts as a center for the exchange of ideas and literature.

In the United States, public groupings are more common, though most are small and often short-lived. One of the most significant is the San Francisco-based Temple of Set, established in the 1980s and claiming a four-figure membership. It draws on the Egyptian deity of Set or Seth, the god most commonly associated with drought and famine. The Temple makes use of ancient motifs of Seth, the closest the Egyptians came to a personification of evil but a god who nevertheless occasionally showed a kindly face.[9]

The Temple was developed by dissident members of the Church of Satan, perhaps the best known of all satanist groups. The two factions split over the extent of commercialization in the Church of Satan and in particular over the flamboyant personality of Anton LaVey, its founder. A guru with a taste for publicity and an unerring instinct for making headlines, LaVey launched the Church of Satan on April 30, 1966, the spring equinox and a date sacred to pagans and witches around the world. He achieved minor celebrity status by interesting the Hollywood actress Jayne Mansfield in his "Church" with its relaxed attitudes to sex and drugs and its elaborate rituals. LaVey studied his subject carefully, poring over various tracts on witchcraft. The result is a predictable cocktail of upturned crosses, naked women, orgies, mock holy wafers—which are "consecrated" according to reports by being inserted into a woman's vagina by a phallus. A former animal trainer and carnival organist, LaVey published *The Satanists' Bible* in 1969, outlining three main rituals with permissive platitudes thrown in for good measure. The book sold worldwide and remains the inspiration of many satanist groups.

The publicity surrounding the horrific Sharon Tate murder in 1969 pushed LaVey into the limelight again. Tate, eight months pregnant and wife of the film director Roman Polanski, hairdresser Jay Sebring, Polanski's friends Wojiciech Frykowski and Abigail Anne Folger, and student Steven Parent were butchered by followers of Charles Manson. Calling themselves Satan's Slaves, Manson's group—or "family," as they liked to refer to themselves—stabbed Tate through the stomach, killing her and her unborn child. Police found the bodies arranged as if part of a satanic ritual and the word "pig" scrawled in blood on the walls. The "family" had close ties with a local neo-Nazi satanic organization, the Ordo Temple. Manson—who was not present at the murders but was later judged just as culpable as the followers he had inspired—was also linked by some with the Church of Satan. There was talk that the killings had been carried out under the influence of drugs according to details gleaned from LaVey's "bible."

In interview after interview, LaVey has made it clear that for him, when you strip away the window dressing and the desire to make money through shocking, the Devil is only a metaphor, a means of getting in touch with humanity's darkest inner desires. "Satan is a symbol, nothing more. He's a symbol of man's carnal nature—his lust, greed, vengeance, but most of all his ego. Satan signifies our love of the worldly and our rejection of the pallid, ineffectual image of Christ on the cross."[10] LaVey is certainly inspired by images of the Devil. In an interview he once ascribed some of his "insights" to a spell as a photographer with the San Francisco police: "I saw the vilest side of nature. People shot, women and children killed by hit-and-run drivers, drug overdosers in profusion. It was disgusting and depressing and I asked myself, 'How can there be a God with all this suffering?' And I actually came to detest and abhor the sanctimonious attitude of people who chirped up with the age-old saying about death and disaster being God's will."[11]

LaVey's status as America's best-known satanist has been challenged of late by Robert DeGrimston. Founder of the Process Church, he has turned an obsession with brutal murderers into a religion. With a theology that Christ and Satan have become fused into one destructive figure, the Process Church has devoted its energies and incantations to the "Son of Sam" killer, David Berkowitz, currently serving 365 years in prison for a series of six murders in the boroughs of the Bronx and Queens in New York.

Many believe, however, that such an exotic theology and belief are a smoke screen and that the Devil is nothing more than a cover for illegal activities. The writer Maury Terry suggests in *The Ultimate Evil* that the Process Church is at the heart of an extensive satanist network across America with centers in California, Texas, and New York.[12] He links the network to both the "Son of Sam" murders and the Tate killings. Both Manson and Berkowitz, he says, were associated at different times with Process. He further alleges that satanists work closely with drug dealers, pornographers, and organized crime. According to Professor Carl Raschke, who teaches religious studies at the University of Denver: "Satanism is to a drug cartel what New Age training is to a lot of corporations. It creates a magical worldview, filled with absolute terror and the most macabre forms of cruelty and violence, in order to ensure loyalty among the operatives of international drug trafficking."[13]

Professor Raschke was speaking in the aftermath of the Matamoros case in April 1989. Mexican drug squad police in the border town of Matamoros raided an outlying ranch that they believed was operated by a drug cartel. In and around a tin and tar paper shack on the property, they found the mutilated bodies of fifteen people. Some had been beheaded, others slashed and burned, others had their hearts and eyes torn out, their ears and testicles ripped off. Police believe their deaths had been part of satanic rituals and their organs had been used to concoct potions. Such barbarity against victims snatched at random off the street had served to keep the operatives of the cartel loyal and silent.

The Witches

The temptation to link witchcraft with satanism is strong, and encouraged by a whole genre of horror films and novels. Yet where satanism is for the most part a reaction to Christianity, witchcraft is, its practitioners insist, something entirely different. Many of the ideas central to the modern witchcraft movement predate Christianity. In its present incarnation, though, organized witchcraft is a relatively recent phenomenon, dating back to the 1930s and 1940s. Two distinct trends coexist—high magic, based around mystical tradition and a "tree of life," which purports to be a timeless source of all knowledge; and a simpler witchcraft of spells, potions, and magic. The first is more theatrical, more tolerant of Christianity, and takes on the trappings of a "Church"; the second is more inclined to hostility to organized religion. Precise definitions, however, are dangerous since individual magicians operate as they choose. What is important here is that neither variety is overly interested in the Devil.

Those who have studied modern witchcraft are convinced that it should not be regarded as wicked or evil, but rather as a religion. Susan Greenwood, an anthropologist at Goldsmith's College, part of the University of London, sees witchcraft as "a belief that puts people in touch with the seasons and the natural world with positive benefits. It can reconnect man with nature. It is holistic, confronting both the good and the bad forces within each one and aiming to restore balance. The concept of an outside Devil therefore has no place."[14] She confirms that some witches, returning to pagan ideas, have revived ancient figures like the horned god of the north, but have done so as an originating force in nature—usually a female one—who is worshiped for herself rather than in any demonic way.

Renewed interest in witchcraft began in the 1920s. In 1921 Margaret Murray, an anthropologist from University College, London, published her *Witch Cult in Western Europe*,[15] which endorsed the notion of a secret society of witches from pre-Christian times, and suggested that it was still functioning, though in a much weakened state. Dr. Murray's work has now been discredited—most damningly by Norman Cohn in *Europe's Inner Demons*,[16] which demonstrated that the idea of a witch conspiracy was a sixteenth-century fantasy fueled by the Inquisition. However, at the time of publication, her book prompted a revival of public interest in witchcraft. Among those to feed it was Dion Fortune—pseudonym of the occultist Violet Firth—who in 1927 founded the Fraternity of Inner Light and in 1935 published *The Mystical Qabalah*, both aimed at promoting interest in magic and magicians as part of an ancient pagan tradition.

Dr. Murray had categorically dismissed any link between witchcraft and satanism, but in the hands of Montague Summers—who published *History of Witchcraft and Demonology* in 1926—and Aleister Crowley, her research was distorted and the two subjects became once again intertwined in the public's mind. Crowley dwelled on the dark side of magic in *Book of Law*[17] and *Magick in Theory and Practice*,[18] both of which remain popular to this day with dabblers in the occult. Like the writings of Anton LaVey (who studied Crowley's texts), both books contain cocktails of ancient rituals with the author's own particular flourishes. In the case of the first book—written after Crowley claimed to have received a message from the Egyptian god Horus in the Cairo Museum while on his honeymoon—the tone is that of a prophet sharing the new dawn with his people. And in the second, Crowley's own fascination with sexual experimentation comes to the fore.

Both make repeated references to Satan and to blood sacrifices to dark forces. In the early 1920s a young devotee, Raoul Loveday, visited Crowley's "temple" on the northern coast of Sicily. He died after, according to his wife, Betty May, killing a cat and drinking its blood during a frenzied orgy of sex and drugs. The resulting outcry led, in 1923, to Crowley being expelled from Italy. He died penniless in 1947—a prayer was offered to Satan at his funeral, as he had instructed. His reputation, however, lives on while the Ordo Templi Orientis, a secretive magic group that he led in the 1930s, remains active both in the United States and Europe.

LaVey, Crowley, and others have given witchcraft a bad name. Both fit into the classic category of misfit and rebel, who find in satanism a way of breaking out of their background and of shocking and drawing attention to themselves. In recent years a great deal of effort has been expended by those who would prefer that witchcraft be seen as something as beneficial to society as Christianity or Buddhism or Judaism. A measure of their success in finally banishing the air of something sinister came in 1994 when Leeds University appointed its first pagan chaplain. Twenty-nine-year-old Susan Leybourne works alongside the eleven other (mainly Christian) chaplains and leads students in marking the winter and summer solstices as well as offering healing services. For the most part, news of her appointment was welcomed—a mark of a new toleration. But the Vicar-General of the local Catholic diocese of Leeds could not resist a few traditional words of wisdom to defend his corner. Ms. Leybourne's activities, he complained, "declare God redundant and offer instant salvation by magic."[19]

TWELVE

An Unconfirmed Sighting

> The topic of ritual abuse is a subject tearing the
> mental health profession apart in America.
>
> —Lawrence Wright

I n recent times the name of the Devil has been heard often and
insistently in connection with allegations of satanic-ritual
abuse on both sides of the Atlantic. In North America and subsequently throughout Europe, a series of high profile cases has
revived the age-old fear that in the midst of an otherwise
"normal" society are interlinked clusters of satanists who break
every rule in the book with impunity.

The allegations have been lurid and shocking—bestiality,
incest, young girls raped and then forced to see through the
resulting pregnancies so that their babies could be used in blood
rituals. These allegations have been made before. The Romans
believed the early Christians capable of similar depths of
depravity. The *Malleus* was sure that alleged witches were up
to much worse. The Jews were branded child-killers in medieval times.

LaVey and Crowley, influenced by the *Malleus*, hint darkly in
their texts at human sacrifice. *The Satanic Bible* has a section,
"On the Choice of Human Sacrifice," that begins by dismissing

the use of animals or infants since both are uncorrupted.[1] It then proceeds to advocate the satanist's "right" to destroy blighted lives—such as those of the emotionally damaged, maladjusted, or neurotic. LaVey, who had studied the techniques of the Third Reich, makes the point in the context not of physical sacrifice but of placing a curse on his victims. In *Magick in Theory and Practice*, Crowley writes of "Blood Sacrifice" and while mentioning animals, suggests that "a male child of perfect innocence and high intelligence is the most satisfactory and suitable victim."[2] Such provocative statements—which do not appear to have been put into practice by Crowley himself—have given the writings of these two unsavory characters a sinister frisson in recent times when the specter of Devil worshipers preying on young flesh has dominated headlines and challenged credulity.

Satanic rituals have a certain appeal to those pushed by their own psychological needs to the margins of society. Pedophiles must be counted among such individuals and a practical link is suggested by some of the court cases concerning abuse. A man was sentenced at Worcester Crown Court in 1990 for having unlawful sex with a fifteen-year-old girl and her younger sister. He had used rituals to frighten them into silence and to emphasize his power and had told the two girls that he was a high priest. The judge spoke of the "pretence of witchcraft or black magic." Another man, jailed in London in 1987 for sexually abusing fifteen boys and girls at different times, was alleged to have used an "altar" for his crimes within an inverted pentagram drawn on the floor with the blood of one of his victims. Both "rituals" could easily have been picked up from any of the occult manuals or novels. In both cases the Devil, or the suggestion of him, was used to justify the abusers' actions.

Cases of sexual abuse of children have become disturbingly common in the past two decades. A survey published at the launch of the Young Minds campaign in London in May 1994 estimated that between fifteen and thirty percent of all sixteen-year-old girls have experienced some kind of sexual abuse.[3] However, it has been the series of high profile allegations of satanic-ritual abuse that have caused greatest unease. While few care workers and child psychologists would today deny that abuse takes place, and that on rare occasions it can be accompanied by the trappings of a ritual, the question of whether there is an organized conspiracy of Devil worshipers who abuse children is one that excites as much debate as was once aroused by the existence of a medieval network of witches. A number of the cases have come to court, but very few have stood up to close scrutiny. The problem is that "evidence" is hard to define and harder still to provide. In satanic-ritual abuse allegations, it is usually one child, or group of children, helped (and some would say encouraged or led) by social workers, therapists, and police officers, who point a finger at otherwise respected citizens and accuse them of the most heinous crimes.

Some experts believe the stories that have surfaced are all part of a childhood fantasy. Bill Thompson, lecturer in criminology at Reading University, has been outspoken on the subject: "I am still waiting and so are the British public for the new information and evidence to show that satanic abuse exists anywhere outside these people's minds. . . . Give me your five-year-old and I will have him talking about witches after three or four hours. After three or four days the witch will have been you."[4] But child therapists like Valerie Sinason—editor of *Treating Survivors of Satanist Abuse*—start and end with the patient.[5] "Therapists are primarily concerned," Sinason wrote recently, "with a patient's emotional truth, regardless of whether it is corroborated by external reality."[6] The two sides in this argument have become polarized—either look for confirmation and approach these survivors' accounts with sympathy and an inquiring mind, or take what patients say at face value. If they believe it happened, then it happened. It is a debate that has split the social work profession.

The Survivors

Survivor stories first began to surface in the 1980s. At the very start of the decade came the publication in North America of *Michelle Remembers*, a harrowing account written by a young Canadian, Michelle Smith, and her psychiatrist, Lawrence Pazder—later her husband—of the atrocities committed against her in a satanic coven that included her mother. Smith claimed she had blotted out the memory of such terrible events until helped by Pazder to "recover" them. Smith's book was followed by a rash of others and accompanying television programs. Lauren Stratford's *Satan's Underground*, published in America in 1988, became a paperback bestseller. It was especially popular among Christian fundamentalists who found in her story of satanic-ritual abuse confirmation that the Devil was real and alive. Stratford wrote of being raped at the age of six by a laborer as her adoptive mother looked on; being involved in pornography with animals when she was eight; and running away and joining a satanic cult at twenty. There she drank human blood and witnessed rituals where youngsters were abused. She claimed that three of her own children were killed in such rituals.

Stratford appeared coast-to-coast on national television and found fame among the media evangelists who took up her story to plug their own view that the world had fallen into wicked ways and needed to be reborn in Christ. Sex and Satan were inextricably linked in that decline and fall. However, Stratford's sister, an eminently sane Christian missionary, challenged her account of their childhood. Then Lauren was taken to task by the respected Christian magazine *Cornerstone* as a deluded, sad young woman with a history of making accusations of sexual abuse and self-mutilation. The original publisher withdrew the book, though it continued to circulate under a new imprint.

Stories of past episodes of satanic activity were soon matched by contemporary cases. Perhaps the most notorious—and one of the longest and most expensive in American legal history—

concerned the Virginia McMartin preschool at Manhattan Beach in California. Peggy McMartin Buckley, her son Raymond, and five other child-care workers from the preschool were accused of molesting hundreds of children who had been entrusted to them over a ten-year period. The children spoke of satanic rituals— animal sacrifices and sexual abuse inside churches. They were counseled by Michelle Smith. Although there was no other evidence than the children's testimonies, their parents demanded that these recollections be believed without question. The courts resisted, resulting in most of the charges being dropped, and others ending in acquittal and verdicts of mistrial.

The collapse of the case did not halt talk of the Devil and a network of his followers preying on children. If anything it promoted it. The suggestion that there was no smoke without fire was often quoted as mental health-care professionals and Christian evangelicals, by tradition mutually hostile, sought together the Devil in the nation's soul. While there were other cases involving children, their attention became focused on adults who had been prompted by events like the McMartin trial to "remember" terrible episodes in their past. The question of "recovered memory" became central to establishing whether the Devil lived on.

In 1988 an influential academic paper, "A New Clinical Syndrome: Patients Reporting Ritual Abuse in Childhood by Satanic Cults," was published by Walter C. Young and Bennett G. Braun, both psychiatrists, and Roberta G. Sachs, a psychologist. The three authors had interviewed thirty-seven "survivors" of satanic-ritual abuse. Their stories overlapped in many details— drugs, abuse, torture and mutilation of animals and people, victims being buried alive in coffins, the sacrifice of adults and babies, ceremonial marriages to Satan, girls impregnated during rituals and then forced to sacrifice their baby to the Devil. This is also all found in *Michelle Remembers*. "The lack of independent verification of the reports of cult abuse presented in this paper prevents a definitive statement that the ritual cult abuse is true," the three authors concluded. They went on: "Despite the fact that some patients have discussed ritual abuse with other patients, and the fact that patients have had contact with referring therapists who may have provided information to them, it is our opinion that the ritual abuse was real."

The paper gave intellectual and scientific authority to survivors' claims. It also immediately became a matter of dispute. Dr. George K. Ganaway, program director of Ridgeview Center for Dissociative Disorders in Smyrna, Georgia, told the 1991 American Psychological Association that hypnosis—often used with "survivors"—made people suggestible and fantasy prone. "Experimental hypnosis evidence indicates that memories retrieved in a hypnotic trance state are likely to contain a combination of both fact and fantasy in a mixture that cannot be accurately determined without external corroboration." Dr. Ganaway's earlier paper, "Historical versus Narrative Truth" had put forward a theory of "screen memory"—that imagined satanic rituals might be a way of taking the pain out of actual abuse by putting it in a dramatic fantasy setting. In other words he believed that abuse may have happened, but that it was not satanic.

The notion of screen memory is not, however, linked to burying memories of actual events and therefore must be distinguished from recovered or false (depending on your point of view) memory where, after a period of amnesia, forgotten instances are brought to the surface, usually with the help of hypnosis. False Memory Syndrome has entered the vocabulary. In the United States there is a 12,000-member False Memory Society made up in the main of those parents who have been touched by what they consider unjust accusations. In Britain some 400 people have joined a parallel organization.

Recovered Memories

In *Treating Survivors of Satanist Abuse*, Valerie Sinason likens the skepticism that has greeted survivors' stories to the cool reception given to the first attempts to reveal the nature and extent of physical child abuse in the 1970s and sexual abuse in the 1980s.[7] Both are now generally accepted and Sinason believes that survivors' stories soon will be too.

Her hopes received a fillip in January 1995, when a report for the British Psychological Society showed that nine out of ten senior psychologists who took part in a survey believed that "recovered memories" of traumatic experiences are sometimes or usually "essentially accurate." However, the report was inconclusive because two-thirds also believed that false memories were possible and none was asked to provide evidence. One working party member suggested that false memories could result from a child growing up in an atmosphere of "overt sexuality" that fell short of sexual abuse but that would lead to confusion and uncertainty.[8] In the United States, this polarized debate has moved on from the high profile cases of the late 1980s and early 1990s to a broader debate about recovered or false memories. The pros and cons were extremely closely examined in Olympia, Washington, in a case subsequently reported at length in the *New Yorker* by Lawrence Wright in May 1993.[9] His conclusions have had a profound and largely negative impact on the credibility of survivors' stories.

At the center of the case is Paul Ingram—at the time of writing the only man in jail in Britain or America for satanic-ritual abuse. Ingram pleaded guilty, though he has subsequently withdrawn his confessions and is attempting to bring a retrial. A respected member of the local sheriff's department, a past chairman of the local Republican Party, this father of five was a pillar of the community in Olympia. Though he and his wife had originally been members of the Roman Catholic Church, they had latterly joined the Church of Living Water, a Protestant fundamentalist denomination. To everyone who knew them, the Ingrams were good, God-fearing people. In November 1988 the image was shattered forever. Paul Ingram was accused by his daughters, Ericka and Julie, then twenty-two and eighteen years old, of abusing them. When questioned by his colleagues in the sheriff's department, he was at first bewildered, and later said that he did not remember anything but if his daughters said it was true then it must be. Pressed by detectives, he confessed to having sex with both his daughters, but couched his admission in conditional tenses as if he were describing the actions of another person.

Hovering in the background was the pastor of the Church of Living Water, advising Ingram that if he owned up to the crime in his heart, his memories would come flooding back. Four days after his arrest Ingram was exorcised in traditional fashion by Pastor John Bratun, who called out the spirits of sexual immorality and gluttony. Ingram tried to be sick into a waste-basket in the middle of the room. He wanted to regurgitate the devils who had possessed him but he couldn't.

Though Ericka's recovered memories grew ever more detailed and shocking, it was Julie, her younger sister, who first implicated a group of her father's friends in an organized ring of abuse. She said that the men who gathered at the Ingrams' home to play poker had forced themselves on her and her sister, while their father looked on.

Ingram, meanwhile, had started remembering rituals whose details conformed with the standard imagery associated with the Devil. He had sacrificed a large black cat in a fire. Julie and Ericka confirmed this, and went on to accuse their mother of participating in satanic rituals. She was less ready than her husband to believe in events she could not recall and fled Olympia with her youngest son. Ingram continued to trawl his memory and dredged up more scenes of ritual sex in the barn. Ericka responded in kind with talk of horns, blood, robes, the stabbing of a baby, chanting. Both sisters talked of their own abortions. They had become pregnant during the abuse and when it was discovered were taken by their father for a termination. When, however, a doctor was called in, there was no sign on Julie or Ericka of the operation. Though it can leave no marks, Ericka had spoken specifically of scars. The girls also recalled intercourse with animals, orgies in the woods, babies sacrificed. It could have come straight out of the pages of Lauren Stratford's autobiography, and it was established that shortly before making her accusations, Ericka had joined various other members of the family in watching a television show about satanic-ritual abuse. As the investigation wore on, she became more and more assertive, her revelations more and more lurid. She claimed her baby had been aborted with a coat hanger and cut up and rubbed all over her body.

The case began to puzzle detectives. Details, dates, incidents that could be verified failed to stand up to test. Dr. Richard Ofshe, a social psychologist from the University of California at Berkeley, was called in to give an expert opinion. In a controlled test, he prompted Paul Ingram to relate incidents that could not have happened. Ofshe left unconvinced by any of the Ingrams. Ericka, he concluded, was a liar and Julie easily led. The prosecution case was shaky, but Paul Ingram saved them the trouble of testing it by pleading guilty to six counts of third-degree rape in May 1989. By July he had recanted, but it was too late. He was sentenced to twenty years in prison. None of the others implicated by the Ingram girls was tried, though they still live under a cloud of suspicion. The Ingram family is now split up.

The question of the veracity of Ericka and Julie Ingram's recollections lies at the core of the argument about recovered memory syndrome. A large question mark hangs over the whole issue. Other explanations—from teenage hysteria and the damaging influence of Protestant fundamentalist Churches, to watching too many films and television programs about the Devil, abuse, and possession—have been offered.

The Ingram case was not an isolated example. Why there was such a rush of cases in the late 1980s and early 1990s remains a mystery. It may be a simple case of one domino knocking down the next. The episode shares many common features with the sort of wave of hysteria that prompted the witch craze of the late medieval period. But there are differences too. In the witch craze it was the strong—the Church—punishing the weak—usually marginalized or inadequate individuals. In many of the satanic-ritual abuse cases, the roles are reversed. It is the weak—children—accusing the strong—their parents. Male inquisitors tended to accuse women of witchcraft. In this twentieth-century witch-hunt, the survivors are more often women who are charging men with wrongdoing.

Transatlantic

Where America led, Britain followed. Materials from the United States began circulating among social work professionals in the United Kingdom, detailing concerns about the growing number of ritual abuse allegations. They made a profound impact on trainee social workers in the social science departments of several northern universities. At Reading University in 1989, the American therapist Pamela Klein held a seminar to "alert" child-care workers to be on the lookout for a satanist network.

Inevitably, those put on their guard soon found what they were looking for. In February 1991, on the island of South Ronaldsay, the most southerly outcrop of the Orkney chain off the north coast of Scotland, nine children, aged between eight and fifteen, were seized by police and social workers in a dawn raid and flown to a place of safety on the mainland. Their parents, and the local Church of Scotland minister, the Reverend Morris MacKenzie, were accused of "lewd and libidinous" abuse of the children. Social workers believed that the minister headed a satanic-abuse cult that met at a disused quarry under cover of night. When his house was searched they carried off the long, black, hooded cloak he wore as protection against the biting winds as he went about his parish visits. They also seized a Celtic crucifix with a broken arm, suggesting it was some kind of satanist blasphemy. Its ancient, gargoylelike image of Christ on the cross confirmed the raiders' worst fears.

The children were held for five weeks before the judicial process intervened and ordered that they be returned to their families. A subsequent inquiry under Lord Clyde—held at a cost to the British taxpayer of £6 million—placed the blame for this debacle on the overzealous social workers who put words into the children's mouths. Evidence showed that during interviews the children had been led, in an often brutal and unsubtle manner, into saying what the social workers wanted to hear. There was no suggestion that the two young women who handled the case, nor their male boss, were in any way malicious—they were simply misguided. Confronted with one large family of disturbed youngsters in South Ronaldsay, they became convinced, despite all advice from wiser heads to the contrary, that they were dealing with a manifestation of the Devil's work.

The Orkney case was not the only one to cause a storm in Britain. It came after seventeen children had been seized by social workers from a run-down area of Rochdale in 1990 to protect them from satanic-ritual abuse. A judge later dismissed the charges and ordered that the children be sent home. In Nottingham and Manchester allegations of Devil worshiping abuse did not stand up to scrutiny, though there was undoubtedly a strong current of deprivation, dysfunctional behavior, and even neglect among some of the families involved. It was as if conventional social work manuals had been thrown out of the window and replaced by a bible that said every case of abuse and deprivation must have a satanic element.

Jean La Fontaine, Professor Emeritus of Social Anthropology at the London School of Economics, was commissioned by the British government to investigate whether satanic-ritual abuse was real or fantasy. Her report, *The Extent and Nature of Organised and Ritual Abuse*, was published in 1994. Restricted to England and Wales and hence excluding the Orkney allegations, Professor La Fontaine looked into 211 cases reported between 1988 and 1991, of which eighty-four involved allegations of ritual abuse. She decided that satanic-ritual abuse implied "a ritual directed to the worship of the Devil. Satanist carries the same implication. Allegations may not indicate the intention of the ritual or indicate that it is focussed on the Devil, so it seemed more accurate to use the broader 'ritual abuse' for all the cases in the study."[10] Professor La Fontaine found material evidence of ritualized abuse in only three of the cases she studied. "In each case the activities were created and led by one man who abused the children. He had also abused children without rituals. None of the three men concerned learned the rituals from belonging to an occult group." They may have picked them up, police believe, from books found at their homes. The rituals were used, the professor concluded, "to justify it [the abuse] and to intimidate and silence the victims." This was not a question of Devil worshipers, but rather of cunning and perverted men employing strategies to get away with their crimes. Where, then, did the children who had made the allegations of satanic abuse get the idea from? Professor La Fontaine's report criticized those who questioned the children for posing leading questions, putting pressure on them, and finally putting words into their mouths. In some cases, a child's silence was interpreted as "an indication that there are evil forces at work," while the professor points out that among many of the older children involved, there was a long and recorded history of abuse. "They are damaged individuals, with a known history of various forms of abuse, neglect or family problems." The social workers decided that the degree of disturbance was so great that it must have been the result of something similarly grave. No such co-relation can be made, Professor La Fontaine contends, and their conclusion—that it was the result of satanic-ritual abuse—was therefore flawed. In examining who was responsible for misdirecting social workers, the professor identified in her report two groups—evangelical Christians and "unreliable" specialists whose claims and qualifications "are rarely checked."

In her final report Professor La Fontaine alluded to a continuing undercurrent of belief that the Devil is a real and tangible force as a factor explaining why the idea of satanic-ritual abuse became credible. "A belief in evil cults is convincing because it draws on powerful cultural axioms. People are reluctant to accept that parents, even those called social failures, will harm their own children, and even initiate others to do so, but involvement with the Devil explains it." It was a classic case of demonization. "Demonising the original poor and linking them to unknown satanists turns intractable cases of abuse into manifestations of evil." It doesn't remove the perceived threat by demonizing a group, as history demonstrates, but it provides an easy explanation. It might have been useful to ask why children were disturbed, whether parents' unemployment, bad housing, mental illness, or any one of a whole list of other causes might be playing a part. Instead, talk of the Devil provided the answer.

In America too the series of satanic-ritual abuse cases and the controversy over recovered memory has been placed in a broader social context. The 1980s saw the reassertion of traditional values. In his analysis of the speeches of Ronald Reagan, Paul Erikson shows that the President was fond of delivering what amounted to sermons. America had a divine mission, authenticated by the Bible, the Soviet Union was the Antichrist and an "evil empire."[11] In such an atmosphere, talk of satanic-ritual abuse fit neatly with the prevailing world view. In its own perverse way, exaggerating and encouraging stories of satanic-ritual abuse served to reassert the coherence and authority of fundamentalist perspectives in society. The Devil was real and evil. The loss of traditional values had led, the argument goes, to sexual excess and letting in the Prince of Darkness.

One feature of this fundamentalist crusade is especially relevant to the sort of allegations heard from Julie and Ericka Ingram. The mass of antiabortion literature, handed out to impressionable schoolchildren, spared no detail of fetuses torn from the womb in a torrent of blood and gore. When asking where the details that accompanied accusations of satanic-ritual abuse came from, such promotional material cannot be ignored.

Though the antiabortion crusade continues and fundamentalism remains strong, the political climate in America has changed since the 1980s. There is a different president with little sympathy for the Christian right and its cherished ideas. Some centers—notably the Huntingdon Beach Therapy Center in California—continue to promote the idea of recovered memory and present those who have uncovered satanic-ritual abuse as evidence, but the tide of opinion is moving against them. Without publicity, the number of new cases coming forward has dropped significantly.

The same is true in Britain where Professor La Fontaine's report was widely accepted as authoritative and as closing a disturbing chapter in the history of social work. Again there are those—at London's Tavistock Clinic, for example—who continue to press the case for recovered memory, but their voice grows progressively weaker. This twentieth-century witch-hunt lasted only a decade. The hysteria it generated and the lurid imagery that accompanied it demonstrated yet again that Satan still has a place in popular culture. In seeking out the inner demons afflicting a troubled society, people are all too ready to find an external Devil.

THIRTEEN

A Trickster in Modern Clothing

> We know that the tail must wag the dog,
> for the horse is drawn by the cart;
> But the Devil whoops, as he whoops of old:
> "It's clever, but is it Art?"
>
> —Rudyard Kipling,
> *The Conundrum of the Workshops*

A world without extremes of good and bad would be, Milton suggested, bland and meaningless. He reserved scornful words for what he described as "cloistered virtue," the goodness of Adam and Eve in the Garden of Eden before they were put to the test. Those same extremes that fascinated the Puritan poet have continued to exert a great pull on writers and artists in the twentieth century, despite the darkness that has descended on the Devil in the mainstream Churches. For many celebrated novelists, Satan remains an engrossing and elastic metaphor through which to explore that gulf between virtuous and wicked actions and individuals. And in cinema, that decidedly twentieth-century medium, the Devil has found a new champion. It has been a mutually beneficial relationship. The Devil serves directors, script writers, and novelists well in their attempts to put a face to evil. Through their books, plays, and films, they have in their turn given new life to Satan, the iconography, and the legends that surround him in the popular psyche.

The novelist Alice Thomas Ellis, a devout and very traditional

Roman Catholic, is among those who have identified this twentieth-century trend: "The rise of moral relativism has made the task of the novelist extremely difficult since if fiction is to be interesting it must concern itself with good and evil. The denial of the existence of the Devil implies the nonexistence of angels and, if you go far enough, of God himself. This position makes fiction, as well as everything else, pointless. The grey avowal that 'we are all guilty' and pretty well much of muchness does not make for a ripping yarn."[1]

Though Satan in all his many guises and manifestations has been explored, modern writers and artists have in the process placed a new and particular emphasis on identifying what the Devil looks like. Traditional and contemporary images have been tried and rejected in the search to produce a single, commonly agreed face for Satan in the twentieth century. Yet as the millennium approaches no consensus has been arrived at. While Milton and Dante have arguably provided the definitive literary portraits of the Devil and heaven respectively, no one artist or filmmaker can claim to have produced a definitive image of the Prince of Darkness. The challenge remains.

To suggest that Satan is in any way or form a reality remains shunned. Indeed in the early part of the century, the Devil went through one of his lowest periods of popularity with writers and artists. The modernists, who came to the fore in the post–First World War era, found little of merit in the traditional figure of Satan. In their determination to avoid reproducing the images of the past, they decided that Lucifer the literary metaphor had passed his sell-by date. It was an ambiguous rejection. Some of the outstanding twentieth-century novelists—including several who were at some time deemed modernists—were drawn to the subject of human evil and explored it in traditional terms. Christian writers, in particular T. S. Eliot and Graham Greene, both self-confessedly doubtful in their faith, returned to the topic of good and evil time and again. The poles they contemplated were no less extreme than those that had intrigued Milton. Indeed in his apparent relish for humanity's postlapsarian misery, for all its

fleeting moments of great nobility, Greene seemed to be con-
juring up a vision of hell on earth with occasional but poignant
glimpses of heaven.

The Polish-born but English-based atheist Joseph Conrad
(1857–1924), by contrast, created Mr. Kurtz in *Heart of Darkness*, a novel unflinching in its portrayal of an evil world. Kurtz is
a company agent orchestrating the slave trade in the Belgian
Congo. He has set himself up as a god, creating his own
kingdom where he could, as the narrator Marlow puts it, give
vent to "the colossal scale of his vile desires." This was a living
hell with the Devil presiding. Conrad located the source of
Kurtz's evil within him and more broadly within the whole colonial system. At the start of the novel Marlow is driven to distraction by two women who sit knitting—one with white wool and
the other with black. Good against evil is a recurring image with
evil by far the more powerful. Alongside this theme of an evil
world, there is an unmistakably supernatural tone to the novel. A
heady cocktail of witch-doctoring, African devilry, and unbridled
sensuality in the person of Kurtz's African mistress give *Heart of
Darkness* a sense of external menace, of something greater than
the human capacity to do evil.[2]

Others have also dressed up the Devil in modern clothes,
leaving just a few of his traditional physical attributes as clues.
The Master and Margarita, by Mikhail Bulgakov (1891–1940),
was begun in 1928 but not published until 1966 due to official
disapproval. The authorities read into Bulgakov's account of the
exploits of the sinister and distinctly satanic Woland and
Azazello a poor reflection on Soviet society. In their exchanges,
the two debate the need for evil to prompt good, its place as part
of the very fabric of human existence. Woland—dressed in a
black soutane, "his mouth twisted into a grin"—asks: "Where
would your good be if there were no evil and what would the
world look like without shadow? Shadows are thrown by people
and things. There's the shadow of my sword, for instance. But
shadows are also cast by trees and living things. Do you want to

strip the whole globe by removing every tree and every creature to satisfy your fantasy of a bare world?"[3]

Bulgakov used a Devil-like character to fuel a wider debate on evil. There is no question of accepting the Christian Devil as a reality. In the works of C. S. Lewis (1898–1963), an atheist who described his own conversion to Christianity in 1929 as "reluctant," the Church's teaching on Satan is taken more literally at the same time as being given a popular face-lift. Lewis's genius was to appeal at the same time to a Christian audience and a wider readership more interested in eternal questions of evil. The apparently superior charms of the Devil and their would-be seductive power are extolled but put firmly in second place to his ultimate failure, to the irresistibility of God and goodness, in the writings of this Oxbridge scholar. Lewis's *The Screwtape Letters* (1942) takes the form of one side of a correspondence between a senior figure in hell and his nephew Wormwood, a young demon with a soul to capture. Lewis paints a comic landscape of hell—not unlike an Oxbridge college, some later commented—peopled by demons who rejoice in names like Glubose, Scabtree, Triptweeze, Slubgob, Toadpipe, and Slumtrimpet.

Behind the jokes and the well-mannered demonic characters, Lewis takes the threat posed by evil seriously. "There are two equal and opposite errors into which our race can fall about the devils," he wrote in his introduction to *The Screwtape Letters*. "One to disbelieve in their existence. The other is to believe and to feel an excessive and unhealthy interest in them." The book tries to reconcile the two. Lewis identifies sexual pleasure as one source of conflict between good and evil, but later and memorably he was to tackle the question of personal suffering, most often a stumbling block to belief in a good and loving God, in *Mere Christianity* (1952) and *A Grief Observed* (1961).

Though Lewis gave the Devil a certain charm, he still left him with no face. Another writer to take the threat posed by Satan very seriously was the Russian novelist Fyodor Dostoyevsky (1821–1881). He presents the Devil as a high-born gentleman fallen on hard times when he appears to Ivan Karamazov in *The Brothers Karamazov*:

> This was a person, or more accurately speaking a Russian gentleman, of a particular kind, no longer young . . . with rather long, still thick, dark hair, slightly streaked with grey and a small pointed beard. He was wearing a brownish reefer jacket, rather shabby, evidently made by a good tailor though, and of a fashion at least three years old that had been discarded by smart and well-to-do people for the last two years. . . . In brief there was every appearance of gentility on straitened means. . . . He had no watch, but he had a tortoise-shell lorgnette on a black ribbon. On the middle finger of his right hand was a massive gold ring with a cheap opal stone in it.

There are common elements here but there is also the traditional suggestion that Satan is a master of disguise, able to sneak in unnoticed in his faded clothes, apparently a spent force, unable to harm anyone, but suddenly ready to pounce. Dostoyevsky seems to believe that the Devil is more than a metaphor, that he is at large in the world. In delving into the human capacity for evil at its most disturbing, Dostoyevsky's bleak and pessimistic vision does not explicitly rule out an incarnate Devil.

Thomas Mann (1871–1950) took up the themes of the trickster in modern guise in his 1947 reworking of the theme of *Doctor Faustus*. Adrian Leverkuhn, a musician who sells his soul to Mephistopheles in return for twenty-five years of creativity, is confronted by "a man, rather spindling . . . a sports cap over one ear, on the other side reddish hair standing up from the temple; reddish lashes and pink eyes, a cheesy face, a drooping nose with wry tip. Over diagonal-striped tricot shirt a chequer jacket; sleeves too short, with sausage-fingers coming too far out; breeches indecently tight, worn-down yellow shoes. An ugly customer, a bully, a *strizzi*, a rough. And with an actor's voice and eloquence." The traditional elements are given a modern form while their incongruity suggests something misplaced or sinister. In the course of his dialogue with Adrian, the character changes dramatically. "As I looked straight at him meseemed he was different, sat there no longer a rowdy losel, but changed for the better, I give my word. He now had on a white collar and a bow tie, horn-rimmed spectacles on his hooked nose. . . . Soft thin hands as well, which accompany his talk with gestures of refined awkwardness, sometimes delicately stroking his thick hair at temples and back." By continually reinventing the devilish image, Mann suggests that neither the Devil nor evil itself can be pinned down. Indeed his work emphasizes the point that as in other ages there is no stereotypical disguise for Satan in twentieth-century literature. Mann's "Devil" is everywhere and nowhere, glimpsed only in the reflection of humankind.

Caught on Film

The writings of Greene and Lewis have been popular with filmmakers. The movies have played a particular role in maintaining a place for Satan in today's world that many describe as post-Christian. Its most lasting effort, though, has been the struggle to put a face to the Devil.

Vincent Price brought the weight of his back catalog as king of the horror movie to *The Story of Mankind* (1957). Ralph Richardson added a classic touch in *Tales from the Crypt* (1963). Stanley Holloway had him more of a disgruntled vaudeville performer in *Meet Mr. Lucifer* (1953), while Donald Pleasence perhaps came nearest to carving out a role for himself as the personification of menace on screen with a string of evil roles including that of the Devil himself, playing chess with Max von Sydow's Christ, in *The Greatest Story Ever Told* (1965). More recent attempts to steal Pleasence's crown include Linda Blair's portrayal of Satan as inhabiting the body of an innocent little girl in *The Exorcist* (1973); Tim Curry as a supernatural spaceman in

Legend (1985); Robert De Niro as Louis Cyphre, munching on raw eggs and looking out impassively from behind his pointed beard in *Angel Heart* (1987); and Jack Nicholson in *The Witches of Eastwick* (1987) as an updated version of the Devil of medieval romps, with much manic rolling of eyes and his trousers down.

Familiar parts of the Devil's legend have been reworked by filmmakers. *The Devil and Max Devlin* (1981) is one of many giving the pact story another outing while *The Devil in Miss Jones* (parts 1 and 2) uses hell as the setting for sexual license in seventies soft-porn. A traditional Prince of Darkness plays a minor role in *The Devil Rides Out* (1967), Hammer Films' screen adaptation of Dennis Wheatley's cult novel. A rich young man becomes involved in a satanic ring and only the timely intervention of his father's oldest friend saves him from making a pact with the Devil, who appears on screen in the familiar guise of horned, goat-headed, half-man, half-beast. Blood sacrifices, nocturnal orgies, child sacrifice, witchcraft, and the hellfire clubs dress up a routine thriller—with the obligatory love interest, car chases, and crowd scenes—as something more sinister. The film demonstrates how, for many filmmakers, the Devil has simply become another of the stock characters—along with Frankenstein, Dracula, and Hell's Angels—of the science fiction/horror genre.

The Exorcist, based on William Blatty's novel of the same name, marked a turning point in such films. The story of a twelve-year-old girl and her possession, it features exorcism, levitation, and blood and gore, but all were accentuated by the use of state-of-the-art special effects. Another quasisatanic novel, Ira Levin's *Rosemary's Baby* produced one of the most memorable screen depictions of evil, in the hands of director Roman Polanski. The tale of a housewife convinced that she has been impregnated by the Devil, it is thought-provoking and relies on the deep fascination and fear of anything satanic in the viewer's mind to suggest, hint, but never preach that there may be evil forces abroad. Tragically, one of the reasons that *Rosemary's*

Baby remains in the public mind is that it was followed by the murderous attack on Polanski's pregnant wife.

In the wake of the Matamoros killings, John Schlesinger's 1987 film, *The Believers*, acquired a new and unwelcome reputation.[4] Mexican police discovered that members of the murderous drugs cartel had repeatedly watched the movie and its account of a New York cult that conducts human sacrifices to gain money and power. The movies may have failed to put a single face to Satan, but in the attempt it has shown its audiences some of his least attractive aspects.

FOURTEEN

In the Psychiatrist's Chair

> I have said I have met Satan, and this is true.
> But it is not tangible in the way that matter is
> tangible. It no more has horns, hooves and a
> forked tail than God has a long white beard.
> Even the name, Satan, is just a name we have
> given to something basically nameless.
>
> —Dr. M. Scott Peck, *People of the Lie*

The novelist Evelyn Waugh once believed himself possessed. The Jesuit historian Philip Caraman tells an instructive story about the author and Catholic convert. In January 1954, on a long, lonely sea voyage to Ceylon, Waugh was plagued by voices and a persecution complex. On arrival, he flew straight back to London and summoned Father Caraman. He asked the Jesuit to exorcise him, convinced that he was possessed. "I told him," Father Caraman recounted to the writer John Cornwell, "that I had no objection to exorcising his presumed demons, but that I would like first as a matter of precaution to get a doctor to look at him." A psychiatrist was summoned and pinpointed the problem as Waugh's sleeping pill, a cocktail of alcohol and barbiturates. When he changed this, the voices went away.[1]

The intervention of medicine and science has steadily reduced any lingering role for the Devil and possession in the twentieth century. With the continuing growth in our understanding of the brain and psychological impulses, the idea of an external force of evil becomes further sidelined—even by priests. Church exorcists routinely refer those claiming possession to psychiatrists while medical professionals are usually involved in the few exorcisms that are still carried out by the mainline churches.

Sigmund Freud led the way in both attempting a clear scientific refutation of the idea of the Devil and explaining why the figure of Satan was so attractive to humankind. In 1923, in "A Seventeenth-Century Demonological Neurosis" Freud examined a case from the height of the witch craze and the various accusations that were made at the trial. He believed that accounts of witches frantically copulating at nocturnal sabbats with a Devil who possessed an extraordinarily long penis was proof of his own theory that sexual repression lay behind most of humanity's neuroses. The charges leveled against the witches, he argued, were revealing only in what they said of the repressed sexuality of those doing the accusing and, more generally, of the society that was prepared to believe them. The Devil was a symbol for all that men and women secretly desired in a sexual sense, but what they could not openly admit for a variety of social and religious reasons. The more the Devil was despised and attacked, the deeper the repression became. Pent-up sexual fantasies were projected onto a group of alleged Devil worshipers—in the seventeenth century the witches and more recently any secret group like the Masons or satanists.

Freud likened the Devil to the negative side of the father-figure. In his 1923 study, he explained God as a father-substitute in relation to humankind, exalted but occasionally distant and hard to understand.

> The unresolved conflict between, on the one hand, a longing for the father, and, on the other, a fear of him and a son's defiance of him, has furnished us with an explanation of important characteristics of religion and decisive vicissitudes in it. . . . Concerning the Evil Demon, we know that he is regarded as the antithesis of God and yet is very close to him in nature. His history has not been as well studied as that of God, and his prototype in the life of

the individual has so far remained obscure. One thing, however, is certain: gods can turn into evil demons when new gods oust them. When one people has been conquered by another, their fallen gods not seldom turn into demons in the eyes of the conquerors. The evil demon of the Christian faith—the Devil of the Middle Ages—was, according to Christian mythology, himself a fallen angel and of a godlike nature. It does not need much analytical perspicacity to guess that God and the Devil were originally identical—were a single figure which was later split into two figures with opposite attributes.

In those opposites Freud saw reflected the ambivalent relationship of individuals with their fathers. Both God the father and personal fathers can often be remote, Freud held, and both therefore push their children to fill the resulting void by creating Satan. "Thus the father," Freud wrote, "is the individual prototype of both God and the Devil." Satan is a personification, not of evil in the abstract, but of repressed, unconscious drives, of the negative in humanity. The frightful fiend was, in Freud's opinion, an often unacknowledged part of all of us. The unconscious element is vital, working as a kind of malign counter-ego to the conscious rather as the Devil traditionally reflects God.

By relocating and redefining the Devil in the unconscious, Freud changed the whole nature of the debate over Satan. While close examination of evil tendencies flourished in the light of Freud's pioneering work, the Devil was largely sidelined, save on a metaphorical level, as one sign of a problem or sickness rather than the cause. It was not just the Devil who underwent redefinition—belief in God and religion in general, Freud argued, were a neurotic response to "the crushing power of nature," an illusion conjured up to deal with fear of dying.

Carl Jung (1875–1961), Freud's most influential disciple, was by contrast a profoundly religious man who took an independent line on religion. He rejected the Freudian evaluation that it was all neurosis and he suggested God and the Devil were not simply metaphors used to explain away human emotions and urges but myths that have an important function in themselves. In *Modern Man in Search of a Soul* (1933) Jung proposes that God and the Devil are two sides of the same coin—not a single deity as understood in the ancient world, but part of the fullness of the reality of the cosmos, which he referred to as the pleroma. He pioneered the idea of humanity possessing a shadow that ran in tandem with our good side. "How can I be substantial if I fail to cast a shadow?" he asked. "I must have a dark side also if I am to be whole; and inasmuch as I become conscious of my shadow, I also remember that I am a human being like any other. The shadow belongs to the light as the evil belongs to the good and vice versa." Without darkness, light has no definition.

The shadow as Jung described it should not be seen as another metaphorical way of describing evil, the psychiatrist's version of the Christian Devil. Jung's shadow is an identifiable force, the human unconscious, what is repressed within each of us and what is beyond the bounds of conventional or imposed morality. It could be applied to individuals, groups, and whole movements and trends in history, as indeed it has been to the Holocaust and Nazi Germany. He identified in the unconscious a collective element that transcends the individual and embraces all of human history. In particular, Jung studied symbols and found that ancient cultures with no links had developed remarkably similar myths and stories of bright, beautiful gods fighting dark, horned demons. Often he found that the imagery was almost identical. He noted how often the serpent recurred as a symbol of evil, from the tempter in the Garden of Eden to Naga, the serpent who was among the chief of Lord Krishna's enemies, to the snakelike monster who torments Hercules in Greek mythology and the huge worm that kills the Nordic hero Sigmund. He argued that the structure of the brain had evolved in the same way throughout humankind, whatever the geographical location, and in the unconscious were "archetypes." Chief among such archetypes was the myth of a Devil-like figure that then becomes a reflection of a malign, destructive strand within a timeless, collective unconscious, liable at any time to assert itself.

Jung also tackled the question of how a good, loving, and omnipotent God could allow evil and suffering. In 1954 he produced *Answer to Job*. God, he held, was above and beyond any human attempts at categorization. To deem God good or bad, loving or destructive was to impose human limits on what is a limitless spirit. By excluding evil from the Trinity of God the father, God the Son, and God the Holy Spirit, Christians were creating a false separation. Jung proposed that evil must be debated, examined, and raised from the unconscious to the conscious if it was to be tackled effectively. When exposed to light, darkness loses its terrifying quality. Philosophers and professional psychologists who have come after Jung have taken up his challenge by discussing evil as the product of humanity rather than as a metaphysical abstraction.

Much effort has been expended trying to distinguish between different types of evil. The clearest line that has been drawn is between natural and moral evil, but even here there is some muddying. Natural evil, identified as those inimical natural phenomena—earthquakes, floods, hurricanes—whose cause or source is a mystery, has traditionally been blamed by Churchmen on God's wrath with sinful humanity. Science has increasingly provided answers to the mysteries behind such "natural" phenomena. Floods and storms are not always inexplicable. The destruction of the environment may play some part and thereby move the argument into the territory of moral evil—that is what has been caused by the actions of individuals or groups acting with free will and reason.

When it comes to moral evil, there is much less consensus. Some medical professionals refuse to use such vocabulary, some are dubious, and others spray the words around like buckshot. In the field of psychology a bewildering range of "models" abound to explain behavior that used to be put down to the Devil—the biological, the psychological, the psychobiological, the sociological, the sociobiological, the Freudian, the rational-emotive, the behavioral, the existential, and so on. Psychiatry too has its definitions.

Edward Chesser is a psychiatrist and director of the cognitive behavior therapy unit at the medical school of University College, London. He sees evil and mental disorders as very different concepts and prefers to concentrate on the latter.

> If we take murder as an example of a possible evil act, it may be an understandable reaction to events that evoke high emotional arousal—crimes of passion, revenge or in response to extreme provocation for example. The motivation is understandable. It may not be sufficient reason in society's or indeed in a jury's mind to justify the murder, but it is a motive. Then there are those murders committed for reasons of sexual gratification, the sadistic murder. And thirdly there are the apparently motiveless murders, random killing in which some mixture of low self-esteem, inadequacy, feeling wronged by society, may be background factors. These are more often considered evil acts as they are more difficult to understand and forgive, though tender-minded people might think that non-understandability indicates mental abnormality rather than evil.[2]

The more senseless the crime, the easier society finds it to describe the act and the perpetrator as evil or mad. Yet Chesser suggests psychiatrists have to concentrate on behavior and motivation, find a reason—be it brain disease, a functional psychosis like schizophrenia, or a neurosis or personality disorder. He admits that sometimes they end up with no word to use to describe the patient's problem.

> The range of mental illnesses is finite, our understanding is finite. We only see things as illnesses that current experts say are illnesses. Patients with a psychotic illness may have a delusional belief that they are controlled by the Devil.

Patients with a trance or possession disorder may act and feel as though they have been taken over by the Devil. People who have shown a lifelong propensity to callousness, gross irresponsibility and aggression may be regarded as having anti-social personality disorder but not a mental illness. What we don't understand today and therefore call evil, we may one day in the future have a name for.

Chesser has little time for talk of the Devil, but others are less certain. John Costello, once a Catholic priest and now a psychiatrist working in private practice in London, regards the Devil as a reality, but only insofar as he exists in people's minds.

And that image extends into reality. Perhaps it is that they need a counterbalance to God—or that there is a counterbalance to God. I don't know. Do I believe in God? Yes. I see the God image in all of us. Whether God is out there I don't know but I believe because of what I see. You can apply the same to the Devil. I know that people need God. And from my work I know that they need the Devil too.[3]

Some psychiatrists refer to such dual needs as "splitting." They see it as a defense mechanism that allows often disturbed people to divide things up into good and evil, harmful and unharmful, God and Devil.

Scott Peck is unafraid to label people evil. The Harvard-educated psychiatrist, author of the best-sellers *The Road Less Traveled* and *The Different Drum*, has a broad following that ranges from seminarians to psychology students to those who pick up their reading matter on railway bookstalls. In another volume, *People of the Lie*, he writes:

If one wants to seek out evil people, the simplest way to do so is to trace them from their victims. The best place to look, then, is among the parents of emotionally disturbed children or adolescents. I do not mean to imply that all emotionally disturbed children are victims of evil, or that all such parents are malignant persons. The configuration of evil is present only in a minority of these cases. It is, however, a substantial minority.[4]

Three different psychiatrists, three shades of opinion, though at heart they all reflect a common endeavor to understand what distinguishes the twentieth century from times that favored the rack and the stake. Partly it is a question of vocabulary. Peck defends his recourse to the emotive word "evil" by claiming that "to name something correctly gives us a certain amount of power over it. . . . We are powerless over a disease until we can accurately name it."[5] Others do not share his diagnosis, though mainstream psychiatry continues to treat patients for whom it can find no precise scientific formulation.

Peck believes that at the heart of the problem of defining evil and evolving a convincing psychology is the divide that grew up between religion and science at the time of Galileo. The two effectively decided to have what he calls a "nonrelationship" where natural and supernatural were split, with religion taking full control of the latter. In that division of spoils, evil has remained in the supernatural sphere, explained away with recourse to the Devil and traditional imagery. Only in the second half of the twentieth century have there been attempts to bridge the gap. "With few exceptions, scientists have not even sought visitation rights," Peck writes, "if for no other reason than the fact that science is supposed to be value-free. The very word 'evil' requires an *a priori* value judgement."[6]

CONCLUSION

The Eternal Question Mark

> I searched for the origin of evil, but I searched in
> a flawed way and did not see the flaw in my very
> search.
>
> —Saint Augustine, *Confessions*

Christianity brought the Devil to the public's attention. Though the notion of an evil spirit, an evil demigod, or an evil god is as old as life itself, the Church fashioned those figures into a fearsome and omnipresent personification of all that was wrong with the world, with a fervor unimagined in Judaism, Islam, or any other creed except perhaps Zoroastrianism. As it rose to the height of its earthly powers, Christianity carved out a special niche for the Devil in the conquest of pagan peoples, in maintaining its hold on the faithful and in vanquishing the rebels and reformers in its midst.

In the latter half of the twentieth century, however, mainstream Christianity has gone quiet on Satan, unsure of its opinions and assailed by science and skepticism in equal proportions. The Devil's creators are going through their own period of self-doubt and in their anxiety to reform themselves have grown to question his continued usefulness. But they are unable to make the decision to pension him off, fearful of its consequences. So

Satan, once fed and sustained by religion, has been left in limbo, a skeleton in the cupboard.

The main reason for such equivocation is that the Devil is not without champions. He still has a constituency on the fundamentalist fringes among those whose Christianity is often medieval in its worldview. The marginalized, the disturbed, and the sick, those who feel for whatever reason excluded from or at odds with contemporary society, also feel an affinity with the Prince of Darkness. He was the first rebel in the cosmos and has become the symbol of their rebellion against the society that excludes them. And those who care for the marginalized and many more who are simply bemused by local, national, and world events are sometimes seduced into believing that Satan is a catchall reason for the suffering they confront.

As the activities of Archbishop Milingo in Rome and a thousand syncretic cults in Africa and Latin America demonstrate, the Devil retains, for some, his popular appeal. Science and reason, mechanics, mathematics, and sociology cannot provide all the answers, medicine and psychiatry cannot cure all ills, and so people are attracted to the irrational, the supernatural, a buried but not entirely forgotten part of our collective pasts. The Devil continues to eke out his days in this twilight world of superstition and strange cults whose activities are blown out of all proportion in the popular imagination.

He has other, more wholesome sources of sustenance. One provider of continuing vitality for Satan is the world of popular culture. From Gilgamesh through apocryphal literature, down to Dante, Milton, Goya, Delacroix, and Byron, the Devil has been a figure of fascination for artists and writers. The twentieth century may have seen a waning in this, as in other areas of Satan's portfolio, but nothing to match his eclipse in the mainstream Churches. Indeed, with the help of popular novelists like Dennis Wheatley, filmmakers like Roman Polanski, newspaper headline writers, and even the caricaturists on television game shows,[1] the Devil has assumed a persona independent of formal religion, appealing directly to the public.

In educated circles it may be politically correct to talk of sickness—individual or societal—but Satan lives on as a way of dealing with what would otherwise be unspeakable, unimaginable, or intangible. There is recognition of something more—beyond the destructive capacity of each of us, in society, in humanity, in mobs, in groups, beyond the power of physicians to heal—a great power that was once called the Devil and that, for lack of any better alternative, remains so for many. All that went with it—the demons, the sulfur breath, the horns—may now be a source of amusement but the name, with its one-letter modification of the word "evil," and the satanic whispers, continue to be heard. The Devil is no longer a monster with horns, the ghoul of medieval art, but a faceless, impersonal evil spirit, the Satan.

Once theologians debated the Devil's origins while those in the pews knew only to be scared of his influence. That same academic/popular divide can be seen today. Scientists and psychiatrists search for definitions of natural and moral evil. Yet for many, evil defies a formula of words or categorization. They can only point at it. They know it when they see it, often in the horrified response to some act so terrible that is quite beyond the human psyche to understand. In the perpetrators of terrible crimes that beggar belief, many see Satan reflected. They have become his face and his image: murderers like Rosemary West, Myra Hindley, and Ian Brady in Britain, Charles Manson in the United States, and Paul Bernardo and Karla Homolka in Canada.[2]

In the aftermath of the Oklahoma City bombing of April 19, 1995, the chief suspect Timothy McVeigh appeared on the cover of *Time* magazine under the headline "The Face of Terror." The intention could not have been clearer had horns been drawn on the picture. McVeigh provided a focus for America's confusion and desire for vengeance at a time of shock and disbelief. He was accused of doing something people could only describe as evil—small children were among the 168 people killed in the blast. When arrested he showed no remorse.

Brady and his accomplice, Hindley, jailed for life in the spring of 1966, ensnared, assaulted, and then murdered a series of children around the northern city of Manchester, burying their bodies on the nearby moorland. In the ensuing three decades the names of the "Moors Murderers" have been inseparable from the qualifying adjective evil. It began at the trial as details of their crimes were revealed and in particular when a tape recording of the last tortured hours of ten-year-old Lesley Anne Downey was played in court with Hindley and Brady showing no sign of remorse. Robert Wilson, a young reporter at the trial, later wrote a book about the two called *Devil's Disciples*, whose title summed up the popular perception:

> There was an aura of evil about the couple which is very difficult to put your finger on. It mainly manifested itself in Myra Hindley, with the hard-faced way she gazed at everybody, an almost arrogant way she looked around the court-room. The biggest thing that occurred to me about the evil of the two was that they were so calm about it all, as if they'd done nothing wrong. That was the really frightening aspect of it all: it made one wonder how many other people walk around doing evil things, without realising, or thinking, or having any remorse, or believing these things to be evil at all.

Wilson went on to link this bemusing and horrifying evil with the Devil:

> There was a general presence of evil around Brady and Hindley that transferred itself to everyone in the court-room. There was this aura that was almost demonic about them. I think the word "devil" was used more than once to describe them afterwards. There were times I looked at this pair, and I too was reminded of the Devil. This was after the veneer had slipped aside, and for the first time, their terrible souls were bared to the world.[3]

There is a strong element of projection here. It was only when the details of their crimes emerged that Hindley and Brady seemed evil. Before then neighbors had regarded them as a little strange perhaps but "ordinary" was the word most often used. It is that sudden transformation of the couple next door into infamous murderers and sadists that is so terrifying. Though Hindley today, pressing for parole, appears in every way a reformed character to those who visit her, there is something about her that means those courtroom revelations can never be eclipsed nor the unnerving air that surrounds her be dispelled.[4] Criminologists would suggest that this sort of "evil" is subjective in the extreme, existing solely in the eye of the beholder, and that there are many scientific and social reasons for criminal behavior. They are a long way from winning over the public.

That connection—some would say confusion—of evil and the Devil seen in Wilson's courtroom recollection remains character- istic of most debate about evil. With the word "evil" bandied about in a vague and imprecise way—often to describe people or events that many would not consider as meriting the descrip- tion—the Devil retains a power. In a leading article written on May 20, 1982, in response to the Argentinian invasion of the Falkland Islands, the *Times* (London) used the word "evil" no less than ten times. Under the headline "The Still Small Voice of Truth," it held forth on "the immense power of evil in the world and the fact that mankind as a whole—nations, societies, and groups—are all capable of becoming merely instruments of that evil." While many would accept that the Argentinian invasion was illegal and an affront to Britain's sovereignty, evil might be judged too strong a word. By such overuse, it has been debased.

The Devil, by contrast, remains beguiling and shocking in both his cultural and religious manifestations. And by being so hard to pin down, faceless, trading under a variety of names and guises even in the New Testament, ever-changing, never quite written off, the Devil continues to hold our interest. Dostoyevsky suggested one reason for this human fascination with the Devil in *The Brothers Karamazov*: "If the Devil doesn't exist, but man has created him, he has created him in his own image and likeness."

It is a chicken and an egg. While the Devil lurks in the background evil cannot be properly debated. And until it is properly debated and defined without traditional myths, legends, and metaphors, while people continue simply to point it out, the Devil will always have a constituency.

That image of the Devil, the metaphor of the Devil for a general evil, and the myth of the Devil that pervades Christian society remain with us. Greater understanding of the human condition and the contemporary world may have already enabled many of the niches where once the Devil lurked to be exposed to the light and given a new and scientific explanation. Yet others remain. Exorcisms, for instance, have declined significantly and those claiming possession are now sent off to doctors but there are still those one in 500 or one in 600 cases[5] where clerics are convinced they are seeing the extraordinary—genuine possession.

It may be that science will one day find the explanation and devise a treatment that absolutely and definitively does away with the Devil. It may even be that his allure fails as Western society in particular becomes increasingly affluent and amoral, and no temptations are left that we cannot explore with an easy conscience. We will no longer need the Devil as a rebuke or reproach. George Bernard Shaw foresaw just such an eventuality when he wrote of Eden: "I always despised Adam because he had to be tempted by the woman, as she was by the serpent, before he could be induced to pluck the apple from the Tree of Knowledge. I should have swallowed every apple in the tree the moment the owner's back was turned." In other words the Devil's work will be done when temptation has lost its capacity to fail.

While people display symptoms that defy doctors' explanations, while events take place that have no rhyme or reason and that prompt a peculiar horror, there will always be a question mark. It may be that science does not hold all the answers, that some question marks are part and parcel of the human condition, and that religion and folklore, with science, provide not a solution but a way of coping, balancing each other's shortcomings.

Greater knowledge, less dependency on the idea of a figure of evil, and more on the negative within each individual has brought a more precise delineation of the unknown, the darkness, the shadow. As the old devilish excuses have tumbled, much of what originally attracted humankind to a Devil-like figure remains unexplained. Suffering still perplexes. Brutality is often alarmingly random. Earthquakes and tornadoes kill without any purpose or sense. It may prove impossible to eliminate doubt. For all the progress of the world, too many of the conditions that gave birth to Satan in the first place still exist. It may be a pale, mean, grudging existence for a figure once so magnificent, so menacing, and with a power to rival that of God, but the myth of Satan lingers on, reduced but a partial answer, however irrational and superstitious, for those bewildered by the world in all its complexity.

It is hard to envisage a time when the world will be free of the irrational fear that haunted Samuel Coleridge's Ancient Mariner.

> *Like one, that on a lonesome road*
> *Doth walk in fear and dread,*
> *And having once turned round walks on,*
> *And turns no more his head;*
> *Because he knows, a frightful fiend*
> *Doth close behind him tread.*

NOTES

PART I "A MURDERER FROM THE START"

1 The Family Tree

The epigraph is from *The Devil: Perceptions of Evil from Antiquity to Primitive Christianity* by Jeffrey Burton Russell (Ithaca, 1977).

1. See J. L. Myres, *Herodotus: Father of History* (London, 1953).
2. Seth has proved an inspiration to twentieth-century satanists—see chapter 11.
3. See Russell, *The Devil: Perceptions of Evil from Antiquity to Primitive Christianity.*
4. For a more detailed discussion, see John G. Griffiths, *The Conflict of Horus and Seth: A Study in Ancient Mythology* (Liverpool, 1960).
5. There are many different versions of the epic and unraveling their origins has kept many scholars and archaeologists occupied throughout this century and before. Discussion here is therefore in general and rounded terms.
6. See chapter 2.

7. See detailed discussion of the text in Neil Forsyth's *The Old Enemy* (Princeton, 1987).
8. See Georges Contenau, *Everyday Life in Babylon and Assyria* (London, 1959), for more detail.
9. John Roberts, *History of the World* (London, 1976).
10. Translation from F. M. Cross, *Canaanite Myth and Hebrew Epic* (Cambridge, Mass., 1973).
11. William Albright's *Yahweh and the Gods of Canaan* (London, 1968) and John Gray's *The Canaanites* (London, 1964) offer a fuller discussion of some of the themes touched on in this synopsis.
12. Modern scholars believe that Homer was not a single author and that the *Iliad* may be the work of different pens.
13. See Jacques Duchesne-Guillemin, *The Hymns of Zarathustra* (London, 1952).
14. For further reading, see R. C. Zaehner's *The Dawn and Twilight of Zoroastrianism* (London, 1961).

2   A Jewish Childhood

1. All quotations in this book use the *New Jerusalem Bible* translation, the clearest of those on offer.
2. Quoted in Selina Hastings's biography of Waugh (London, 1994).
3. Modern scholars continue to find food for thought in Job. For example, the founding father of liberation theology, Gustave Gutierrez, has published a short commentary on the Book of Job.
4. See C. V. Wedgwood's *The World of Rubens* (London, 1967).
5. See chapter 9.
6. See Kate Saunders and Peter Stanford, *Catholics and Sex* (London, 1992).
7. See Jeffrey Burton Russell, *The Devil: Perceptions of Evil from Antiquity to Primitive Christianity* (Ithaca, 1977).
8. See chapter 4.

3   Head-to-Head with Jesus

1. This has been a long-running battle among biblical scholars with Markian advocates now clearly in the majority.
2. E. P. Sanders, *Paul* (London, 1953).
3. Neil Forsyth, *The Old Enemy—Satan and the Combat Myth* (Princeton, 1987).
4. See, for instance, the King James Bible.
5. Anton Fridrichsen, "The Conflict of Jesus with the Unclean Spirits" in *Theology*, number 22 (1931).
6. For more on this bizarre theory, see Paul Carus, *The History of the Devil* (New York, 1969).

4   Leader of the Opposition

The epigraph is from R. L. Thompson, *The Devil* (London, 1929).

1. John Roberts, *History of the World* (London, 1976).
2. Quoted in Norman Cohn's *Europe's Inner Demons* (London, 1975).
3. Eusebius's *History of the Church* is available in Penguin Classics.
4. Neil Forsyth, *The Old Enemy—Satan and the Combat Myth* (Princeton, 1987).
5. See M. P. Brown, *The Authentic Writings of Ignatius* (Durham, N.C., 1963).
6. Paul Johnson, *A History of Christianity* (London, 1976).
7. The Second Vatican Council—1962–1965—tried in its declaration *Nostra Aetate* to heal the wounds between the two traditions.
8. Jeffrey Burton Russell, *Satan: The Early Christian Tradition* (Ithaca, 1981).
9. See note 6 above.
10. Ibid.
11. Saint Augustine's *Confessions*, translated by Henry Chadwick (Oxford, 1991).

PART II: THE WHOLE WORLD'S SEDUCER

The epigraph is from an interview with Professor Kolakowski, author of *Conversations with the Devil.*

5   The Horned God of the North

1. Thomas Carlyle (1795–1881) as quoted in *Social England: A Record of the Progress of the People,* edited by H. D. Traill (London, 1893).
2. See *Social England: A Record of the Progress of the People,* edited by H. D. Traill.
3. Quoted in S. J. Watts, *Social History in Western Europe 1450–1720* (London, 1984).
4. It was not until the eighth century that King Offa built a monastery on the site of Alban's martyrdom and thus laid the foundations for the modern-day town.
5. R. L. Thompson, *The Devil* (London, 1929).
6. Principally since J. R. R. Tolkien's 1936 study, *Beowulf: The Monsters and the Critics.*
7. Such mixing of Christian saints and pagan gods can still be seen today in the syncretic cults of Latin American countries. In Brazil, for instance, Saint Catherine enjoys a godlike status in the cult of Candombile.
8. Pope Gregory the Great instructed Augustine of Canterbury to be fierce in holding fast to the bare essentials of Christianity, but to overlook all other abuses and dilution of the faith with other beliefs.
9. Bede's *Ecclesiastical History of the English Nation* is published in Penguin Classics.
10. See R. L. Thompson, *The Devil.*
11. Luther Link, *The Devil: A Mask without a Face* (London, 1995).
12. Quoted in Father Louis Coulange's *The Life of the Devil* (London, 1929).
13. See Paul Johnson, *A History of Christianity* (London, 1976).
14. Saint Benedict's *Rule* (various imprints).
15. Published as *Exorcism* and edited by Dom Robert Petitpierre (London, 1976).
16. A separate order was formally abolished in 1972 by Pope Paul VI

in the flurry of modernization that followed the reforming Second
Vatican Council of the 1960s.

6 The Crusaders' Bogeyman

1. All translations of the *Qur'an* are from Maulvi Muhammad Ali's
   Holy Qur'an (London, 1917).
2. See Nabih Faris, *Ibn al-Kalbi's Book of Idols* (Princeton, 1952).
3. See F. E. Peters, *Muhammad and the Origins of Islam* (New York,
   1994).
4. *The History of al-Tabari*, vol. VI, translated and annotated by
   W. Montgomery Watt and M. V. McDonald (New York, 1988).
5. Ibid.
6. *Impact International*, October 28–November 10, 1988.
7. See also *The Rushdie File*, ed. Lisa Appignanesi and Sara Maitland
   (London, 1990).
8. See John Roberts, *History of the World* (London, 1976).
9. Interview with the author.
10. See J. N. D. Kelly, *Jerome: His Life, Writing and Controversies*
    (London, 1975).
11. See Norman Cohn, *Europe's Inner Demons* (London, 1975).
12. See Jeffrey Burton Russell's *Lucifer: The Devil in the Middle Ages*
    (Ithaca, 1984).
13. Interview with the author.
14. Gershom Scholem, *Major Trends in Jewish Mysticism* (Jerusalem,
    1941).
15. These folklorish aspects are well reflected in the works of Isaac
    Bashevis Singer, who was born in Poland in 1904 and died in
    1991. His many novels were written in Yiddish. In 1978 he was
    awarded the Nobel Prize for Literature "for his impassioned nar-
    rative art which, with roots in Polish-Jewish cultural tradition,
    brings universal human conditions to life."
16. See Russell, *Lucifer: The Devil in the Middle Ages*.
17. Ibid.
18. See Cohn, *Europe's Inner Demons*.

290 Notes

7 The Cathar Heresy

The epigraph is from Paul Johnson, *A History of Christianity* (London, 1976).

1. See Tobias Churton, *The Gnostics* (London, 1987).
2. Quoted by Churton in *The Gnostics*.
3. Both quoted in Norman Cohn, *Europe's Inner Demons* (London, 1975).
4. See J. N. D. Kelly, *Jerome: His Life, Writing and Controversies* (London, 1975).
5. Walter Map's writings are published by the Camden Society, volume 50, 1850.
6. In 1991 an abridged, annotated version of Aquinas's *Summa Theologica* was published in London and New York.
7. See Churton, *The Gnostics*.
8. Ed. Lumiansky and Mills, *Chester Mystery Plays* (London, 1974).
9. Ed. George England, *Towneley Cycle* (London, 1897).
10. See Luther Link, *The Devil: A Mask without a Face* (London, 1995).
11. For a fuller account, see Jeffrey Burton Russell, *Lucifer: The Devil in the Middle Ages* (Ithaca, 1984).
12. Ibid.

8 Hocus-Pocus and the Witch-Craze

The epigraph is from Professor Sir Keith Thomas, *Religion and the Decline of Magic* (London, 1971).

1. The traditional view, endorsing the idea of a Europe-wide witch conspiracy, is best expressed by Margaret Murray in her 1921 book, *The Witch Cult in Western Europe*. This was considered the last word and regularly reprinted down to the 1960s. Modern scholarship has however rejected Murray's view and is nowhere better expressed than in Norman Cohn's *Europe's Inner Demons* (London, 1975).
2. J. H. Elliot, *The Revolt of the Catalans* (Cambridge, 1963).
3. See John Parker, *At the Heart of the Darkness* (London, 1993).
4. Quoted in the various biographies of Luther, including John Todd's (London, 1964).

5. Various versions of the *Mallus Maleficarum* are still available in occultist bookshops—see chapter 11.
6. Quoted in Paul Carus, *The History of the Devil* (New York, 1969).
7. Hencke, *Konrad von Marburg* (Marburg, 1861).
8. See Carus, *The History of the Devil.*
9. See Thomas Aquinas, *Summa Theologica* (London and New York, 1991).
10. This story is examined in great detail in Lyndal Roper, *Oedipus and the Devil* (London, 1994).
11. E. E. Evans-Pritchard, *Witchcraft: Oracles and Magic Among the Azande* (London, 1931).
12. The best account of this tragedy is found in Dr. Christian Meyer's nineteenth-century essay in *Die Gartenlaube.*
13. Aldous Huxley's *Devils of Loudon* (London, 1953) provides an immensely detailed if slanted account.
14. See Thomas, *Religion and the Decline of Magic.*
15. Alan Macfarlane, *Witches in Tudor and Stuart England* (New York, 1970).
16. St. John D. Seymour, *Irish Witchcraft and Demonology* (New York, 1992).
17. E. M. W. Tillyard, *The Elizabethan World Picture* (London, 1943).
18. Paul Boyer and Stephen Nissenbaum, *Salem Possessed* (Cambridge, Mass., 1974).
19. Ibid.

9   Rebel Rebel–a Literary Interlude

The epigraph is from William Blake, *The Marriage of Heaven and Hell* (1791).

1. Desiderius Erasmus, *Handbook of Militant Christianity*, translated by J. P. Dolan (Notre Dame, 1962).
2. Jeffrey Burton Russell offers an extended and excellent treatment of these issues and writers in *Lucifer: The Devil in the Middle Ages* (Ithaca, 1984).
3. *King Lear*, III:iv, 109.
4. Ed. Pat Rogers, *The Oxford Illustrated History of English Literature* (Oxford and New York, 1990).

5. Recent productions have suggested that Iago was a homosexual and was in love with Othello, but there is no concrete suggestion of this in the text.
6. *Othello*, V:ii, 300–304.
7. *Macbeth*, V:i, 38.
8. *King Lear*, IV:i, 36.
9. For more on Dante, see the five-volume *Enciclopedia Dantesca*, edited by Umberto Bosco (Rome, 1970).
10. All quotes are from Mark Musa's translation in Penguin Classics.
11. See also Douglas Bush, *John Milton* (New York, 1964).
12. All quotes are from the 1968 Penguin Classics text.
13. See R. L. Green and W. Hooper, *C. S. Lewis* (London, 1974).
14. See also William Empson, *Milton's God* (London, 1963).
15. The best and most readable survey of the Devil in eighteenth-, nineteenth-, and twentieth-century literature is found in Jeffrey Burton Russell, *Mephistopheles: The Devil in the Modern World* (Ithaca, 1986).

PART III: TOO SOON FOR AN OBITUARY

The epigraph is from Karl Rahner, *Encyclopedia of Theology* (London, 1975).

10   Dead and Buried?

The epigraph is from C. S. Lewis, *A Preface to Paradise Lost* (1942).

1. *Catechism of the Catholic Church* (London, 1994).
2. Professor Leslek Kolakowski, *The Key to Heaven and Conversations with the Devil*, translated by Celina Wieniewska and Salvator Attansio (New York, 1972).
3. The Devil is referred to once in the *Decree on the Church's Missionary Activities (Ad Gentes)*, and three times in the *Dogmatic Constitution on the Church (Lumen Gentium)*. Evil features explicitly rather more, though only eight times, seven of which are in the *Pastoral Constitution on the Church in the Modern World (Gaudium et spes)*.
4. Leo XIII, *Humanum Genus* (1884)—copies of all papal docu-

ments are at the Catholic Central Library, Francis Street, London SW1.

5. Catholic hostility to the Masons is well covered in Stephen Knight's *The Brotherhood* (London, 1984).

6. Paul VI's address was made on November 15, 1972.

7. Ibid.

8. Paul is best remembered for the ultraconservative *Humanae vitae*, which reiterated the Catholic ban on artificial contraception. However, Peter Hebblethwaite's 1994 biography makes a powerful case for Paul's otherwise liberal inclination.

9. November 20, 1988.

10. August 18, 1986.

11. *Catholic Herald*, May 6, 1994.

12. Ibid.

13. Interview with the author.

14. Interview with the author.

15. Bishop Jenkins on the *Moral Maze*, on BBC Radio 4, on December 23, 1993.

16. Quoted in Jonathan Petre, *By Sex Divided* (London, 1995).

17. *Those Tiresome Intruders*, published in the Grove Pastoral Series, with a foreword by the Bishop of Coventry (1990), and *The Case for the Existence of Demons*, published in Holy Trinity Booklets (1989). The Bishop was also interviewed by the author.

18. See *Exorcism*, edited by Dom Robert Petitpierre (London, 1976).

19. Interview with the author.

20. *Weekly World News*, October 18, 1994.

21. Covered fully in Ian Cotton, *The Hallelujah Revolution* (London, 1995).

22. See Jeanette Winterson, *Oranges Are Not the Only Fruit* (London, 1985).

23. See Peter Popham's report in the *Independent Magazine*, July 23, 1994.

24. Archbishop Emmanuel Milingo, *Precauzioni nel ministero della preghiera di liberazione* (Rome, 1980).

25. Covered in a special feature for BBC Radio News, *The World at One*, on February 27, 1995, and in *Marie Claire*, in August 1995.

11   The Underbelly of Society

1. Used, for example, in BBC TV's popular "Do the Right Thing," hosted by Terry Wogan.
2. *New York Times*, October 18, 1994.
3. *Today*, June 18, 1993.
4. Quoted in *Harpers* magazine, December 1990.
5. Eileen Barker, *New Religious Movements* (London, 1989).
6. *Independent on Sunday*, July 10, 1994.
7. See also Alex Bellos's report in the *Guardian*, September 17, 1994.
8. See MTV News report, "I Believe," produced by J. Gelas and broadcast at various times in September, 1994.
9. See chapter 1.
10. Quoted in *Life* magazine, May 1989.
11. The best account of these organizations can be found in John Parker's thorough if slanted *At the Heart of the Darkness* (London, 1993).
12. Maury Terry, *The Ultimate Evil* (New York, 1992).
13. See *Life*, May 1989.
14. Interview with the author.
15. See Margaret Murray, *The Witch Cult in Western Europe* (London, 1921), and Norman Cohn, *Europe's Inner Demons* (London, 1975).
16. Ibid.
17. See Aleister Crowley's "Confessions," edited by John Symonds and Kenneth Grant (London, 1989).
18. Aleister Crowley, *Magick in Theory and Practice*—most recently reprinted in New York in 1969.
19. *Catholic Herald*, December 16, 1994.

12   An Unconfirmed Sighting

The epigraph is from Lawrence Wright, *Remembering Satan* (New York, 1994)

1. See John Parker, *At the Heart of the Darkness* (London, 1993).
2. See Aleister Crowley, *Magick in Theory and Practice*, rpt. (New York, 1969).
3. Some experts would see this estimate as rather high. Some defini-

tions of sexual abuse include things like exhibitionism and sexual remarks, which can bump up the percentages.

4. *Guardian*, February 24, 1994.
5. Ed. Valerie Sinason, *Treating Survivors of Satanist Abuse* (London, 1994).
6. Ibid.
7. Ibid.
8. *Independent*, January 13, 1995.
9. *The New Yorker*, May 17, 1993, and May 24, 1993.
10. Professor La Fontaine's report was published by Her Majesty's Stationery Office in 1995.
11. Paul Erikson, *Reagan Speaks* (New York, 1989).

13 A Trickster in Modern Clothing

1. Writing in the *Tablet*, May 28, 1994.
2. See J. Baines, *Joseph Conrad: A Critical Biography* (London, 1960).
3. *The Master and Margarita*, by Mikhail Bulgakov, translated by Michael Glenny (London, 1971).
4. See chapter 12.

14 In the Psychiatrist's Chair

The epigraph is from M. Scott Peck, *People of the Lie* (New York, 1983).
1. John Cornwell, *Powers of Darkness, Powers of Light* (London, 1991).
2. Interview with the author.
3. Interview with the author.
4. See Peck, *People of the Lie*.
5. Ibid.
6. Ibid.

Conclusion: The Eternal Question Mark

The epigraph is from Saint Augustine's *Confessions*, translated by Henry Chadwick (Oxford, 1991).

1. Used, for example, in BBC TV's "Do the Right Thing," hosted by Terry Wogan.

2. At the time of writing, Bernardo is facing multiple murder charges concerning the kidnapping, killing, and dismembering of various friends and relatives in the early 1990s, including the sister of Homolka. Homolka, Bernardo's wife, has admitted to luring the victims—who were used as sex slaves—and to participating in the killings but is giving evidence against her husband. What has particularly shocked Canadians is the dichotomy between the outward appearance of this attractive, successful, unremarkable couple and their secret activities in the basement of their home.

3. Robert Wilson, *Devil's Disciples* (London, 1986).

4. The author has interviewed Myra Hindley on several occasions for a previous biography of Lord Longford.

5. See chapter 10.

BIBLIOGRAPHY

The Devil and evil in general are vast subjects. This bibliography refers only to the books the author found most enlightening and those that might be useful and accessible as further reading for those wanting to follow up some of the areas in the text.

Armstrong, Karen. *A History of God*. London, 1993.
Arnold, Ralph. *A Social History of England*. London, 1967.
Babuta, Subniv, and Jean-Claude Bragard. *Evil*. London, 1988.
Barker, Eileen. *New Religious Movements*. London, 1989.
Bernstein, Alan. *The Formation of Hell*. London, 1993.
Carus, Paul. *The History of the Devil*. New York, 1969.
Cervantes, Fernando. *The Devil in the New World*. New Haven and London, 1994.
Churton, Tobias. *The Gnostics*. London, 1987.
Cohn, Norman. *Europe's Inner Demons*. London, 1975.
Cornwell, John. *Powers of Darkness, Powers of Light*. London, 1991.
Cotton, Ian. *The Hallelujah Revolution*. London, 1995.
Coulange, Father Louis. *The Life of the Devil*. London, 1929.
Forsyth, Neil. *The Old Enemy—Satan and the Combat Myth*. Princeton, 1987.

Harpur, Patrick. *Daimonic Reality.* London, 1994.

Huson, Paul. *The Devil's Picture Book.* London, 1972.

Johnson, Paul. *A History of Christianity.* London, 1976.

Link, Luther. *The Devil: A Mask without a Face.* London, 1995.

Milingo, Archbishop Emmanuel. *Precauzioni nel ministero della preghiera di liberazione.* Rome, 1980.

Oplinger, Jon. *The Politics of Demonology.* London and Toronto, 1990.

Papini, Giovanni. *The Devil.* London, 1955.

Parker, John. *At the Heart of the Darkness.* London, 1993.

Peck, M. Scott. *People of the Lie.* New York, 1983.

Peters, F. E. *Muhammad and the Origins of Islam.* New York, 1994.

Praz, Mario. *The Romantic Agony.* Oxford, 1933.

Russell, Jeffrey Burton. *The Devil: Perceptions of Evil from Antiquity to Primitive Christianity.* Ithaca, 1977.

————. *Lucifer: The Devil in the Middle Ages.* Ithaca, 1984.

————. *Mephistopheles: The Devil in the Modern World.* Ithaca, 1986.

————. *The Prince of Darkness.* Ithaca, 1988.

————. *Satan: The Early Christian Tradition.* Ithaca, 1981.

Seymour, St. John D. *Irish Witchcraft and Demonology.* New York, 1992.

Spufford, Francis, ed. *The Chatto Book of the Devil.* London, 1992.

Thomas, Professor Sir Keith. *Religion and the Decline of Magic.* London, 1971.

Thomson, Oliver. *A History of Sin.* Edinburgh, 1993.

Traill, H. D., ed. *Social England: A Record of the Progress of the People.* London, 1893.

Watts, Sheldon, J. *A Social History of Western Europe 1450–1720.* London, 1984.

Wright, Lawrence. *Remembering Satan.* New York, 1994.

INDEX